TEARAWAYS

Dr Michael Macilwee works at Liverpool John Moores University and has a special interest in youth crime and disorder. He is the previous author of *The Gangs of Liverpool*, shortlisted for the 2006 Portico Prize for Literature.

TEARAWAYS

More Gangs of Liverpool
1890-1970

Michael Macilwee

MILO BOOKS

First published in March 2008 by Milo Books

ISBN 978 1 903854 76 1

Typeset by Andrew Searle

Printed in Great Britain by
Cox & Wyman Ltd, Reading, Berkshire

MILO BOOKS LTD
The Old Weighbridge
Station Road
Wrea Green
Lancs PR4 2PH
United Kingdom
www.milobooks.com

Contents

The Gangs of Liverpool

1880s
Cornermen
High Rip
Logwood

1890s
Ladder Gang

1900s
Racing Boys

1910s
Clutching Hand (Widnes)
Red Star Gang (Widnes)

1920s
Bucks

1930s
Black Hand Gang
Kelly Gang

1940s
Black Flash Gang
Black Hand Gang
Chain Gang
Commando Gang
Falcon Gang (Wirral)

Forty Thieves
Just William Gang
Kelly Gang
Peanut Gang (aka Park Lane Gang, Forty Strong)
The Ringer
Salisbury Street Gang
Shelter Girls
Skull Gang
Snake Eye's Gang
Throstle Gang

1950s
Black Robe Gang
Bluebirds
Brodie Gang
Congo Gang
Dick Barton Gang
Dillinger Brothers
Holly Road Gang
Midnight Blue Gang
Swallow Gang
Teddy Boys
Tennyson Street Gang

1960s
Alderwood lads
Central lads
The Dodge
John Bulls (Jays)
Shiners

Acknowledgements

THE AUTHOR wishes to thank the following for permission to use images: Ruth Hobbins of Liverpool Libraries for reproducing photographs; Jim Tait of the *Shetland Times*; Gary Evans and James Moore for the 'swallow' tattoo; Brian Willan of Willan Publishing; the British Film Institute.

Quotations reproduced by kind permission of Liverpool University Press include John Belcham, ed. *Popular Politics, Riot and Labour*, John Barron Mays, *Growing up in the City*, and David Murray Lowson, *City Lads in Borstal*. The author also thanks the following: Merseyside Police for permission to quote from Chief Constables' annual reports; Oxford University Press for permission to quote from M. Brogden, *On the Mersey Beat*; Chris Walker from Trinity Mirror for permission to quote from the *Liverpool Echo and Daily Post*; Richard Whittington-Egan for permission to quote from *Liverpool Roundabout*; Virgin Publishing for permission to quote from Norman Lucas, *Britain's Gangland*; James Morton for permission to quote from *Gangland, vol.2*, Warner Books, 1995; Random House for permission to quote from Joshua Greene, *Here Comes the Sun: the Spiritual and Musical Journey of George Harrison*, London: Bantam, 2006.

Thanks also to our Ste and Bobbie Rhys-Chadwick for their help with the fiddly computer bits; the staff at both Liverpool Records Office and the Document Supply Centre of Liverpool John Moores University, for help in obtaining research material. I am grateful to the following individuals: Pat Keeley and Bobby Wilson. Finally, thanks once again to Peter Walsh for his interest in the book.

Every effort has been made to contact the copyright holders of the material included in this book. In instances where this has not been proved possible, particularly with some of the old images, apologies are offered to those concerned. Any omissions will be rectified on notification.

Preface

IN OCTOBER 1947, one of Liverpool's worst villains appeared in court. This 'absolute public menace' was the leader of a gang that terrorised his neighbourhood. Shopkeepers were so afraid of him that when they saw him approach they nervously stood guard over their tills or protected their windows. He was said to be wild and untameable and even his parents admitted that they couldn't control him. The prisoner in question thought that he was untouchable.

His arrogance was not without foundation. As he stood in the dock for the first time, accused of breaking into a shop, he knew that his ten previous offences had resulted in nothing more than a slap on the wrist. Indeed, he would have been punished previously but for one mitigating circumstance. At eight years of age, and three feet eight inches high, he was too young to be charged.

His luck had just run out. He was sent to a remand home pending removal to local authority care, for both his own protection and that of the public.

The tiny felon was only one of a long line of Liverpool tearaways stretching back to the Victorian period. In 2006, I wrote *The Gangs of Liverpool* about the growth of the Cornermen gangs of the 1870s. These were groups of young men, mostly of Irish background, who congregated outside the hundreds of public houses on the street corners of Liverpool. They intimidated pedestrians who had the misfortune to walk past them. The lads would spit, swear, beg for money and occasionally push people off the pavement. The Cornermen became infamous in 1874 after one particular group kicked to death a respectable man called Richard Morgan in Tithebarn Street. His mistake was to refuse to hand over some beer money.

In the mid-1880s, gangs of youths, often employed as scalers at the docks, formed so-called High Rip gangs in the north end of Liverpool. These were altogether a more serious concern since they were organised and ruthless. Armed with knives and belts, they would rob shopkeepers and demand a slice of dockers' wages.

Foreign sailors would be decoyed down dark alleys and savagely mugged. By 1887, the High Rip was in disarray, although the name lived on in Liverpool folklore as a general label for any violent robbers and ruffians.

What follows is the story of Liverpool's young tearaways in the post-High Rip era, through to the end of the 1960s. The term 'tearaways' is used in preference to 'gangsters' as the latter word can be misleading, conjuring up images of American syndicated crime and extortion. It has rightly been pointed out that, in the past, Liverpool gangland activity was at best an inferior version of American racketeering. According to crime writer Norman Lucas:

> On a smaller scale Liverpool became a replica of Chicago's gangland. It was cruder and much less lethal . . . whereas in Chicago's underworld the stakes ran into millions of dollars the 'take' in Liverpool's criminal activities was invariably a matter of a few pounds.[1]

Some Liverpool youths tried to act like big-time gangsters, particularly during the 1940s, but they lacked the organisational skills to make a big impression.

The word 'tearaways', however, sums up the unruliness, impudence and cockiness of Liverpool's young Turks. Historically, Liverpool has produced its fair share of hard cases and cheeky villains, but they have been essentially unorganised and opportunist lawbreakers with a preference for small and intimate criminal partnerships rather than big syndicates. More recently, the boom in drugs trafficking has helped put infamous Liverpool figures such as Curtis Warren at the very top of the country's criminal league table. However, if we leave aside the post-1970s growth of the drugs trade, various commentators have questioned whether Liverpool delinquency was ever highly developed. For local crime reporter, Richard Whittington Egan, Liverpool gangland was always a casual affair:

> Another big difference between the Liverpool and the London crookdom is that whereas vice in London is really big business on an *organised* basis, in this city an alert police-force has always so far succeeded in breaking up the gangs . . . which have from time to

time threatened to terrorise the town. In the main Liverpool's vice does not consist of large rackets in the hand of a few master crooks. It is essentially small time, haphazard, lacking in central organisation and carried out by individual villains each working more or less alone and for his own nefarious purposes.[2]

In support of this thesis, sociologist and academic Mike Brogden described the Liverpool criminal scene:

It is a secondary economy, the economy of the streets with relatively low class crime. Most Liverpool crime relates to casual employment. There are gangs of kids who do a bit of thieving one day, a bit of violence the next and a bit of shoplifting the third. It relates to the economy of the city. Apart from the docks there's nothing worth stealing.[3]

It seems that pre-war Liverpool lacked a godfather figure to rival crime lords such as London's Darby Sabini or post-war Glasgow's Arthur Thompson. There was no single Mr Big at the head of a huge criminal empire, certainly nobody with enough reputation to make an impact on the national scene.

In his annual report, covering the war years, 1939 to 1945, Liverpool's Chief Constable stated, 'Readers of this report will recall references in the press to criminal "gangs" in Liverpool. These gangs are not organised under one leader like the gangs that formerly existed in the U.S.A.'[4] As Chapter 11 of this book shows, historically Liverpudlians have exhibited a fierce defiance of authority. Perhaps this rebelliousness also led to a rejection of any absolute criminal leadership. It is as if proud Scousers have always done their own thing. They bow to nobody.

There are no doubt sociological and cultural reasons why the Liverpool crime scene was historically fragmented and lacking in central organisation. As far back as 1889, the Head Constable of Liverpool, Sir William Nott-Bower, explained Liverpool's peculiar problem: 'Liverpool is a seaport with a population consisting largely of seamen, foreigners, and that floating class of young men, free from all restraints of home life, often with much money to spend, who cannot be made moral by Act of Parliament.'[5] Since the city's population was formed out of so many different ethnic and transient communities, there have been plenty of gangs and family 'firms' but no individual strong or ruthless enough to bring them under tight control. Liverpool's bitter sectarian divide also meant that Catholics and Protestants spent more time fighting each other than combining to form fruitful criminal partnerships.

It is as if Liverpool gangs lacked the discipline, ambition and structure to create lasting criminal empires. These people lived for the moment, drinking and enjoying themselves before they embarked on their next lengthy voyage. The casual nature of dock work also meant that the men were rich one day and broke the next. This disruptive and haphazard lifestyle was not conducive to centrally organised crime.

In the past, a great deal of serious disorder on the city's streets was committed either under the influence of alcohol or in order to obtain money for drink. Liverpool had a great reputation as a heavy-drinking district. After lengthy voyages, ships' firemen would emerge parched from their fiery stokeholds and flock to the numerous bars, desperate to replace in beer what they had lost in sweat. In 1903, one Patrick Melia appeared in court accused of murdering Edward Kelly in a drunken row over money. A witness for the prosecution admitted that the victim was addicted to drink. The judge felt obliged to add, 'It appears that everyone in Liverpool is.'

Drinking and fighting have played a large part in Liverpool's criminal past. As far back as the 1770s, the city had a reputation for anarchic violence. 'Nocturnal riots in the streets were not infrequent,' one anonymous writer commented. 'A number of hot-headed young men were often engaged in these disgraceful frays and the inoffensive passenger was sometimes insulted by them.'[6] The lager-fuelled heirs of these Georgian tearaways can still be seen spilling out of city centre nightclubs each weekend. Yet such recklessness and boisterousness are the very opposite of organised crime. Such shambolic behaviour is hardly conducive to gang disclipine.

Some writers have even questioned whether there were structured gangs of youths in Liverpool, or indeed anywhere else in the country. In 1970, academic David Murray Lowson published a book on the city's borstal boys. He qualifies his use of the word 'gang' by offering a definition: 'Gang – the customary "set" rather than an organised band of anti-social youths of the type met in America, which does not really exist in England.'[7] Residents of some of the rougher Liverpool neighbourhoods might beg to differ.

However, if Liverpool never had any large criminal fraternities to rival London's Kray twins or the mighty American syndicates it certainly had gangs, hundreds of them in fact. What they lacked in terms of organisation and financial clout they more than made up for in terms of ruthlessness and sheer viciousness. Gangs come in all shapes and sizes, from loose and temporary affiliations of crooks to more permanent, tightly knit teams to spontaneous and uncontrollable mobs. Some gangs remain anonymous while others revel in the terror evoked by their name. The motivations also differ from gang to gang. Some are determined to make money while others simply want to beat people up for no reason whatsoever.

At the bottom end of the scale there are juvenile gangs with sinister names such as the Skull and the Snake Eye's, consisting of a few mates banded together to cause a bit of childish mischief. At the other end of the scale there are highly proficient criminal gangs comprising specialists such as safe-blowers, getaway drivers and fences. An individual expert in a particular field is bound to form alliances with others for highly lucrative jobs. Between these two extremes there are plenty of small-scale family teams, made up of brothers, brothers-in-law and cousins. Such gangs often specialise in a particular branch of criminality such as burglary, making counterfeit coins or terrorising the neighbourhood.

The more successful crime families have expanded over the years, bequeathing the legacy of their fearsome reputations from generation to generation. Liverpool boasts quite a few large, lawless families, usually of Irish background, traceable back to the mass influx of immigrants during the famine years of the mid-nineteenth century. Anybody reading through the court reports of old Liverpool newspapers will spot the same surnames cropping up throughout the decades.

As far as gangs go, there are also groups of friends who find themselves embroiled in one-off drunken arguments or violent assaults. To the newspapers reporting their misdemeanours, they certainly look like gangs. There are also teenagers who seek a common identity through a shared love of music and fashion. The Teddy Boys of the fifties and Mods of the sixties are typical examples of this type of youth subculture. This doesn't mean that all these lads are in the same gang. Rivalry and animosity still exist between different factions, particularly those from different districts. Geography is very important to gang members, that sense of pride in belonging to a particular area. Territorial mobs such as the south end's Park Lane Gang, alternatively known as the Peanut Gang, could hold an entire district to ransom.

Some gangs are united by a common religious cause. Sectarian mobs, drawn from the Catholic and Orange communities, become galvanised by their hatred of each other. The IRA, not so much a gang, of course, as a paramilitary organisation, has periodically demonstrated its presence in Liverpool with audacious acts of terrorism.

As a major seaport, Liverpool has had its fair share of racial gangs consisting of Chinese immigrants, West African seamen and other ethnic groups who have banded together both for cultural reasons and for protection in a strange and sometimes hostile city. Local white youths have sometimes formed gangs in opposition to the perceived threat of 'foreigners', or simply as an excuse for a good punch-up. In the aftermath of both world wars, racial tensions have degenerated into bloody conflict on the streets of the south end of Liverpool.

There are also groups who have volunteered to fight political battles. Strikes against employers, for example, have led to street warfare around Scotland Road. Vengeful gangs have also erupted spontaneously in opposition to some suspected enemy such as German Liverpudlians after the sinking of the *Lusitania* in 1915 or local Jews after two British servicemen were hanged in Palestine in 1947. These were not so much gangs as riotous mobs, indulging in opportunist looting and shameful violence.

Local football teams have also attracted the gangs. Passions of sectarian intensity have been transferred to support of Everton or Liverpool football clubs. The sixties saw the emergence of the modern football hooligan as lads vented their anger on referees, rival supporters or simply the fixtures and fittings of homeward bound trains in shocking orgies of vandalism. The sixties also saw the rise of loose bands of disruptive and anti-social teenagers, with no real aims or goals other than a nihilistic contempt for society. Such gangs, if they can be so called, had no hierarchy or structure, no hideout or uniform. They simply roamed the streets looking for trouble and vandalising anything of value in their path.

In the following pages, all these gangs and mobs will take their turn centre stage, over a period that spans changes of century, the birth of socialism, a sectarian civil war, race riots, two world wars, economic depression, a general strike, the creation of the welfare state and various cultural and technological revolutions. Whatever the social or historical circumstances, there have been gangs of tearaways in Liverpool ready to take up the cudgels and make their mark.

1

Knifemen

'HI-E-E-E RIP ... HI-E-E-E RIP.' The long, drawn out rallying call of a gang of late-Victorian brigands would strike terror into the legions of hardened dockers and foreign sailors massed around the waterfront area of Liverpool's north end. For the cry was usually the prelude to a swiping blow from the buckle end of a belt or the sharp rip of a knife. Random violence, brutal muggings and merciless revenge attacks on witnesses brave enough to give evidence against them were the main activities of a gang of youths called the High Rip who terrorised the city's streets and back alleys in the mid-1880s.

Members dressed in a uniform of tight-fitting jacket and bell-bottomed trousers held up by a thick leather belt. A quiff of hair would protrude from underneath a 'bucko' cap, set at a jaunty angle. The gang was so organised and so bold that they thought that they could get away with anything. They usually did. However, during 1887 the gang more or less disbanded and shocking reports of their savagery faded from the newspapers.

Various reasons were put forward for the demise of the High Rip. A huge, tough policeman from the Cheapside Bridewell was said to have put the fear of God into the gang. Legend has it that he once tackled some ruffians by grabbing the leader and turning him upside down. He then swung him around by his feet, knocking down the rest of the gang like skittles. The officer, known as 'Pins', summed up his unorthodox methods: 'I grabs 'em, I pins 'em against the wall and I slaps 'em a bit.'[1]

Another possible reason for the gang's extinction is the action of vigilantes. One such group was the Logwood Gang, consisting of dockers armed with wooden batons. At the end of the working day, they would march over the canal bridges en masse for their own protection. Nevertheless, those on the outside of the crowd still risked being picked off by the High Rip. In one particular battle, staged at the junction of Vauxhall Road and Silvester Street, the High Rip was routed. Buoyed by the result, the ship repairers and foundry men, armed with short lengths of chain, were next to take on the High Rip. When the gang raided a foundry man's house in Gerard Street in reprisal for some earlier affray, they found that the man had anticipated trouble and had taken the precaution of smuggling a crowd of workmates through the back entrance. The High Rip was taken by surprise and, in a short but bloody battle, proved no match for an armed gang of grown men, made muscular by years of hard labour. The East Dispensary in Richmond Row had one of its busiest days.

For some people, it was vigilante action that finally broke the back of the High Rip. Being a member of the gang became a most dangerous occupation and eventually the High Rippers were viewed with derision rather than terror.[2] Others maintained that it was the actions of a notorious flogging judge called Justice Day that wiped out the gang. Short terms of imprisonment were combined with multiple doses of the lash given at the beginning and end of each sentence. It was argued that not many brutes came back for more. In 1926, a slaughterman working at the Gill Street abattoir asked a colleague whether he had been in the High Rip Gang. The man admitted as much and pulled up his shirt to reveal his back, the skin of which was corrugated like a washing board. The elderly ex-hooligan said that after Justice Day had finished with him he decided that crime did not pay.[3]

Sceptical justice campaigners, however, pointed out that the level of violent crime in Liverpool actually increased at the end of the judge's ruthless reign. A more socially conscious explanation is that as conditions improved, young people became better behaved. Education, housing reform and the provision of youth activities were all seen as civilising influences. It must also be added that gang members may simply have grown up, got married and settled down.

However, not all associates of the High Rip suddenly hung up their knives to become law-abiding citizens. In 1887, in one of their worst outrages, the brutes went on the rampage around Scotland Road, assaulting and robbing shopkeepers, even punching a baby in the face. As well as imprisonment, the lads were given sixty lashes. Yet the severity of the punishment did nothing to cure the violent tendencies of at least one of the gang.

Upon his release from gaol, Bernard McCall went back to live with his parents in Bootle. In 1889, a policeman was on duty there when he noticed a man in a bloodied state, obviously the victim of a violent assault. The officer went to the man's house where he found his wife crouching in a corner, also drenched in blood. A strip of flesh an inch and a half long had been torn from the woman's scalp. Her face was severely bruised and she had lost a considerable amount of blood. When she drifted out of consciousness she was rushed to the Bootle Hospital, where she remained for some time.

The battered couple were the parents of Bernard McCall. They had been arguing at home when their son returned and noticed that they had been drinking. 'Beer on the table again,' he cried before swiping it away in disgust. He then viciously attacked his mother and father. Before she became unconscious, Mrs McCall told the constable how her son had threatened to roast her before banging her head repeatedly against the wall and floor. Her husband, who had been hit on the head with a fender, ran outside for the police. If it hadn't been for a neighbour, who rushed to her aid, the poor woman reckoned that her son would have finished her.

In court, Mr McCall was reluctant to give evidence against his son. He claimed that the fender, falling accidentally from the table, caused his injury. Despite his best efforts, Mr McCall could not save his son from an eighteen-month spell in gaol, this time without a flogging.

The prison whippings handed out by the judge might have deterred some gang members but others were so tough, or perhaps so desperate for money, that they carried on their lawless lives regardless. Indeed, some men bore their scars proudly as a badge of honour. Mr T. Bell, former Chief Constable of Bootle, related a story regarding one former High Ripper called Nick who had once suffered a severe flogging after appearing before 'Judgement Day'.[4] For years afterwards, Nick would haunt the dockside pubs demanding free drinks on the strength of his 'hard man' reputation. To intimidate his victims he would take off his shirt and exhibit his scarred back. He would never use violence but the threat was usually enough to terrify some licensees.

One night, Nick entered a pub and stripped to the waist as usual. He approached the bar and demanded a free beer. Although the licensee was new to the district he had heard about the man's reputation and was determined to put a stop to such bullying. Nick laughed when asked to leave. The licensee, a much smaller but stockier man, then bolted the pub doors and for the next five minutes gave the bully the biggest hiding of his life. Apparently from that day on, Nick was the quietest man in the pub. Never again did he parade his scarred back.

Yet the memory of the High Rip lived on in the hearts and minds of the city's ruffians. In 1889, James Mawdsley and William Baker were arrested for being drunk and disorderly in Gordon Street, off Great Homer Street. An aggrieved Mawdsley drew his knife and shouted, 'Now lads, come on, High Rip.' He was disarmed before he could stab the officer and ended up spending a month in gaol. Two years later, Thomas Devany, described in court as a member of the High Rip, received four months imprisonment for threatening to knife a bookmaker at Chester races.

If some of the old High Rippers maintained a violent if isolated stand, a new generation of Cornermen gangs provided a visible and terrifying presence on Liverpool's streets. On 12 September 1891, two letters appeared in *The Liverpool Review* criticising the inactivity of the police. The first pointed out that the area around Leeds Street and Upper Milk Street in the city centre, where Richard Morgan was murdered, was infested with street-corner loafers, either lying in the street drunk or verbally abusing passers-by. Muggings were common and innocent pedestrians ran a gauntlet of fear with apparently no help from the police. The second letter claimed that there had recently been a huge riot in Great Homer Street involving no less than 2,000 people. Some were almost beaten to death. Desperate residents blew frantically on whistles to attract the police yet nobody arrived on the scene until half an hour had passed.

Yet despite the public's view that the police were nowhere to be seen during such disturbances, there was also plenty of evidence to show that officers were often in the very thick of the action. The area around Vauxhall Road, once the favoured stamping ground of the High Rip, was particularly dangerous for patrolling policemen. In 1889, an officer was walking his beat when he noticed James Roche, a well-known young ruffian, standing at the corner of a street on the opposite side. Roche picked up a stone and threw it, shouting, 'I'll do for you.' The missile struck the policeman smack in the face, leaving him with a bloody nose, cut chin and black eye. Roche ran away but was apprehended later the same night during another disturbance in which more bricks were being thrown by groups of youths. At the Police Court, Mr Raffles, the stipendiary magistrate, put it to the prisoner, 'I suppose this is the usual thing in Vauxhall Road?' Roche answered nonchalantly, 'Yes, sir, there was a lot of it last night.'

The north end of Liverpool certainly remained volatile. In May 1889, the area of waste ground between Hawthorne Road and Stewart Road played host to a series of Sunday afternoon betting disturbances. In one incident, a dogfight was staged that left one of the dogs dead. An argument over the result led to a scrap between a local man and a rival from St Helens. After a few blows, the men were separated and a proper contest under 'rules' was arranged for the following week. The fight duly took place with a purse of gold being put up by the spectators. After forty blood-soaked minutes, the St Helens man was beaten into submission. A return bout was then arranged. Such disorder apparently took place week after week without any interference from the police.

Street gambling became a focal point for the gangs. In 1890, swarms of disorderly youths would congregate around St Anne Street and Wilton Street in Islington to play pitch-and-toss, marbles and cards. They would use the pavement and steps as a card table, all the time mouthing the foulest language imaginable. The gangs were feared to be as bad as the Cornermen who infested Roderick Street and other passages running from Soho Street to St Anne Street. Residents complained that there had recently been a stabbing and robbery in the area as well as a number of violent assaults. The police, however, were nowhere to be seen, not that a single officer was of much use in such a rough neighbourhood.

It seems that the card players were not bothered whether they gambled in back streets or front streets. When a policeman was spotted they simply vanished into a network of dens from which there were many escape routes. The residents in the area dared only use their front door, having to keep the back door firmly locked, for if people did use the narrow back entry and accidentally disturb a card game they would be met with a torrent of abuse and even physical assault.

In 1901, thirty-seven people appeared at the Police Court charged with gambling on a Sunday afternoon on some waste ground in Love Lane. A large squad of officers and plain-clothed detectives raided a gathering of about 1,000 men. A variety of games were in operation, including a wheel of fortune, cards and pitch and toss. About thirty of the ringleaders were arrested, including Michael Traynor, the former leader of the High Rip gang.

Sunday gambling occasionally led to violence. In 1913, Patrick MacFarlane was walking along Regent Road in Bootle when he saw a group of men playing cards. He took an interest in the game but began to protest upon seeing a man fleeced out of half a crown. The boss who was keeping the ring told MacFarlane to mind his own business, before thrashing him with the buckle end of his belt. The blows ruptured one eyeball and left MacFarlane almost blind in the other eye.

* * *

An age-old question in the debate about crime is whether the situation is getting better or worse. Politicians, top police officers and newspaper editors often bandy around statistics to prove one thing or another. At a Watch Committee meeting in July 1892, the Head Constable rejected allegations that rowdyism and violent crime were rising in certain districts. He confidently provided statistical evidence from three previous annual reports to demonstrate that crime was in fact decreasing. These reports showed that there was also a drop in the number of people claiming to be too afraid to give evidence in court. Finally, the Head Constable proudly asserted that there was no street in Liverpool where people were too afraid to walk.

Yet the *Liverpool Review* felt that these reports did not reflect what was happening on the streets. For example, despite the claims of the Superintendent of D Division that the Marybone district was comparatively quiet, the journal pointed out the horror of a recent sectarian outrage in that area. During the incident, fifty or sixty heads were broken in an organised faction fight. Piles of stones had been collected beforehand in readiness. A public house was wrecked and the streets left strewn with rocks and broken bottles, which afterwards were collected for recycling in the return bout.

The claim made by the police, that people were safe walking through Liverpool's streets, was also challenged by the journal. It was pointed out that the district stretching from Soho Street to the docks, together with numerous streets in the extreme north and south ends of the city, were filled with street-corner rowdies, using filthy language and obscene jokes. People were still being blackmailed and maltreated by the ruffians, yet none of this was being reported to the police. Such was the reign of terror imposed by the gangs that shopkeepers dared not report robberies for fear of reprisals. As regards witnesses having the confidence to report crime, the journal pointed out that recently a gang was threatened with prison if they continued to molest a woman who had given evidence against them in an assault case.

It was all very well for the police to claim that the situation was improving but the citizens of Liverpool knew what was really going on in their communities. For the *Liverpool Review*, the 'Marybone War' was evidence of 'the savagery and brutality' of thousands of Liverpudlians, which no amount of police public relations exercises could deny. Liverpool's streets experienced many random atrocities, committed by youths simply looking for trouble. Knifings occurred for the smallest provocation. In 1894, while walking past the Rotunda Theatre in Scotland Road, Thomas Maddox, accompanied by a man called Kelly, accidentally knocked against Murdoch Caldwell. A few words were exchanged and a fight ensued with both men rolling in the road. As a crowd started to gather, Kelly joined in the attack by punching Caldwell in the face. Maddox then brandished a clasp knife and 'high ripped' Caldwell behind the ear and on the forehead. Despite cries from the crowd of, 'Mind the knife, he's got a knife,' Caldwell was heard to groan, 'I have got it'. He died shortly after.

Maddox went into the road and callously sharpened the blade on the kerbstone before shouting, 'The first man that comes near me is a dead 'un.' As the police arrived, the attackers ran off but witnesses offered Maddox's name. Arrested two days later, the youth said, 'There's no use denying it. I did it.' However, he also claimed that his mysterious drinking colleague Kelly, who he knew only by sight, incited the assault by saying to him, 'Are you going to be beat Maddox? Here's a knife, stab him.'

In addition to the gratuitous and random beating of strangers, the second great legacy of the High Rip reign of terror was theft with violence. Seamen on shore leave and dockers making their way home on payday were prime targets. As the nineteenth century drew to a close, muggings continued. Even women became victims. Yet it would be wrong to lay the blame for such robberies on organised gangs. The thieves were often desperate individuals accompanied by a mate or two. They might not even have set out looking to rob their victim but simply took the opportunity as it arose.

The March 1894 Assizes saw a whole batch of youths brought up for assault and robbery. Unfortunately, they appeared before Justice Day, the notorious flogging judge. William McNabb suffered four months' gaol and eighteen strokes for mugging a woman in Soho Street; James Elliott and Hugh Gray received six months and two separate doses of fifteen lashes, for highway robbery in Vauxhall Road; William O'Brien received thirty strokes in two instalments for being part of a gang responsible for another violent theft.

The following month, Charles Walsh and James Reilly mugged Annie Tobin. She was walking along London Road when Reilly came up to her and butted her in the chest. He then snatched her bag, containing thirty shillings. Walsh was caught and the next morning, while in custody, he received a parcel of food from a visitor. There was a note hidden inside: 'Keep up your heart Charlie, for there was only five shillings and sixpence halfpenny in it altogether.' It seems that Reilly was trying to con his own mate, since the robbery netted a bit more than that. When the astute Walsh returned the cutlery to his gaolers, a reply was found hidden in a can: 'Tell Reilly I know how much was in it.' The other man was arrested the next morning and charged with being Reilly's accomplice as well as being involved in the theft of a pony and trap from outside a public house. His accomplice in that robbery threatened to knife the publican if he followed them.

In 1895, John Burrows was walking with his sister-in-law along Portland Place, off Great Homer Street. As they passed a gang standing on the corner, one of the men made an offensive remark to the woman. Burrows smacked him but immediately felt a sharp pain in his shoulder. He became faint due to loss of blood and had to be rushed to the East Dispensary. Shortly after, in nearby Fox Street, Charles McFarlane pulled a knife from his boot and boasted to his mates, 'That's the way to do it.'

It would appear that almost every adult male on Liverpool's streets carried a knife. This is not surprising since so many men worked at the docks where a blade was simply a tool of the trade. Smokers also needed penknives to cut up chunks of tobacco. The problem was that as soon as a fight broke out, even a trivial argument amongst friends, the 'shiv' was inevitably produced, often with tragic consequences. These assaults were not the work of organised gangs but individuals born into a culture of casual violence. A brief survey of the stabbings committed in Liverpool in a single year illustrates the hostile and savage nature of the city's streets. For whatever reason, 1896 stands out as a particularly bad year for knifings.

In March, in Brownlow Place, James Cullen stabbed Martin Noon, leaving the broken blade lodged in his shoulder. The victim lay in a critical condition at the Brownlow Hill Hospital until June. The day before the attack, Noon and a friend were in a public house in Boundary Street, off Vauxhall Road, when Cullen came over and asked the men when they were being paid. The next day, after Noon had received his wages, Cullen again approached and demanded the price of a drink. Noon told the man to pay for his own but ended up being knifed.

Assaults on drinking partners were common. David White was sentenced to twelve months with hard labour for knifing John Dick. In June the men had been drinking all day when an argument broke out. White knocked his friend down and then punctured him twice in the back. A similar stabbing assault between drinking partners took place in Liverpool two days later. Next, a black man called Walter Barker was sentenced to four months with hard labour for stabbing James McCarthy in June. Barker saw his victim in Duke Street, near Hanover Street, and accused him of snitching on him to the police. He threatened to stab McCarthy if he did such a thing again. Later that day, the pair met again. This time Barker caught McCarthy by the throat and threw him down before running off. McCarthy followed his attacker but Barker turned around and knifed him. At the police station an unrepentant Barker stated, 'I'm sorry I didn't put it into his neck instead of his back.'

Also in June, Thomas Brady knifed William Maguire. The victim was standing on a Toxteth street corner arguing with another man. Brady interfered and kicked Maguire to the ground. The man got up and chased Brady, eventually catching him. However, as they struggled, Maguire felt that he had been nicked. Brady ran away, dropping the knife. It was then discovered that Maguire had been wounded once in the head, twice in the shoulder and once in the arm, none of the cuts being serious.

In July, while walking along Canning Street, John O'Neill met a man called Thomas Capon. Both men lived in adjacent Frederick Street. O'Neill asked his neighbour for the price of a drink but the man refused and the pair ended up fighting. A policeman separated them but an hour later while O'Neill was standing on the corner of Canning Street, Capon approached him, jabbed him in the chest and ran away. O'Neill was taken to the Southern Dispensary and then on to the workhouse hospital in Brownlow Hill where it was discovered that he had a puncture wound just above the heart. Meanwhile, Capon voluntarily went to the detective office in Dale Street and admitted, 'I have come to give myself up. I have stabbed a man in the left breast and I think he is dead. This is the knife I done it with.' Ironically, Capon was wanted as a witness to the following stabbing outrage that also took place in July.

John Gibbons, known as 'Scotty', was walking along Frederick Street when he met Richard Williams and John Hilton standing on the corner. Hilton was the man who earlier robbed the pony and trap and threatened to stab the pursuing publican. As Gibbons passed, Williams, who was carrying a knife, started scuffling with him. Hilton shouted, 'Stick it in, Dick.' Seconds later, Gibbons had been fatally skewered in the heart with a blow so forceful that it sliced through his fifth rib. It seems that the attackers had a history of trouble with a friend of the victim. On an earlier occasion, Hilton, armed with a knife, had threatened Gibbons with the words, 'Now Scotty, you are just in the right neighbourhood for a doing over.' Despite a plea of self-defence, Williams was found guilty and sentenced to death, although he was later reprieved.

Just before midnight on 15 August 1896, a PC Connor was on a corner in what was once High Rip territory when he came across a drunkard called Henry McGarry. As the man was using bad language, Connor told him to move on. McGarry knocked the officer to the floor. The policeman jumped up and was forced to draw his baton, which he then used on McGarry's head, beating him to the ground. As the injured drunk staggered up he muttered, 'All right, Mr Connor, I'll go quietly.'

The pair walked calmly to the bridewell when McGarry unexpectedly renewed his attack. The policeman attempted to draw his baton but found it snatched from him. The pair again ended up wrestling on the ground when James O'Rourke joined in by beating the constable on the head with a stick. While the officer lay face down, Patrick Loughlin stabbed him a few times in the back. The victim, no doubt full of adrenalin, had no idea that he had been injured, despite a couple of the wounds being three inches deep. A baying mob formed and McGarry managed to escape. Despite his injuries, the constable pursued his prisoner and eventually tracked him down to an outhouse where he held on to him until help arrived.

Back at the Chisenhale Street Bridewell, PC Connor fainted due to shock and loss of blood. He was rushed to the Northern Hospital where it was discovered that he had suffered seven stab wounds in addition to a severe blow to the head. McGarry was taken to the hospital to be present when the injured policeman completed his statement. On the way, McGarry enquired, 'What's to do? Is he dying?' He callously added, 'I wish I had killed him. I am willing to swing for him.' Loughlin was later seen sitting on a doorstep where he boasted about stabbing a policeman. He claimed that he had delivered seven stabs although only five had 'got in', the other two being wounds he had inflicted on himself during his frenzied assault.

At the Assizes, McGarry was found guilty of unlawful wounding and sentenced to thirteen months with hard labour. Loughlin was put away for seven years for wounding with intent. O'Rourke was found not guilty.

On a Saturday night in September, some policemen attended a disturbance in St John's Place, off Northumberland Street. James Mahon went into his house and threw a bottle at the officers from an upstairs window. He then rushed out the door and began stabbing at them, ripping one of their tunics. Also in September, John O'Dwyer knifed Joseph Deboe in the eye and assaulted a man called Judge, after a Saturday night fracas in Paul Street, off Vauxhall Road. He explained to the police, 'It was a row between us. I was double banked.' Around this time, James Hughes wounded Christopher Whartley in Virgil Street. The victim was arguing with a woman when Hughes interfered. It was suggested that the men sort out their differences with fisticuffs. Whartley said that he didn't mind as long as the fight was fair. However, Hughes then stabbed him twice in the head.

In the same month a policeman was knifed in Great Newton Street, off Brownlow Hill. PC Cannon was standing on the corner when John Kinsella approached and asked for directions to Doran's pawnshop. The man went on his way but then came back and for no reason sliced the policeman's stomach and thigh. Despite his injuries the officer managed to hold onto his attacker until help arrived. It was revealed in court that there were several witnesses to the crime but they did nothing to help the victim. Inspector Strettall expressed his dismay at the dangers of policing Liverpool's streets: 'This is the worst of it: officers are nearly losing their lives for the protection of the public. When people are about and officers are almost dying in the street, nobody seems to take any notice of it.'

As the century drew to a close, the knife remained the weapon of choice for Liverpool's ruffians. In 1897, two men were standing on the corner of Tithebarn Street and Highfield Street when a drunkard approached and demanded money. One of the pair replied that he had none but they were so afraid that they allowed themselves to be searched. Frustrated at finding nothing, the drunk pulled out a knife and warned, 'If you don't give me three-half-pence I will put this knife through you.' A man of his word, he then stabbed one of them.

* * *

The new century began much as the old one had finished, with violent street robberies and gratuitous knife attacks on both the police and public. In 1900, two men mugged a woman called Edith Moore. One attempted to snatch the woman's purse while the other put his hands over her mouth to silence her. The poor woman was then assaulted and robbed. A public-spirited cyclist pursued the thieves and arrested them. At the police station, one of them claimed, 'I would not have done it, only I was out of work and had nothing to eat.' In court, the judge's solution was to put him on a prison diet for the next three years.

In the same year, a PC Behan was patrolling his beat when Mathew Heffey rushed up to him and gashed him in the arm and thigh. Heffey was found guilty and sentenced to five years. However, the case did not end there. Just before Heffey appeared in court, his cousin approached a man called George Boyle and urged him to attend court and speak up for Mathew. Boyle refused, explaining that he knew nothing about the case. On the day of the trial he nevertheless received a witness summons at his home, which he ignored. Days later, Boyle was sitting in bed when the cousin entered the room and threatened, 'You did not appear for my cousin at the Assizes where he got five years and I will do five years for you.' He then stabbed Boyle over the eye. The victim already had his arm in a splint and was unable to defend himself.

The police remained fair game for violent assaults. On an evening in December 1900, Richard Skelland was fighting with a man in Upper Harrington Street in Toxteth. Two policemen separated the brawlers and they went on their way. However, as the officers walked away, the rough-looking Skelland ran after them and cracked one officer on the jaw. He was arrested after a violent struggle during which a hostile crowd gathered and threw bricks at the police. One PC was struck in the face, later losing the sight in one eye.

The pitch-black alleys of late night Liverpool continued to provide the ideal conditions for violent street robberies, especially from defenceless women, though the number of incidents gradually decreased as the century progressed. As housing and social conditions improved and employment opportunities increased, young men largely moved from the street corners to engage in other more worthwhile pursuits such as education, sport and politics. Thanks also to better policing, the bloodshed on Liverpool's streets was considerably reduced and the city became a more civilized place to live. By and large, people stopped being beaten over the head or knifed and robbed as they made their perilous journeys homewards through dark back alleys.

By 1904, the Head Constable's annual report was proudly boasting of a decrease in the use of the knife on Liverpool's streets. Part of the reason for this was the demolition of the old back-to-back courts where victims had no escape from their attackers. Also, such incidents were hidden from the eyes of the police, who seldom patrolled the courts. The February 1904 Assizes boasted a list of only twenty-two prisoners, the shortest for many a year. One journal, with tongue in cheek, put the improvements down to 'the increasing goodness, generosity and sympathy which are evident everywhere'.[5]

Nevertheless, isolated assaults could still bring to mind the savagery of the High Rip. In 1909, four members of the Summerville family from Harold Street in the south end dished out a vicious sustained attack on the police. The incident erupted after PC Gibbs went to William Summerville's house to serve him with a summons for disorderly conduct. The man accepted the piece of paper with a polite, 'Thank you.' However, as the officer turned his back he was hit on the head with a poker. Henry Summerville, William's brother, then struck him on the forehead and behind his ear with a carving knife. Both weapons were dropped and the men's mother, Emma, carefully retrieved them and took them back into the house.

Other men then came out armed with a poker and an axe. John Kean punched the officer but he bravely managed to hold both him and William Summerville against some railings. However, Kean then bludgeoned him with a poker on the side of his face while Hugh Barr also cracked him on the back of the head with the blunt side of the axe. The policeman dropped to the floor. The men ran back into the house as two other officers rushed to the scene and took William into custody. However, Kean then kicked the prostrate officer between the eyes while Mrs Summerville ran out of the house with a kettle of boiling water. Some concerned neighbours prevented her from pouring the contents over the poor man's head but not before she had managed to deliver a good kick to the officer's ribs.

The barbaric intentions of Emma Summerville demonstrate that Liverpool women were not averse to outrageous savagery. A disturbing parallel to the violence of the Cornermen was the amount of merciless brutality displayed by women.

2

The Amazons of Liverpool

'THE NEXT TIME I meet you, you bastard, I'll bite your nose off. You will then have lost a nose as well as a finger.' Such were the seasonal good wishes issued on Boxing Day 1888 to Margaret Garretty as she strolled along Great Homer Street. The spiteful threat came from an old adversary called Catherine Curl, who was out walking with her daughter, Catherine Umbers.

It seems that Curl had bitten off Garretty's finger in a previous battle. For this she was convicted and ordered to pay costs. Having neglected to do so, she was imprisoned for three months. Curl's daughter, who seems to have inherited her mother's sadistic nature, went one better by suggesting, 'No, don't bite her nose off; throw vitriol over her and blind her, so that she will have to be led about by a dog and string.'

The terrified Garretty ran away and informed a constable, who advised her to issue a summons. In a subsequent court appearance, Curl denied the allegations and produced witnesses to show that for the entire day in question she was minding a child with measles. It was also alleged that Garretty was in the habit of calling after Mrs Curl in the street, shouting, 'Cannibal!' and, 'Where's your jail cuckoo?' The latter remark was a reference to a child Mrs Curl had given birth to while serving her sentence. There had, in fact, been a long-standing feud between the women. However, the word of the complainant was believed and Curl was bound over to keep the peace for six months.

Reports of female 'cannibalism' were not uncommon. In 1912, one woman tried to sue another who had allegedly bit her thumb in a fight. Septic poisoning set in and the thumb had to be amputated. The poison spread and her arm also had to come off. In court, however, it was established that the amputee had in fact been the aggressor and had punched her rival in the mouth, knocking out two of her teeth. That was how she sustained the wound to her thumb. The case was dismissed.

Catfights amongst women occurred regularly in the bleak courts and back alleys of Victorian Liverpool. Another female fibber claimed that a rival had torn out chunks of her scalp. From the witness box, she brandished a clump of hair as evidence. A sharp-eyed magistrate pointed out that the locks were the wrong colour.

Some of the violence on Liverpool's streets involved acts of revenge on those brave men, women and even children who were willing to appear in court as witnesses to crimes. This would create bitter animosity and often result in ferocious retaliation on the so-called 'grass' or 'snitch'. Members of the public were also targeted for daring to prevent crimes. Sometimes revenge was wreaked simply because somebody felt aggrieved or slighted by another's actions. The High Rippers were infamous for violently preventing the public from interfering with their criminal activities. As the nineteenth century drew to a close, women became as bad as men when it came to dishing out merciless acts of retribution.

Indeed, the press blamed the High Rip for the following outrage. Judging by the level of violence used, the men and women involved could well have been bona fide gang members. In 1889, a constable was on afternoon patrol in the Soho Street neighbourhood in Islington. He noticed an unruly crowd of people outside a house and went to make inquiries. It seems that Polly Sweeney had an old grudge against Margaret Lloyd and had gathered together a bunch of twenty roughs to storm the woman's premises. The men proceeded to break up the furniture and ornaments and smash all the windows.

The offenders fled as the officer approached but on a nearby corner John Downey was captured. The constable put it to him, 'You are the ringleader of this lot. I want you for smashing this house.' A defiant Downey allegedly replied, 'I won't go. I will hang for you first.' Another constable turned up to aid the arrest but Downey put up a terrific fight. He shouted to his colleagues, 'Men, will you see me taken this way? Have none of you any knives or belts?'

Aided by an opening volley of bricks and bottles, the posse returned to rescue their colleague. As the police struggled on the ground with their prisoner, Downey pulled out his own knife and sliced an officer across the forehead. Someone else kicked the wounded officer while he lay on the ground. The policeman managed to get on his feet only to be felled by a flying bottle thrown by Polly Sweeney herself. As he hit the ground a second time, another man and woman allegedly resumed the kicking. The second constable was 'high ripped' behind the ear with a sharp knife before being brutally beaten.

Despite his injuries, the second policeman managed to keep hold of Downey and drag him to the bridewell, assisted by some colleagues who had rushed to the scene. The rest of the gang were rounded up later, although one harpy cracked another constable on the nose as she was being arrested. The gang appeared at the Police Court and were remanded for a week. The case then disappears from the newspaper records and it is therefore unclear whether any of them were found guilty.

Children were also fair game for a vengeful beating. In 1894, a pack of rough-looking young women, all aged between sixteen and twenty-one, were charged with wounding twelve-year-old William Nutting in a ferocious attack. The previous day, the boy had given evidence in court in a case in which a man called Edward Wedgewood was sentenced to six months' imprisonment for stabbing Annie Ford. After the verdict, a detective overheard some women standing outside the court ominously promising that, 'Before the evening is out there will be another assize case.'

After leaving the court at St George's Hall, Annie Ford went for a celebratory drink with the young William Nutting. Mrs Wedgewood, the convicted man's wife, rushed into the alehouse, shouting, 'Here they are.' She then struck Ford in the face while another woman joined in the attack, screaming 'Oh you swine; you are drinking the blood money.' The terrified lad managed to escape.

Later that day, Mrs Nutting sent her son to the shops. However, as he walked along Smithdown Road in Wavertree, carrying a basket filled with meat and potatoes, a gang of women ambushed him. They shouted, 'Oh! Oh!, Here he is. He can afford to buy cakes and sweets out of the blood money.' The women then knocked Nutting down and kicked him unconscious. They even took the joint of meat from his basket and beat him about the head with it. A witness ran over to rescue the boy but was threatened with the same treatment. He said it looked like the women were playing football with the boy's body. As they ran away, the attackers shouted, 'There is your twelve shillings blood money.' At the Royal Infirmary it was discovered that three of Nutting's ribs had been broken. He remained poorly in the hospital for ten days.

Police arrested four of the women in a house in Bancroft Street. Some of them were relatives of Wedgewood, the man in prison. As the constable entered, one shouted, 'If you take one you will have to take the lot; we were all in it.' A woman called Ada Walker then assaulted two policemen as they tried to take the suspects into custody. She struck one officer on the back of the head with a piece of wood and then threw some mud and stones, most of which found their target. Walker had previous convictions for assaults on the police and was sentenced to two months with hard labour. The other women denied attacking the boy but when they were taken to the Infirmary the patient managed to identify them.

At the Police Court, three other women were also charged with assaulting the lad. When a policeman arrested Annie Wedgewood, the aggrieved woman produced an illustrated copy of the *Police News*, complaining, 'You need not have put this in the *Police News*. None of us had hats on.' The court erupted into laughter. Wedgewood was sentenced to twelve months' imprisonment with hard labour at the Assizes in May 1895. Her accomplices received between three and ten months. As the sentences were read out, the women shrieked and howled at the injustice. The commotion held up proceedings for some time. Even when the prisoners had been removed below the court they could still be heard yelling.

For some women, violence was second nature. In 1894, a hawker called Mary Ann Connolly and a woman named Brennan were accused of the manslaughter of Mary Ann Mullarkey and a separate assault on another woman. It is not clear what provoked the attack but the victims had obviously done something to upset their attackers. Mullarkey was walking home carrying a jug of beer when her two assailants chased her into the house and thrashed her with pokers. She sought treatment at the dispensary but later died of blood poisoning as a result of her infected wounds. Despite claiming that Brennan was responsible, Connolly was found guilty.

The household poker was the weapon of choice for aggrieved residents of Drinkwater Gardens, a narrow alley in the Islington district. If ever a place was misnamed it was this dreadful slum. With not a flower in sight, the passage was bounded by tall, smoke-begrimed houses, which leaned towards each other as if to offer mutual protection and support in this most dangerous of districts. Smashed windows were stuffed with rags and paper. Broken chimney pots, worn-out steps and filthy courts only added to the misery of the place. The police were no strangers to the squalid area and the nearby East Dispensary was ideally situated to minister to the steady stream of poorly, injured and sickly inhabitants. Malnourished and half-naked children with pinched features made regular journeys to the pubs, returning with cans and jugs of refreshments for their parents. By evening the effects of the liquid were seen in the uproar in the neighbourhood. Booze-fuelled residents with scores to settle would reach for the poker at the first sign of trouble.

In 1895, one drunken quarrel ended in tragedy. A marine fireman called Daniel Wedekind was enjoying a drink with a female friend in a public house in St Anne Street. It was alleged that a man called Owen Green entered the pub and demanded a drink. Wedekind refused and was threatened by Green, who promised that he would have a woman from Drinkwater Gardens see to him. Feeling intimidated, Wedekind and the lady moved on to another alehouse, where Green again accosted him.

Upon leaving the pub, the couple entered Drinkwater Gardens, where Green and a woman called Mary Roxburgh confronted them. Words were exchanged and as the two men fought, Roxburgh rushed at Wedekind and smashed a bottle of porter in his face. She then thrust the jagged remains into the man's eyeball. In a cruel twist of fate, he was already blind in the other eye as a result of an earlier accident. Not that it mattered. The victim, now totally blind, was rushed to the dispensary and then on to the workhouse hospital, where he died under the anaesthetic during an operation to sew up his wound. Green was later discharged from court while Roxburgh was found guilty of unlawful wounding.

In 1901, William Evans and Margaret Stevens, a father and daughter from Kirkdale, were found guilty of callous assaults on their lodgers, Susannah Holland and her husband. One evening, Holland had cooked some fish for her partner when a drunken Stevens entered her room and ate some of the meal. The aggrieved Mrs Holland warned Stevens that she would have to pay for the fish but the drunk picked up a kettle of boiling water and emptied it over the poor woman. The victim's screams brought William Evans rushing to the room where he picked up a hatchet and attempted to crack Mrs Holland on the head. Unfortunately, the scalded woman's husband took most of the force of the blow, his wife nevertheless sustaining a small wound.

In court, Mr Evans' defence argued that this was his client's first offence and that he should therefore be treated leniently. He was fined forty shillings. His daughter received six months with hard labour, a sentence met with outrage. Stevens, who had behaved in an aggressive manner throughout the hearing, broke into a torrent of foul-mouthed abuse. She threatened the magistrate, police and the victim before being dragged kicking and screaming to the cells.

Drink was behind much of the violence in the slum districts of Liverpool. Almost all the habitual drunks were deemed to be of the lowest classes, most of them women. It was said of these poor creatures, 'They are products of ignorance and poverty, wrecks of humanity, to whom drunkenness is the greatest, if not the only, pleasure in life.'[1]

In 1905, thirty-three-year-old Margaret Sweeney, armed with a sweeping brush, smashed the windows of both a pub and a house in Islington. When arrested, Sweeney flung herself to the floor and promised to shatter every window in the street. She was charged not only with criminal damage but also with being a habitual drunkard. In court, several policemen testified that the woman was continually violent when drunk and was a danger to other people. Since 1897, she had amassed forty-nine convictions for drunkenness and wilful damage. Sweeney, however, explained to the court that she did not drink, 'that much'. She admitted to touching a drop only when there was trouble in the family. Unfortunately, she must have belonged to a very troublesome family. She also claimed to be a hard-working woman despite having no occupation.

The jury decided that she was indeed a habitual drunkard. The sentence handed down by the judge was not so much a punishment as an opportunity for Sweeney to straighten herself out and redeem herself. She was imprisoned for ten days and afterwards detained for three years at the Lancashire Inebriates Reformatory at Whalley. A journal of the time felt that although punishment could not make people sober, the law could at least help point people in the right direction. As the unhappy woman left the dock, she unleashed a volley of abuse, aimed mainly at the police. Even when out of sight, in the corridor below the court, she could still be heard screeching a piercing yell before bursting into a tuneless song that gradually faded as she approached the dark, dank cells.

At the beginning of the twentieth century, random and gratuitous violence, fuelled by drink and aided by sharp knives, also began to fade. After the heyday of the High Rip, street muggings steadily declined. However, gang violence was never completely eradicated but merely took on new forms as the century progressed. The street corner gangs split into smaller teams as lawless youths began to look for more artful and cunning ways of making money. For some thieves, better education meant the ability to plan and commit more intelligent crimes. As the city's geographical boundaries expanded, so did the opportunities for theft. Liverpool's tearaways needed to keep one step ahead of the game.

3

Robbery after the High Rip

FOR THOSE TOO squeamish to crack somebody over the head or stick a blade in their ribs, there were plenty of other ways of making a dishonest living on Liverpool's streets. Mugging was a crude form of theft, likely to net only a small amount of money from fellow slum dwellers. The penalties were also severe, as the frequent punitive whippings illustrate. Floggings were given to prisoners only if the robbery took place *with* violence.

Picking pockets was less risky. Beating up victims in the street attracted attention and possible retaliation whereas a good pickpocket could come and go unnoticed. There was always the possibility that a mugging could go wrong and end up in a murder case, with hanging as the inevitable result if convicted. If done cleverly, picking pockets involved no threat of violence for either the thief or the victim. The nature of the crime meant that it was suited to individuals although there were also gangs of pickpockets, known as bottling teams, who would swarm the crowds at fairs and horseracing meetings.

At the end of the nineteenth century, Liverpool was noted for being a magnet for thieves from the rest of the country. In addition to the usual influx of stowaways, sailors and foreign paupers, the city was also attracting skilled 'cracksmen' from London who committed daring burglaries, particularly of jewellers. London-based pickpockets and thieves also poured into Liverpool when the going got too hot down south. By 1904, the Head Constable of Liverpool, in his annual report, was still warning about the dangers posed by 'undesirable aliens', in other words, brigands from other areas.

In 1895, a team of international pickpockets settled in Liverpool but probably wished they hadn't. John McHarvey and George Edwards were wanted throughout the world but it was in Liverpool that they finally faced justice. Edwards was a professional dipper. Little is known about him since he constantly refused to give the authorities any details of his life. Between 1878 and 1879, he picked up convictions in Glasgow and Edinburgh. He was also implicated in the theft of jewellery worth £200 from a shop in Deansgate, Manchester. As a result, the devastated jeweller committed suicide. Edwards also had convictions in the Isle of Man. In 1892, he went to America. After getting into trouble in New York he moved to Chicago in an attempt to 'work' the World's Fair. After being recognised as a pickpocket, he was driven across the Atlantic back to England.

McHarvey came from Melbourne, Australia. Police believed him to be the son of the oldest confidence trickster in Victoria but so far he had escaped any serious convictions himself. He travelled to England in 1893 and along the way met Edwards. Their modus operandi was the old-fashioned pocket dip. The pair would loiter outside banks waiting for an easy touch.

In 1895, a young clerk for a firm of wool brokers was sent to the North-Western Bank in Dale Street to cash a cheque for £229. On receiving the money, the lad placed the cash in a notebook, which he then put in an outside pocket of his coat. On his way past the Exchange, McHarvey pushed past him. Almost immediately the clerk noticed that the book and money were missing. He notified a nearby policeman and then returned to the bank to have the numbers of the notes recorded. Detectives were given a description of McHarvey and within an hour the officers went to a public house in Everton where the men were arrested.

It seems that around noon, the pickpockets entered the kitchen of the alehouse where the manager was sitting. In celebratory mood, McHarvey ordered three drinks and a cigar. It was then that the detectives entered and arrested him, followed by Edwards who, on seeing the police, had quickly nipped out into a back room. After taking the men into custody the detectives searched the public house and found the notebook and some of the money. The rest of the cash had been stuffed between the rafters and slates of the back room. McHarvey was found to be carrying several fake notes and bogus cheques, including one for £25,000, something that caused much laughter when the men appeared in court.

McHarvey, together with an accomplice called George Wilmore, also faced another charge. Wilmore was McHarvey's former partner in crime in Australia. When the colonies became too hot for him, he also moved to England. Both Wilmore and McHarvey used various aliases, which made it difficult for the police to pin any previous convictions on them. Both men were believed to be the heads of gangs of dangerous criminals.

In a neat confidence trick, McHarvey boarded a Liverpool boat to Belfast. Just as the ship was about to sail, he claimed that he owed his friend Wilmore some money. Pretending that he hadn't got the cash immediately available, he borrowed it from a passenger but then jumped from the ship as it left the dock. The victim was left sailing away wondering at his own stupidity.

The judge declared that the prisoners were incorrigible thieves who had unfortunately settled in Liverpool. Although they had got away with their crimes all over the world he intended to shorten their criminal careers. Edwards was sentenced to ten years and McHarvey to eight years. Wilmore got five years. Despite the lucrative pickings of this international gang of professional thieves, most local pickpockets netted only small amounts of money. Typical was a seaman who, in 1900, was relieved of £3 on payday. As he passed the corner of Hopwood Street and Vauxhall Road, a gang surrounded him and dipped his pockets.

As knife crime and street robbery decreased, thanks largely to better policing, burglary increased. The economic growth of the city saw entrepreneurs boosting their wealth through thriving business opportunities connected with the docks and accompanying industries. These rich merchants began to move to bigger and grander houses in the more affluent suburbs such as Allerton and Aigburth. They were able to fill their homes with expensive ornaments and jewellery. In response to this, the focus of Liverpool's thieves began to change. Why rob a shilling from a poor drunk in Scotland Road when you could net a small fortune by travelling a few miles from the city centre? Big-time, out-of-town burglary was born.

House burgling had two great seasons. In the winter, residents went to bed early leaving the house at the mercy of thieves. In the summer, the wealthy went on holiday, leaving the premises in the charge of servants who were not so watchful. In 1892, the so-called Ladder Gang pleaded guilty to burglary in West Derby. Thomas Wilson and James Gatton made elaborate preparations to gain access to the house. They tied cords across the coach road, presumably to hinder any approaching traffic, before fastening the doors of the house, no doubt to prevent anybody running out and raising the alarm. Finally, they used ladders to climb up to the balcony. As can be guessed from their modus operandi, these were not opportunist burglars but hardened professionals with previous form.

When arrested, the men were found with a wish list of intended victims, including such illustrious names as Lady O'Hagan and Sir William Fielden. They must have studied the newspapers looking for promising targets. The gang also admitted to burglaries in Wigan, Warrington and Stockport. In court, they denied that they had rained down stones on the heads of the policemen below as they were being arrested. They pointed out that as the officers removed the ladder, some loose rocks were accidentally dislodged from the roof. The pair received seven years' imprisonment.

In 1897, three of Liverpool's cheekiest burglars were caught in a house in Canning Street, just south of the city centre. The wealthy owner had gone away and had asked the police to keep an eye on his property. At five o'clock in the morning, a constable noticed that the premises were occupied. Together with another policeman he entered the address and found Joseph Fitzsimmons and Henry McKenna under a bed. Edward Fitzsimmons was found in another room where a pile of clothes and ornaments had been neatly piled up ready for removal.

The men denied any intention of burglary. They explained that they had been on their way home from a drinking session the night before when they saw the door to the property open. They decided to go in and sleep off the effects of the alcohol. Indeed, McKenna claimed that when the officer woke him up, 'he thought he was at home with his poor old mother', a statement that caused much laughter in court. Joseph Fitzsimmons suggested that the real burglars had fled the property, leaving the door open. He explained the fact that they were trembling when arrested, as being due to the effects of the drink. The judge, however, thought that hiding under the bed was hardly consistent with innocence. The brothers received six months and McKenna four.

The cheek of Liverpool burglars was legendary. In 1891, a public house in Regent Road, Bootle was broken into. While the publican's family slept soundly upstairs, thieves entered the bar parlour, lit a cosy fire and stayed for several hours finishing off the spirits. In 1907, a house in Stoneycroft was ransacked while the occupants were on holiday. Clothing and boots were targeted. However, the thieves didn't just take the posh new suits; they first changed out of their own dirty rags and left them behind in the drawing room. Over thirty years later, when a man burgled a house in Eldon Place, he not only stole goods but also cooked himself sausage and eggs.

While the Fitzsimmons brothers were proving themselves particularly inept at burglary, another pair of Liverpool brothers was showing a more professional approach to the dishonest craft of breaking and entering. In 1897, following the arrest of three men in London, one of Liverpool's most successful burglary teams was smashed. One man was caught in the capital after a frantic five-hundred-yard chase, after which the arresting officer was thrown to the ground and assaulted.

The men were charged with committing a series of daring burglaries in Lancashire and Cheshire over the previous six months. The crimes were carried out in such a professional manner that Liverpool police were baffled and left without any leads. The arrests led to the recovery of jewellery and silver plate worth about £1000. Two of the men responsible for handling the stolen goods, and possibly for the burglaries, were brothers, Lawrence and Herbert Murrell, or Morrell. They went under the name of Brown and passed themselves off as successful Liverpool merchants.

In London, they made acquaintance with William Thwaite, a 'potman' in a public house, and asked for his help in getting rid of the stolen property. Thwaite later turned Queen's Evidence and exposed the workings of the gang. It seems that the goods were stolen in the North West, transported by rail to London and finally disposed of by Thwaite using a network of pawnbrokers. He received five shillings and sixpence a day for pledging the goods. Sometimes he was unsuccessful and the suspicious pawnbroker held onto the items, refusing payment. The total value of all the property stolen over the six-month period was estimated to be £4-5,000. Today, that would be worth over £400,000.

Thwaite revealed that a larger team carried out the burglaries, using a horse and trap to carry off the stolen property. Wealthy houses in Anfield, Newsham Park, Sefton Park and Egremont were targeted. Shops such as Russell's Ltd, of Cazneau Street, were also hit, netting a number of valuable watches and clocks. Detectives from Liverpool travelled to London and were able to identify a large proportion of the property, in particular a valuable presentation piece of plate silver stolen from the home of a minister.

After receiving information, London detectives visited Camden Town Railway Station, where they found in the cloakroom a large tin chest sent to the capital from Lime Street Station in Liverpool under the name of Brown. The box contained seventy-six dozen knives and forks of the best quality silver, a haul taken from a single raid on a shop in Scotland Road. Gold and jewel rings, silver plate and a number of clocks completed the booty, which weighed one and a half hundredweight.

The Murrells were committed for trial on charges of burglary. Also related to their arrest, a young man called Edmund Carter was charged with various burglaries. It was alleged that he was also responsible for sending the box of booty to London. At Liverpool Assizes, the brothers were found guilty of handling stolen goods. Lawrence received ten months with a six-month consecutive sentence for another offence. Herbert was imprisoned for twelve months.

In 1911, Lawrence Murrell was back in court accused of being part of another gang of burglars. Murrell now ran a cocoa room but, since old habits die hard, he was suspected of handling stolen goods on the side. He was arrested after a spate of housebreaking in Lancashire. Most of the premises were entered through bedroom windows left open by men pretending to be window cleaners. The judge remarked that there were no more dangerous crooks than dishonest window cleaners. Murrell received three years' imprisonment.

As the twentieth century progressed, technological advances inspired new types of robbery and fraud. In 1904, a Liverpool-based Frenchman made an arrangement with a local bookmaker to accept his bets from Paris. The Frenchman, who was secretly staying in Liverpool, used a forged telegram in an attempt to fool the bookie into believing that he had placed his bet before starter's orders. In fact, he had waited until the race had finished before choosing his horse. Putting £6 on a 10 to 1 winner, he then forged the time of the telegram before sneaking it into the bookie's office.

In 1913, Samuel Howard used the anonymity of the telephone to conduct a novel fraud. First he would enlist the services of a boy with a handcart, whom he would pick up in the street. He would enter a telephone box and ring a large-scale wholesaler. Pretending to be a retailer from another big firm, Howard would order cases of brandy or sugar. He would then pay the boy to collect the goods. The firms were duped into believing they were dealing with another legitimate business.

The ingenuity of thieves was countered with more modern systems of security. As shopkeepers became more security conscious they began using safes to store their valuables. However, robbers simply adapted to the task. Whereas some burglars were able to work alone, the heavy work involved in safe-theft required the combined efforts of a small team.

In July 1902, thieves targeted a number of Liverpool businesses housing safes. The crime wave began when Wade's Coachbuilders, of London Road, was forcibly entered and the safe wrecked by sledgehammers. However, the thieves stole only a few gold and silver medals won at agricultural shows. A timber merchant of Boundary Place was next to be hit. A safe weighing 10 cwt was moved from the general office to a more private, soundproof room where the thieves managed to rip open the side of the box but found only a set of books of no value. A smaller safe was also cracked but that too contained only books. A hospital collection box, containing plenty of cash, was overlooked, either because the thieves had a conscience or were too busy looking for bigger treasure. Finally, a clothing firm was burgled but not much was taken.

If stronger safes were immune to sledgehammers, then thieves had to look for more advanced methods of opening them. Early in the century, Liverpool's Head Constable, Albert Dunning, remarked that the growth of education was having little effect on crime rates. Robbers were simply becoming cleverer at committing crime. Safe breakers, for example, now used electric arcs instead of jemmies.

There were also other methods. In 1902, a Glasgow team travelled to Liverpool to target the premises of a pawnbroker of Upper Duke Street. Nitro-glycerine was used to blow the safe. First, the men took some carpets and placed them around the safe to deaden the sound of the explosion. However, the operation was unsuccessful and the safe's mechanism was merely twisted. The thieves abandoned the raid and fled.

Thieves were always looking for new ways of getting money. While cash and valuables were being locked away in sturdy metal safes, some unknown Liverpudlian realised that similar amounts of money and cheques were being openly transported around the city in nothing stronger than a hessian sack. In 1901, Liverpool experienced the first mailbag robbery in its history. A postman was collecting the mail from post boxes in the fashionable residential district of Mossley Hill when a man blinded him with pepper and relieved him of his sack. The man stumbled about in great pain, his eyes streaming. When he had regained his sight, the thief and the sack had disappeared. It was estimated that about ninety letters were stolen, some containing postal orders. The empty postbag was later discovered in Sefton Park.

* * *

The general public also became the target of audacious thieves. Unscrupulous conmen found increasingly elaborate ways of parting people from their money, usually with their consent. Travelling gangs were behind the mock auctions that took place periodically in the city. To pull off the scam, the men would rent an empty shop for a short period. It was important that the swindlers moved from town to town before they were found out. The auctioneer or 'patter man' would use every psychological trick in the book to play upon the gullible public's desire for a bargain. 'Here you are sir, you are lucky today, it's the boss's birthday and he is giving away a gift' was a typical opening line. Decoy purchasers, known as 'outside men', would bid for genuine articles at bargain prices, enticing the crowd to make their own offers.

However, what the crowd would bid for would usually be flashy rubbish, a lot of it made for shop display rather than practical use. Imitation silver tea sets and worthless metal cigarette cases washed over with 'silverine' were favourite items, proving the old proverb that all that glistens is not gold. The outside men would congratulate the successful bidder and make him feel as if he had done well for himself, before hustling him out of the premises, leaving him no time to examine the worthless tat. If a customer returned to make a fuss, there would be a ruffian known as a 'plug ugly' to threaten him with violence if he didn't shut up. Most dupes put it down to experience and never visited another auction. However, there were always plenty of other mugs to keep the scam going.

In 1900, two men were passing an auction room in Lime Street and were attracted by the unbelievable offers. Henry Spiro, the auctioneer, enticed the audience with various items of jewellery. He claimed that he was advertising the goods for a firm and was willing to give away a few presents. He asked the audience to give him some money, promising to return it with a gift. Several people handed over a shilling and received their shilling back plus a pair of cuff-links. Spiro raised the stakes by increasing the amount to five shillings. People gave their cash and received it back with a brooch. The amount was increased to ten shillings and people were delighted to be handed back their money along with a bracelet.

Henry Baker, of Birkenhead, was attracted to the offer of a watch for a sovereign, with the sovereign being handed back, of course. The proposal was so good that Baker bid two sovereigns to receive two watches. The sovereigns were wrapped up with the watches in paper packaging and handed back to the bidders; or so they were led to believe. When Baker opened up his packages he found two halfpennies and a shilling. The watches were each worth about eight shillings.

In court, a witness, who was also a jeweller, explained that the watches were what were known as 'flat catchers' and were unreliable as timekeepers. The cheap metal was similar to that of the worthless rings used in another popular scam. The rings would be deliberately dropped in the street by swindlers and then sold off as 'gold' to the first gullible 'flat' that came along. Spiro received three months with hard labour.

Protection rackets were another form of scam. The following example does not compare with the rackets of organised crime in America but was a rather amateurish local attempt to obtain cash through fear. In 1913, two clerks demanded money with menaces from a firm of auctioneers based in Church Street in the city centre. The men sent a letter supposedly from an organisation called the Ancient Order of Bucks, offering the patronage of the 'Order' in exchange for an honorarium of £5. The offer included the goodwill of members who would attend the sales and make the bidding brisk. However the letter went on to become more menacing: 'It is not so much what members would do if the "Order" secured you patronage, as what will happen if you desire to proceed without our aid.' The letter then threatened that the auction room might be cleared by the use of a small quantity of a certain powder, probably gunpowder. The court decided that the letter's message – pay up or be blown up – was a stupid practical joke and the men were found not guilty.

Mailbag theft and auction scams remained rare while burglary continued. The summer of 1907 saw Liverpool hit with a tide of break-ins, both domestic and commercial. The targeted properties were again situated in the more wealthy suburbs, a world away from the dank and dismal courts and back alleys that were the scene of many nineteenth-century muggings. The regular beat policing that enabled the cramped city centre streets to be kept largely under control was not as effective out in the suburbs. Homes and shops had been entered in all directions, yet the police were left baffled and without a clue. At the end of June, a large quantity of valuable silver plate was taken from South Albert Road, off Ullet Road. Days later, a grocer's shop was targeted, losing a large proportion of its stock. More silver plate went from Newsham Park, followed by property from Walton Breck Road and jewellery from Ivy Leigh, Tuebrook.

Many burglary teams consisted of brothers. In 1907, John and Charlie Doherty broke into a jeweller's shop in Dale Street in the city centre and allegedly stole goods worth £200, including 230 gold rings, twenty-eight gold watches and twenty-four gold muff chains. A policeman on patrol noticed Charlie standing near the shop with his back to the shutters. Shortly after, he called to his brother who was inside, 'Come on Johnny.' As the policeman approached to investigate the matter, Charlie sprinted towards the Town Hall. A voice from inside the shop shouted, 'What's up Charlie?' Receiving no answer, John jumped through the fanlight from where he had entered the premises, straight into the arms of the waiting constable. Charles was arrested the next morning but not before the goods had been disposed. None of the jewellery was ever traced.

In court, the defence questioned whether any robbery had taken place at all, since none of the items had ever been recovered. The implication was that the goods might not even have existed, leaving scope for an insurance swindle. However, both men were found guilty. It was believed that John Doherty had been going straight since 1899 but was led astray when his brother came back on the scene. He was sentenced to nine months hard labour. Charles, described as a habitual and clever criminal, received five years.

Also in 1907, another pair of brothers, Joseph and William Blackburn, broke into a pawnbrokers shop in West Derby Road and stole nineteen watches, some rings and other jewellery to the value of £50. From information received, detectives staked out Moor Lane, Fazakerley early the next evening. After three quarters of an hour, they observed the brothers digging in a cornfield. They then saw them conceal two baskets in a different part of the field before leaving. The detectives found the baskets but they were empty. They then started digging in the same spot as the thieves and found a sack full of the stolen jewellery.

As darkness closed in, the crafty detectives substituted the treasure with broken bricks and reburied the sack. They then returned to their vigil where another colleague later joined them. At three o'clock in the morning, as dawn was breaking, the detectives decided to replace the bricks with the jewellery and put the sack back under the sod. At nearly half past five the brothers returned to retrieve their baskets and dig up the plunder. The detectives suddenly pounced on the astonished men. 'It's a fair cop. We will go quiet,' uttered Joseph Blackburn.

In court, the men's defence argued that there was not the slightest evidence that his clients had committed the actual robbery. However, they were found guilty and sent down for two years.

The value of the motorcar as a tool for robberies was illustrated as early as 1915. The car brought new opportunities for burglars. The increased mobility meant that thieves could now travel far and wide looking for suitable jobs. It also meant that the local police were usually at a loss for suspects. In December, a house off Smithdown Road was broken into. Various items, including two expensive brooches, were taken.

By chance, the next day Manchester police called at a house to arrest a man for an unrelated crime. While they were there, Max Kilmanovitch paid a visit. As his pockets were suspiciously bulky, the officers decided to search him. Amongst various items of jewellery, they found the two brooches from the Liverpool job. Kilmanovitch claimed that a man called Billy Firth had given him the articles. He pleaded that he was hard up and added, 'Don't do me any harm and I will get you the three men tonight.'

The police accompanied the man to his home in Miles Platting, Manchester, where he also ran one of his many watch repair shops. The businesses were in fact fronts for his criminal activities. The constables began to search the house and found a loose floorboard, underneath which was a cigar box containing the works of twenty-four watches without the cases. One of them belonged to a Liverpool man whose house had been robbed earlier. Further searches under the floorboards uncovered an arsenal of burglar's tools, including a jemmy, three melting pots, chisels, skeleton keys, lamps, cartridges and rubber shoes. In a bin in the backyard there was a fully loaded five-chambered revolver.

It seems that there had been an epidemic of housebreaking in Liverpool, Manchester, Leeds and Blackburn. Houses were hit while the occupants were out shopping or at church. Kilmanovitch was one of a team of thieves who raced from job to job in a motorcar. At Liverpool Assizes, he was found guilty and sentenced to twelve months' hard labour followed by deportation. The judge announced that he would have given him longer but he didn't see why this country should maintain him.

Whereas burglars preferred to work unnoticed, often in the dead of night when residents were asleep or offices unoccupied, distraction thieves relied on busy, crowded environments to carry out their brazen work. In 1890, a team targeted a public house in Tetlow Street, Walton. The men used an old scam, known as the 'bird trick', to net the cashbox, a bowl and some loose money. Frank O'Neill and John McKellar went into the parlour leaving James Murphy and Frank Cartwright having a drink at the bar. The men sat in the parlour, then called over the landlady, Mrs Stirraker and her daughter, saying they would like to show them a bird.

McKellar then opened a paper bag and let loose a canary. One of the men pretended to do his utmost to catch the bird while his friend kept his back to the door in order to keep the women in the room. During the distraction, the other two men situated in the bar stole the cashbox and money. Mrs Stirraker eventually realised what had happened but was roughed up as she tried to prevent the men escaping.

The police soon apprehended the men who were all prolific thieves. O'Neill was described as a 'professional criminal', McKellar was known as a dangerous man who had once threatened to murder somebody, while Murphy had form in Manchester where he was known under different names. McKellar received ten years' imprisonment while O'Neill got seven years. Unfortunately, the prize exhibit, the poor bird, died on the first day of the Assizes.

Professional distraction thieves could not stay in one place for too long. The very nature of their work meant that they had to keep moving both to avoid being recognised and to prevent places becoming accustomed to their particular scams. James Trott was a travelling distraction thief who specialised in thefts from banks and post offices. In 1899, he entered the Bath Post Office and asked an official at the desk to show him the location of a certain railway station on a map he was holding. After the official and a colleague had pored over the map without success, Trott abruptly took his leave. It was then discovered that a packet containing two £5 notes and some gold was missing from behind the counter. The package had been placed twenty-two inches inside a wire partition so Trott must have been considerably skilful and flexible in reaching for it.

A year later, Trott turned his attention to the Bank of Liverpool in Water Street. A clerk had been sent to deposit £810 at the Bank of England nearby. As he put the bundles of notes on the counter, a stranger tapped him on the arm and asked him how he could get to Victoria Street. After the clerk pointed out directions he turned around and noticed that the money was missing.

There was no stopping Trott, for the next day he obtained postal orders for £12 from two post offices in Manchester. He then went to another post office in the neighbourhood and cashed them. Such behaviour was very unusual and after police made enquiries, Trott was arrested on his second visit to the post office. Although he had previous convictions, in court it was suggested that older men had led him astray.

In 1911, Charles Smethurst and William Jones employed a tried and trusted technique to rob a milliner in County Road, Walton. Smethurst went into the shop and asked for change of sixpence. After he left, Jones entered and quickly came out again. Minutes later, the men were seen outside counting and sharing some money between themselves. It seems that when Smethurst entered the shop, the doorbell rang, warning the shopkeeper that she had a customer. It was later discovered that the bell mechanism had then been broken; leaving Jones the opportunity to slip in unobserved and steal ten shillings from the till. The men were caught and found guilty. Jones was sent away for twelve months but Smethurst, as the ringleader, received three years. He addressed the judge from the dock:

> Smethurst: 'Thank you, my lord, and I wish you a merry Christmas!'
> Judge: 'Take him away.'
> Smethurst: 'And if I should not be out before, I wish you three merry Christmases.'

He then had to be forcibly removed from the dock.

In 1917, two thieves staged a classic distraction robbery at a jewellery shop in the city centre. They entered the store and asked a lady assistant to show them a tray of rings. One of the men failed to see anything he liked but offered to show the assistant a beautiful ring in the window. As he opened the door to allow the lady to step outside, his accomplice sprinted from the shop with the rings.

Other thieves employed more subtle methods. In 1918, several Liverpool jewellers were the victims of a new scam. A prospective customer would ask to see a tray of plain gold rings. After closely examining a few, he would make his excuses and leave. Later, the jeweller would discover a cheap brass replica had replaced one of his expensive rings.

Another distraction scam was known as 'at the wash'. In 1918, Liverpool was hit with a spate of such robberies whereby the thief waited until a gentleman, preferably a well-heeled one, went to the washroom of a hotel or restaurant. The intended victim would normally take off his coat to wash himself. The thief, who was usually also well dressed, would do likewise and hang his coat on the next peg. While the victim splashed his face with water, the thief would quickly finish his own ablutions and as he took his own jacket, would carefully slip the wallet out of his victim's coat. In one incident, £400 was taken. Restaurants were forced to put up notices warning of the practice.

In 1924, the Bank of Liverpool was once again the victim of a cheeky distraction theft. Just before closing time, a shipping insurance clerk placed treasury notes to the value of £100 on the counter. A man in the queue then tapped him on the shoulder and directed his attention to a ten-shilling note on the floor. As the clerk stooped to pick up the note the stranger made off with the man's money. Although there were plenty of customers waiting to be served, nobody saw the man disappear.

Filching wads of notes from bank counters was undoubtedly more profitable than stealing wage packets from seamen. It may also have been seen as more morally acceptable. For really big rewards, however, bank fraud was a better option. As the nineteenth century drew to a close, and the economy of the city grew, there were more lucrative gains to be had from bigger crimes requiring a little more intelligence, cunning and planning. Indeed, the twentieth century kicked off with one of the biggest and most spectacular crimes seen in Liverpool. Once again, the Bank of Liverpool was targeted.

4

The Great Liverpool Bank Fraud

MUGGINGS AND STREET robberies have their origins in poverty and social deprivation. In nineteenth-century Liverpool, such crimes involved poor people robbing fellow paupers. People have to survive somehow and this was nowhere more urgent than in a Victorian society where social welfare was largely voluntary and haphazard and the conditions in the workhouse so grim that most people avoided it.

Yet some thefts were motivated by more than starvation and impoverishment. The years between 1870 and 1900 saw an increase in working-class prosperity. This was reflected in a greater choice in clothes and food. Yet such social and economic improvement did not mean that people no longer had any need to steal. For some, it meant that that there was a greater variety of things to steal and more choice as to what to spend the stolen money on.

As people became better educated, some moved into clerical work, of which there was plenty in Liverpool, serving the growing industry of ship owners, insurance companies, banks and importers and exporters. It was only a matter of time before some lowly clerk saw an opportunity to take a slice of the riches that surrounded him. Here, thousands, if not millions, of pounds would be at stake.

One of the biggest cases was the Great Liverpool Bank Fraud. Over a period of twelve months in 1901, a gang bled a bank of almost £170,000, a sum that a century later would be worth over £13 million. Thomas Peterson Goudie, a £150-a-year ledger clerk at the Bank of Liverpool (later known as Martins Bank), was the insider responsible for this 'crime of the century'. Goudie was a well-educated single man aged about twenty-eight. He was five feet seven inches tall with a square build, dark hair and a sallow complexion, with a square, clean-shaven jaw. He spoke slowly with a Scottish accent. Originally born in Lerwick, Shetland, of a Scandinavian mother, he led a sheltered life and did not see a train until he was twenty-one. Bored with the austerity of such a remote place, Goudie moved to Liverpool to experience the excitement of the city. He lodged close to the south end docks.

Goudie didn't fit in. Indeed, he liked to keep his distance from people. He rarely drank with any companions. A man of regular habits, he was at home most evenings by eleven o'clock. He did form one youthful friendship with a man equally passionate about football and together they attended cup games. However, the friendship waned as the clerk changed his passion to horse racing and gambling.

Goudie didn't dress outlandishly. In fact, the comment was made that his watch and chain were not of a quality befitting a man of his social position. Before he became involved in the crime, the odd supper party or occasional visit to the theatre were his only entertainment. Weekends were spent at home reading and smoking his pipe. All in all, he was a man most unlikely to be involved in a major fraud.

However, Goudie also lived another life, dramatically different to the drab routine of a frugal bank clerk. To his betting friends, he was known as Peterson. He frequently placed large bets on the horses although to offset suspicion he would have others put the bets on for him, since bank clerks were not allowed to gamble. He often went to racecourses with a group to whom he entrusted large sums of money to do his betting. It was not uncommon for him to spend £200 on one race. He began betting on horses in 1897 and within a year he was behind with his rent and seriously in debt to a moneylender.

In 1899, Goudie was forced to support his gambling addiction, and attempt to recoup his losses, by indulging in some relatively small-scale fraud at the bank. He took the decision to forge a cheque for £100, hoping to use some of the money to win back and replace what he had stolen before it was missed. Unfortunately, his run of bad luck continued and he was forced to forge more cheques. By October 1900, he had defrauded the Bank of Liverpool of £2,100.

Although the seeds of Goudie's self-destruction had already been sown, his downfall was finally sealed by a chance encounter with a group of racecourse ruffians. On a trip to Newmarket, Goudie bumped into a couple of 'racing boys'. This was the term used for gangs of unscrupulous criminals, permanently on the lookout not so much for a good horse as a suitable 'mug'. The placid, naïve and nervous young Scotsman fitted the bill perfectly. The crew included a Bradford bookmaker called Thomas Kelly and a con artist cum bookie's runner called William Stiles, who posed as a rich man. After they discovered Goudie's occupation, Stiles and Kelly persuaded him that there was a fortune to be made through betting. The gang in fact cheated Goudie by pretending to put bets on for him. On one occasion, the bank clerk should have won £2,000 but when he asked Kelly for the money he claimed that Stiles had borrowed it. In a few weeks, he had been duped out of £64,000.

In order to commit the fraud, Goudie operated on the account of a soap manufacturer called Hudson. He forged his name on a cheque to an imaginary customer. When the cashed cheque was returned to the bank, he neglected to enter it in Hudson's account. Goudie started with small cheques but graduated to bigger amounts such as £30,000. About twenty-five forged cheques in the name of R.W. Hudson were issued.

The fraud deepened when a couple of other racing boys came up from London to Liverpool to join the scam. They had discovered the identity of Kelly's dupe and were determined to have a slice of the action. The team included a bankrupt bookmaker from America, James Mances, and a swindler, Laurence Marks. Together with a professional light-heavyweight boxer from Brixton called Dick Burge, the men hatched a plot to further fleece the bank clerk. They traced Goudie and confronted him, threatening to inform the bank if he did not help them. The hapless Goudie not only had to send cheques for bogus bets to Kelly and Stiles but also fund this other group of blackmailers. In a couple of weeks, the terrified clerk had stolen another £91,000. Burge and Mances were involved in cashing the cheques in London. Burge received £38,500, Mances £36,750 and Marks £15,000. Goudie ended up with about £750, which he predictably lost on the horses.

Goudie began to spread the frauds over the accounts of several firms. These accounts were in the ledger for which Goudie had responsibility. When the cheques, having been paid, were returned to Liverpool to be debited to the various accounts, Goudie would simply omit their entry in the ledger while also destroying the cheques. He thereby created a huge hole in the accounts and it was only a matter of time before it was discovered. It was common practice for banks to furnish their London agents with a list of the cheques cashed. One particular list sent from the Bank of Liverpool to London was returned as incorrect as it failed to mention a cheque for a substantial sum. Goudie was questioned but explained away the single discrepancy as a mistake.

The fraud could well have continued for a lot longer but one day the bank manager asked to see Goudie. It was over some trivial matter but the clerk was afraid that the game was up. He decided to flee from his desk on Thursday, November 21. It was speculated whether he intended in the future to attempt one final swindle before going missing. Clearly when he went on the run he was totally unprepared; he even left his hat behind. His belongings were left at his lodgings while his personal savings of £600 lay untouched in another bank in the south end of the city.

Goudie's description, together with details of a £250 reward, was circulated throughout the country, particularly to hotels and shipping offices. Amateur detectives by the thousand contacted Liverpool police with suspected sightings and suggestions as to where he might be hiding. London, Paris and Brazil were amongst the fanciful locations identified. A suicide theory gained hold but was replaced by the belief that Goudie had already escaped Liverpool and was very much alive. A man answering to his description did board a small vessel and was supposed to have hidden in her bows but a search failed to find the stowaway. It was then believed that Goudie had stayed in Liverpool all day Friday when his description had not yet been issued to the public. Information was also received that he was in the habit of carrying around a large sum of money. This emergency stash of £5 notes had been sewn into the lining of his waistcoat.

What actually happened was that while his ledgers were being examined on November 21, Goudie ran hatless via Back Castle

Street to the Old Ropery and sheltered in a dock gateman's hut. Explaining that he had lost his own headgear in a rush to see some friends, Goudie asked the gateman for the use of a cap that was hanging up. He then left the hut and remained about the docks until evening when he visited an accomplice called John Aitken, a clerk in a betting club. Together with Aitken and a bookie's runner, Goudie went to Park Lane to buy some clothing to aid his disguise. The men took Goudie to the overhead railway and accompanied him on a trip to Seaforth where they left him to make his own way.

The next day, posing as a seaman by the name of Johnson, Goudie obtained lodgings with the Harding family in an artisan's cottage in Bootle. Mr Harding was a crane driver with the Mersey Docks and Harbour Board. The rent of his house was a bit beyond his wages and for this reason he let out his upper and lower front rooms. The house was situated as far as possible from Goudie's regular lodging in the south end of the city. This gave him some anonymity. Also, whereas Goudie normally lived in a respectable neighbourhood, his Bootle accommodation was in a rougher part of town, not the sort of place where a bank clerk would normally choose to stay. The place was in a secluded cul-de-sac, tucked away from road traffic. It provided Goudie with a degree of obscurity, despite being only half a mile from the local police station. The cottage was situated at the foot of Miller's Bridge, which shadowed the house and provided a welcome degree of cover. Most importantly, the hideout was near to the docks in case he needed to make a quick escape.

After one night, Goudie left suddenly, saying that he was going to board a ship. He then went missing for four days before returning to the same lodging. It seems that he was checking out accommodation in Southport but thought that the place was too small. He informed the Harding family that he was unable to sail as he had fallen on deck and injured his leg. The supposed injury gave Goudie the perfect excuse for no longer venturing outdoors. Instead, he lay on the couch in his reasonably comfortable front room or on his bed, no doubt staring with a heavy heart at the motto pinned on the wall: 'Ills have no weight and tears no bitterness.' So agitated and strange was he in his behaviour that Mrs Harding feared that her lodger would commit suicide.

On the evening of November 28, a man claiming to be a doctor visited Goudie. Mrs Harding, however, had her doubts about this mysterious visitor, who was in fact Goudie's friend, John Aitken. Being aware from the newspapers and posters that there was a man on the run, a train of suspicion led her to inform the police about her lodger. A photograph of Goudie printed in the newspaper bore some similarity but the poor woman was still full of doubts. It was she who had purchased, at Goudie's request, some warm underwear. The rough undershirts were not the type that would normally be worn by a bank clerk, but, of course, Goudie was passing himself off as a seaman. Nevertheless, it seems that the clerk, who of course came from the cold north, had a preference for rough underwear, even for work. This fact didn't go down well with his colleagues at the bank who thought that he dressed far below his station.

When James Cumming, the Chief Constable of Bootle, learned of Goudie's whereabouts he immediately sent two detectives to arrest him. On Monday, the Bootle borough police found their man in bed. He had a stash of about £278 and a supply of clothing suitable for a lengthy sea voyage. What the unkempt but clever Goudie didn't have on him was any sort of written identification that would betray him to the authorities. However, his boots were at the foot of the bed. They bore the maker's name, which tallied with the description the officers had been given. As Goudie opened his mouth to speak, he displayed his artificial teeth, a further clue as to his real identity. A dejected Goudie knew the game was up. 'I am the man you are seeking,' he admitted. Later, a representative of the bank properly identified him.

Less than two days after Goudie's arrest, the pioneer British filmmakers Mitchell and Kenyon staged the world's first crime reconstruction. Using the actual location and some of the individuals involved, the filmmakers showed Mrs Harding going to the police to inform on her lodger. Another shot showed an actor playing Goudie being escorted from the house by two plain-clothed policemen.

Mr and Mrs Harding later gave an exclusive interview to the *Liverpool Mercury* newspaper, revealing their suspicions about their lodger. They claimed that when they alerted the authorities they did so out of a sense of duty rather than in hope of the reward. They even refused cash offers to be photographed and tried to stop their home being sketched by the newspapers. The police had tried to keep the couple's identity a secret but the sight of uniformed officers constantly coming and going attracted a large crowd and threw an unwelcome spotlight on the family. Word soon spread and the Hardings provoked the hostility of neighbours who did not like living near to a 'grass'. A policeman had to be stationed on Miller's Bridge with special responsibility to protect the family. However, despite initial reluctance, the Hardings eventually claimed their reward. Their home was later wrecked and the family had to flee.

The details of the embezzler's arrest were wired to New Scotland Yard in London. The reply was that officers would be sent to take Goudie back by train to the capital for trial. On his way to the Dale Street lock-up, the prisoner told a detective, 'There was only one man in the world who knew where I was, John Aitken.' Little did he know that it was the woman with whom he lodged who finally blew his cover, even though Aitken had only a few shillings in his possession and could have done with the reward.

It was believed that Goudie's accomplice, Laurence Marks, jumped overboard on a ship bound for Folkestone from Boulogne. He had originally fled to the Continent but sent telegraphs to his friends and the police promising his return to England. Luggage labelled with his name was left on the boat and it was concluded that he had jumped into the sea rather than face the consequences of his crime. When a steward opened the luggage he found a note expressing the owner's intention of committing suicide. However it was also suggested that Marks employed a man to board the ship and leave the luggage in order to hoodwink the French police. Nobody on the vessel saw anybody jump. Mances also escaped. He was last seen in France in November 1901.

In February 1902, Goudie and the fraudsters stood trial and were found guilty. The judge passed sentence on the bank clerk by making the following point: 'You have not the ordinary excuse which so many criminals have that necessity drove you to crime. There was no necessity.' The judge added that he did not know whether to marvel more at 'the wickedness of Goudie's folly or the folly of his wickedness'. The fact that Goudie benefited little from the fraud was of no consequence. He was sent to Parkhurst, on the Isle of Wight, for ten years with hard labour. He eventually became prison librarian but developed a heart infection and a gastric ulcer and died in custody in 1907, aged thirty-four. The only mourners at his funeral were a prison officer, a curate and an undertaker. Upon discovering who was being buried, a lady who was visiting the cemetery bought some flowers to place on the coffin.

Kelly and Stiles were found guilty of conspiracy and let off lightly with sentences of two years' imprisonment. Burge, however, also received ten years with hard labour. As proof that malefactors can change, on his release from prison Burge became a well-known figure in the sporting world. The lengthy sentence ruined his own boxing aspirations but after his release he became a top boxing promoter, putting on title fights in Liverpool and London. At the outbreak of the First World War, he enlisted in the Sportmen's Battalion and was quickly promoted to sergeant. He put on many charity concerts and exhibitions for the Red Cross and injured troops before dying of pneumonia in 1918.

In February 1902, Liverpool was rocked by another fraud case, although a much smaller version of the one committed by Goudie. The case began twelve months earlier with George Gibson, a nineteen-year-old clerk working at a shipping office in South Castle Street. One of his duties was to collect considerable sums of money and bring them to the cashier to be entered into the books. However, the clerk made friends with two older men, Arthur and Frederick Spragg, described as undesirable types not unknown to the police. The brothers led the young man astray, first taking him to billiard halls where Gibson was seen to spend more money than he could ever have earned. The three men were next seen almost every night gambling at the casinos of major hotels.

The brothers then told the young man that they had an infallible system of betting on the horses. Arthur Spragg was in fact a travelling bookmaker. Gibson was told that they could make huge sums of money if only they had enough cash to speculate. The system was an old one and said by experts to invariably fail.

It involved doubling the bet on every loser. Gibson agreed to fund the system by taking the firm's money that he should have cashed in. He started with small amounts but over the months he graduated to taking bigger sums such as £100. Soon he had stolen nearly £1,000.

Inevitably, the shipping firm's books did not balance and Gibson became suspicious that an audit would soon take place. Like Goudie, he decided to flee, as did his two companions. One brother went to London and the other to Smethwick, near Birmingham, taking the young clerk with him. Detectives searched high and low around Liverpool but eventually received information of the men's whereabouts. Contact with detectives in Birmingham and London led to all three men being arrested.

The Liverpool Bank Fraud and the shipping office swindle were exceptional crimes, both in the amounts of money stolen and the reasons behind the theft. Unlike most Liverpool crime at the time, both frauds seem to have been motivated by greed and an addiction to gambling rather than abject poverty. Making money through embezzlement involves a certain amount of ingenuity, nerve and sheer brass front to carry off the deception.

Perhaps a simpler way to make money is to literally make your own money.

5

Coining Gangs

COINING, OR MAKING counterfeit money, was a popular offence with a long history. However, the crime was viewed as despicable by both the authorities and the ordinary people who were being defrauded. In its most primitive form the scam involved making a plaster of Paris mould of a coin and filling it with heavy metal. In Victorian times, pewter mugs, stolen from alehouses, were often used as a source of material. The dud coins would then be sold on to gangs of 'smashers', many of them women, who would pass them on to shopkeepers. Articles would be bought that required change from the dud coin.

In a nice irony, the public houses that supplied the base metal would sometimes find themselves victims of the racket and would end up with the missing pewter mug returned as a fake half-crown. Some shopkeepers nailed such coins to the counter in order to deter future attempts at fraud. The smashers were careful not to walk around with too much fake money. Being caught with a single dud coin could be explained away; having a pocketful would lead to a lengthy sentence.

Raids on the premises of coiners could be as dramatic as modern day drug raids. The coiners would attempt to destroy evidence of their activities while the door was being broken down. They would smash the moulds and throw newly made coins into the fire to melt. Sometimes the police were greeted by molten metal being thrown at them or they would be attacked with chairs to buy time while evidence was destroyed. However, in Liverpool, most coiners seem to have gone quietly, admitting their guilt at the nearest opportunity. Female partners of coiners would often plead that they were working under their husband's direction in order to escape responsibility for the crime.

The ploy didn't work for the wife of Jimmy Carroll, the so-called 'King of the Coiners'. In 1880, Elizabeth was imprisoned for ten years for carrying a 'bucket', or bag, of her husband's fakes. She was spotted touring the shops around Heyworth Street, dishing out base florins to a team of smashers. One of the gang failed to keep 'nix' for the 'Ds' (detectives). The Carrolls came to Liverpool from Dublin and soon set themselves up as expert counterfeiters around the Scotland Road area. It was a family affair. Carroll's three daughters, Catherine, Susan and Ellen, also had criminal records for coining offences. In one raid on a house off Vauxhall Road, Ellen was caught trying to flush the evidence down a drain. In 1890, seventy-two-year-old Jimmy, not long released from his own ten-year stretch, was again arrested for possession of some poorly made half-crowns. The magistrate felt that the elderly man had lost his touch.

In 1892, another team of coiners appeared at the Liverpool Assizes. Ada Bedford, Catherine Burns, Thomas and Mary Lyon, together with Stephen Barton, were accused of manufacturing thirteen base half-crowns and attempting to spend two of them. Bedford and Burns were caught trying to use the coins and, when searched, were found to have more counterfeit money in their possession. The pair then incriminated Barton and the Lyons. Information given to the police led to a raid on a cellar in Collingwood Street, off Scotland Road, where the other prisoners were found. In the cellar, and also in a property in a court off Burlington Street, equipment for manufacturing the coins was discovered. One key fitted the doors to both houses. In a reversal of the usual plea, Mary Lyon admitted her guilt and claimed that Thomas didn't know what was going on. All five were found guilty with Thomas being recommended for mercy on account of his previous good character. The gang received sentences ranging from three months to three years, with Barton bearing the brunt of the judge's wrath.

Not even lengthy prison sentences could deter some hardened counterfeiters. In 1895, James Greaves, aged sixty-six, and his partner of a few months, Elizabeth Hodgson, aged forty-seven, were found in possession of a quantity of base coins. Greaves was a professional counterfeiter who had served two previous sentences of fifteen and ten years for producing dodgy money. He served only a part of the second sentence and was released on licence in 1894 only to go back to what he knew best. He was in fact a shoemaker by trade and could easily have found work but chose to put his skills to more lucrative use. Greaves was sentenced to eighteen months imprisonment to be followed by the remainder of his ten-year sentence. It was acknowledged that Hodgson was under the bad influence of her partner and she was sent to prison for only four months.

Not only coins but also paper money was forged and passed into circulation. In the early 1900s, a travelling bunch of thieves from London, including Robert Ferry, Stanton Strange and John Wallace, were seen loitering suspiciously in various streets in the city centre. Detectives put the gang under surveillance. A man called William Dixon was walking through Lime Street on his way to board a train to London when John Wallace engaged him in conversation and offered to accompany him on his trip to the capital. First, Wallace invited Dixon for refreshments at the Adelphi Hotel. He then asked the man for change of some notes to pay for the drinks. However, Dixon smelt a rat and refused. He then noticed that Wallace went off with two other men. On another occasion the tricksters were seen at the Princes Landing Stage watching a ship depart. A policeman observed Robert Ferry accost a passenger and ask for change of a £50 note. Again, the man refused to be taken in.

Detectives saw them visit several hotels in Lime Street. When arrested, the men had in their possession several 'flash', or fake, bank notes. In court, the men's defence argued that the fake notes were being kept merely as curios and were not meant for spending. The magistrate rejected the men's claim that they were in Liverpool on holiday and sentenced them to three months with hard labour.

A variation of passing off fake money was passing off dodgy precious stones. In 1908, Henry Richardson went into a jeweller's shop in Islington and produced a stone, which he claimed was a diamond that had come loose from his ring. Since he was desperate for cash he wanted to sell it. The jeweller had only £7 spare but Richardson offered to accept the money and return for the balance. He never did go back, and the stone, on closer inspection, turned out to be a mineral known as zircon.

In an economic depression, when cash was in short supply, the need to make money was more important than ever. As the century progressed, the technology for producing counterfeit money improved considerably. In 1927, police raided a house in Everton and seized a printing press, paper, dies, chemicals, an enlarging camera and plates used to make counterfeit one pound notes. There were even tools for creating watermarks. As the detectives raided the property, a sheaf of notes had just rolled off the press. One man attempted to escape but was caught by a squad of officers who had surrounded the premises. When searched, he was found to have fifty-two fake notes in his possession. In the house, his accomplice could only state, 'What can I say? It's all here for you.' The men were part of a professional team that had been operating nationally for about two months. In one of their pockets was a letter, addressed from London and signed by a mysterious figure called 'M'. It read: 'Those things were too wet for disposal last Saturday. We dried them on Sunday. We stopped working in Sheffield and we moved here on Monday, and shall be home on Friday to prepare those others for Glasgow.' Four men were imprisoned for their part in the operation.

Upper-Pitt Street, off Great George Street, was the location of another coining factory. When police raided a lodging house in 1929 they found four men sitting around a glowing fire on which sat an iron pan full of molten metal and a ladle. In front of the fire were three plaster moulds containing five counterfeit half-crowns in the process of cooling off. One man was sentenced to three years for making the fakes while his companions received twelve months for being in possession of the counterfeit coins and the implements used to manufacture them.

Rather than go to all the trouble of manufacturing genuine looking coins, an easier alternative was to create tokens that could be used in vending machines in place of money. Obvious targets of this scam were cigarette machines, often found in railway stations or outside shops. The manufacturers soon got wise and fixed the machines so that the coins had to pass various tests before they were accepted. Nevertheless, some machines accepted coins more readily than others.

In 1931, the McNeil brothers were caught after a tobacconist in West Derby Road decided to set a trap after coiners had repeatedly targeted the vending machine on the wall outside his shop. The shopkeeper fixed a contrivance by which any bad coins would fall into a special tray at the back of the machine rather than pass through successfully. He had also marked some packets of cigarettes so that they could later be identified. The shopkeeper then waited all evening in the pitch-black shop while two policemen kept watch in the street.

Just after midnight, a dodgy sixpence passed through the machine into the tray and the shopkeeper quickly opened the door to find the brothers standing outside. The policemen then stepped forward and searched one of them, finding the marked packet together with some counterfeit coins. Putting aside family loyalty for a moment, the man explained, 'I did not make them. I got them off my brother.' He was also found to have some cigarettes, which he admitted obtaining from a machine in Walton Road. A search of the man's house revealed coining equipment.

In court, the police admitted that the men, both seamen, had very good characters but had been out of work for months. In fact, in 1926 one of them had been awarded a gold medal from the President of the United States for his heroism in rescuing members of the crew of a shipwrecked coastguard cutter. Nevertheless, he was imprisoned for twelve months while his brother received ten.

In 1931, several shopkeepers around Ratcliffe Street noticed that they were receiving counterfeit florins. Following investigations, detectives discovered that the money was being distributed through St Anne's Institute, a lads' club in Islington. A youth called McEvoy, aged about sixteen, claimed that William Clemenger had asked him if he wanted to make some easy money. The lad jumped at the chance and was given some counterfeit coins to spend. He was told to keep the duds in a handkerchief in case they rattled, a sure sign that they were fakes. Over the next two months McEvoy and Clemenger went out twice a week to spend the money in selected shops. Clemenger also advised McEvoy to pass off the coins to newspaper boys but the lad showed his moral scruples when he pointed out that those lads worked hard for their money. Eventually, Clemenger tried to get the lad to start making his own coins. He even offered him a mould and suggested taking occupation of an empty cellar. However, McEvoy thought it was too risky and refused. Clemenger accused him of getting 'windy' and threatened to find a new partner.

On 12 December 1931, William Clemenger and his brother Patrick called at Prescot Street police station. William declared, 'Paddy has told me all about the snide job. I have been in touch with a number of the gang and I have got these two counterfeit half-crowns from one named McEvoy.' Clemenger then asked what it would be worth if he worked for the police on the job of tracking the counterfeiters. A detective offered him £5 and expenses to gather information about the maker of the coins. Patrick Clemenger was also given a few pounds for his assistance. William then offered the names of four of the gang. Three days later, he told the police that three men were about to take over a cellar in order to make some moulds. Clemenger then accused a man called Healey of being the one with the motorcar who brought the coins into the city for distribution.

On one occasion, when the detective went to meet Clemenger, two colleagues shadowed him in a taxi. These officers afterwards saw Clemenger talking to a man called Connor who was later searched and questioned. He had in his possession ten fake coins, which he claimed Clemenger had given to him. For the police, the penny, counterfeit or not, was beginning to drop. They now realised that Clemenger was the very man responsible for making the snides. After a surveillance operation, police raided his house in Lower Milk Street, off Tithebarn Street, and found in the top rooms some plaster of Paris, moulds and other equipment used to make florins. As Clemenger entered the room he admitted, 'All right, the game is up,' although he afterwards tried to wriggle out of trouble by claiming that all along he had been working for the police on their instructions. Later, in his cell, he called to his detective handler, 'How is my wife. I do not care about myself. I am going to plead guilty.'

On December 27, Healey walked into Rosehill Police Station to give himself up. He said, 'I know you have got Connor and you will only get me later. Have you got Clemenger yet?' The police did indeed have Clemenger. At the Assizes, he was found guilty and sentenced to three years' imprisonment. Healey and Connor were bound over.

The success of the coiner depended upon the swindler getting the coins past increasingly alert shopkeepers. In 1932, Frederick Mellor tried an alternative approach, the very opposite of the usual coiners' modus operandi. Rather than make his own coins, he aimed to obtain ready-made fakes from shopkeepers. Mellor went into a tobacconists shop in Lime Street and told the lady assistant that he was the Chief Inspector of the Liverpool C.I.D. For added authenticity, he even carried keys with a metal disc attached, stamped with those very words. Mellor was on the short side and was acutely aware that he might not pass for a policeman. He therefore reassured the lady by explaining, 'The police have not got me for my size or looks, but for my brains.'

He inquired whether any counterfeit coins had recently been passed over, adding that he currently had a man in custody for coining offences and wished to see if the shop had any fakes that matched those in the man's possession. Mellor even gave the assistant an official-looking letter asking for any coins to be handed over so that an expert could analyse them. The letter promised that he would return the next day. The assistant refused his request and alerted some real detectives who lay in wait. Mellor came back to the shop carrying a large envelope marked, 'Private. The Chief.' The assistant duly handed him some fake coins and as he left the shop Mellor was arrested and later sentenced to eighteen months with hard labour.

When police raided another house in Burlington Street in 1934, they found in the oven a mould for producing fake florins and two tins containing warm metal. Moulds for making other types of coin were found on the hob together with pliers and a file, used for putting the milled edges on the coins. In a cupboard, police also found a block of tin and some plaster of Paris. The fireplace and floor were splashed with molten metal, final proof if it was needed that the house was being used as Liverpool's answer to the Royal Mint. The occupier could only say to the arresting officer, 'All right. I'll make a clean breast of it. You've got me.'

In 1937, the vending machine scam was still going strong. Three Liverpudlians were arrested after acting suspiciously around the machines in Tithebarn Street and Castle Street. A policeman observed the men repeatedly going back to the same machine for more cigarettes. When searched, one of them was found with twelve packets of cigarettes, twenty-two brass discs and a tool for flattening out pieces of metal.

Variations of coining offences never went out of fashion. In 1941, a husband and wife team were tried at Liverpool Assizes for a fake £10-note scam. Instead of trying to pass off the dodgy notes to shopkeepers, they used a clever alternative. The pair would buy something with the object of receiving a tenner note in their change. They would then deftly substitute the real note for their fake and complain to the shopkeeper, who would be obliged to take back the counterfeit and reimburse the customer with an apology for his mistake. The trick wasn't that good since the couple were eventually caught and convicted.

Coining offences were not the sole preserve of adults. In 1916, two teenagers created a small laboratory in a yard near to their home. After stealing chemicals and glass tubes from his workplace, one of the boys was able to coat farthings with quicksilver to make them look like sixpences. Also in 1916, a group of Wallasey boys would place the metal caps from beer bottles on the tramway lines. The flattened discs were ideal for use in vending machines. No fewer than forty-nine bottle tops were found in one machine at Seacombe. Simpler still, the following year a group of teenage girls were caught using homemade cardboard tokens to obtain bars of chocolate from various vending machines. In court, one parent explained that he thought the girls were making the tokens to 'play shop'.

In 1938 a gang of four boys, aged eight and nine, were caught stripping lead flashing from the roof of the Popular Cinema in Netherfield Road, Everton. One lad claimed that they wanted to make lead soldiers. His mate, the more entrepreneurial of the two, admitted that they were 'going to make half crowns'. In 1941, some teenagers found a tin of paint used for re-plating bathroom taps. They cunningly decided to coat some halfpennies to make them look like shillings before asking a soldier for some change of a fake coin. He realised that he had been duped only after the lads had walked away but he managed to run after them and hand them over to the police.

The ingenuity and streetwise savvy of Liverpool kids has a long history. Schooled in the bleak courts and back alleys, with the ever-present temptation of the docks so tantalisingly close, Liverpool's young tearaways soon learned to look after themselves.

6

From Guttersnipes
to the Black Hand Gang

WHILE THE CRIMINALS of Liverpool were busy devising new
and dubious ways of earning a living, their children were often left
to forge their own paths in the world. In the late Victorian age,
when pocket money was unheard of and food and clothing a
luxury rather than a basic human right, juvenile robbery and
childish scams were not so much criminal choices as a basic
necessity for survival. Typically, juvenile crime involved
youngsters either begging or stealing or turning their hand to some
dodge or other in order to earn enough money to feed themselves
and their families. Newspapers rarely published reports of
vandalism or gratuitous violence. Gangs formed simply in order to
maximize the opportunities for robbery, rather than to fight each
other. Poverty was the obvious cause of such criminal activity. Yet
as social conditions improved, crime continued and new
explanations and solutions were required.

Looking back, it seems grossly unfair that Victorian youngsters
were criminalized simply for trying to keep themselves alive. In
1890, *The Liverpool Review* reported a promising reduction in street
begging in London as a result of the new Juvenile Vagrancy Act,
aimed at preventing cruelty to children.[1] The legislation placed the
responsibility for the child firmly on the parents. Placards
outlining details of the Act were placed throughout the districts
most infested with young beggars. Twenty prosecutions
emphasised the seriousness of the authorities in clamping down
on the problem. The journal hoped that the streets of Liverpool
would see a similar improvement.

Research into the lives of these London 'street Arabs', or
'guttersnipes' as they were also known, revealed that some children
worked alone and earned between tuppence and sixpence a day.

They lived like adults in lodgings, visited the theatre and smoked and drank long before they were out of their teens. Some children took work as salesmen under an employer, even though their employer was sometimes their own age. Others begged in order to provide for their parents and these children were felt to be worse off than those who worked alone. Some of the lads were outright thieves, although they were often the nicest boys in the street, particularly those that stole out of vanity rather than greed. One young 'Artful Dodger' even picked the pocket of the policeman who arrested him 'just to show the gentleman, like, how it was done'.

Yet six months after the Juvenile Vagrancy Act was passed, the *Liverpool Review* began to see problems with its interpretation.[2] It was reported that a bright, cute little fellow was recently charged with begging in Liverpool. The boy was in fact selling matches and was more of a juvenile entrepreneur than a vagrant. He began making a few coppers shining boots. He then invested his earnings in some boxes of matches, which were selling quite well when he was arrested and marched off to Cheapside Bridewell. His mother's opinion was that 'a better lad to a mother never lived'. The magistrate agreed and discharged him. Such a lad would be ruined if he were put amongst the dubious associates of a reformatory institution, for he had the makings of a successful businessman. The journal felt that the arresting officer should have used his discretion. While it was right for the police to keep the streets clear of troublesome young vagrants who preyed upon the public, it was wrong to persecute and criminalize poverty-stricken youngsters who were merely earning an honest living. The authorities were urged to make a distinction between these two classes of children.

In 1892, a journalist spent a day at the Police Court in Dale Street, 'a dingy, uncomfortable, evil-smelling place at the best, but when crowded with the human refuse of the streets and the gutters it is well nigh unbearable'.[3] The picture painted was of absolute squalor, degradation and the utter futility of the juvenile criminal justice system. After the drunk and disorderly cases came the begging cases followed by the juveniles. Raggedly clothed mothers, holding half-starved babies, stood in the dock with their unwashed children. Against them stood the police, School Board inspectors and other officials. Each case followed a similar farcical pattern. A constable would take the stand and announce that he found the child begging or stealing or selling matches. The mother – it was always the mother or sister or aunt, never the father – would then be interrogated. The result would be a fine of half-a-crown with half-a-crown costs. The poor child, who probably never knew what it was to have a whole shilling at one time, was condemned to find the five shillings or face the consequences. Occasionally, the fine would be dispensed with and the delinquent packed off to Hightown in Formby or some other reformatory. The mother would plead with God and the magistrate to give the boy a final chance while the child would scream and beg to be allowed to return home.

The journalist concluded that in all these cases the root cause of the problem was poverty. He criticised the authorities for not allowing the youngsters to be educated for free with decent clothes and a full stomach. Some children were being sent away from school because they were not in a fit state, physically or otherwise, to be admitted. Others were sent home for their fees and never returned. Widows with a couple of children were hit doubly hard. The eldest child would often be kept at home to look after the babies while the mother was out hawking or charring.

It was therefore very difficult for parents who were out all day and night earning a meagre living to ensure that their children were not up to mischief on the streets. Boys and girls were being picked up when their parents thought that they were at home. Indeed, youngsters preferred the warmth, excitement and opportunities of life on the streets to 'curling up on hard boards or flags in a dark, cold, dismal hole of a broken-down shanty off Vauxhall Road or Marybone'. In such circumstances, the School Board inspector or Children's Shelter man was looked upon by the children as a figure of terror, as much the enemy as the police constable on his beat.

At the end of the day's court proceedings, the journalist witnessed a bunch of five boys 'sentenced' to Hightown. It was felt that they might as well have been sent to Walton Prison. Some kind soul bought the lads some scones and the sight of them devouring them was felt to be a testimony to the failures of the present system of juvenile care.

However, the same year, 1892, saw a major piece of social reform in the establishment of the Police-Aided Clothing Associations. The first was in Edinburgh, followed by Birmingham a year later. Liverpool was next in 1895. By 1903, 15,000 children had been given clothes and shoes. In one twelve-month period, between 1908 and 1909, forty ladies working voluntarily helped clothe over 3,000 children. This was an age when, as Liverpool firebrand MP Bessie Braddock observed, 'a kid with shoes was an event'.[4]

It was usually a beat constable who first identified a child's need for new garments. Once the officer had found out where the child lived he would inform his sergeant and the pair would pay the family a visit. After a thorough inspection of the home circumstances, a form was filled in and the relevant clothing provided. However, if conditions in the home were truly bad and the treatment of the child unacceptable, the matter was referred to the Society for the Prevention of Cruelty to Children. A prosecution could then follow.

It was up to the constable to keep an eye on the child to make sure that he or she was wearing the clothes, which were still the property of the Association and only lent out. All the clothing was marked inside with a Liver bird and the letters CDC. The clogs all had their uppers perforated with a pattern of holes in a cross shape. Letters were sent to pawnbrokers and dealers in old clothes warning them against accepting the police clothes. It was in this way that the police became the friend, rather than the habitual enemy, of many slum children. Yet the provision of education and free clothing did not stop juvenile crime. Young thieves were always on the lookout for new ways of making money. For those unwilling to commit street robberies, shop thefts or house burglaries, there were plenty of other opportunities for making quick cash.

In 1897, a couple of enterprising children took advantage of the education system to commit an innovative crime: stealing coats from school cloakrooms as the pupils were having their lessons. John Duffy, aged thirteen, and Frank Gee, eleven, stole fifty-five jackets from various schools in the south end. A wardrobe dealer and several pawnbrokers were convicted of receiving the stolen clothing. The boys received sixpence per coat from the wardrobe dealer or two pence from the pawnbrokers if the coats were tied up as bundles of rags.

Poverty and hunger were not the sole motivations for robbery and violent crime. In the same year, a stonemason was lying in a brickfield off Lower Breck Road, Tuebrook. As he enjoyed forty winks, he heard something whiz past his ear. On looking up, he saw James Caligari, aged fourteen, and John O'Brien, fifteen. As he approached the lads, he noticed that Caligari was carrying a revolver. The stonemason knocked the lad down with a single punch and confiscated the weapon. O'Brien then pulled out his own gun and fired, narrowly missing his target. Johnson succeeded in wrestling the firearm from the second lad but Caligari merely pulled out a third revolver and took another pot shot. Fortunately, the lads were not very good marksmen. The man knocked Caligari down again and was able to escort the battered lads to the nearest policeman. In custody, Caligari explained that a couple of days earlier they had found a purse full of money in Church Street and decided to invest in some firearms. The desire for a bit of mischief was as strong as the need for food.

Liverpool lads were as sharp as tacks. The question of whether a practice was honest or not was rarely allowed to interfere with their entrepreneurial spirit. On a cold wet Monday in November 1901, Mr H. Lee Jones, director of the Liverpool Food and Betterment Association, of Limekiln Lane, near Scotland Road, went on a midnight tour of Liverpool's rougher districts to check on how the other half lived. As he travelled along Scotland Road, Kirkdale Road and Great Homer Street, Jones visited the boys' sections of various lodging houses. The lads were up to all sorts of tricks. Some were involved in a scam whereby they scanned newspaper advertisements looking for jewellery that was offered for perusal without a cash payment upfront. Once the jewellery had reached the lodgings, the flash pieces were sold at even lower prices than those enticingly offered in the advert. They were never paid for. Alternatively, they forwarded the first instalment of five shillings for receipt of an expensive silver watch. The tasty timepiece was then pawned before they moved on to repeat the trick.

It seems that some children were committing crimes not because of poverty but simply for excitement. Times were changing and so was the criminal landscape. Whereas in Victorian times, children became involved in begging and street trading out of hunger and sheer necessity, as social conditions improved so did the motivations for making money. A report presented to Parliament in 1910 showed that selling newspapers was the most popular form of juvenile street trading.[5] In Liverpool, boys could earn up to three shillings and sixpence each night. While it was acknowledged that certain poverty-stricken families benefited greatly from this additional income, it was also found that the boys' cash was spent mostly on sweets, cigarettes and nights out at the music hall. Only a small proportion was ever taken home.

At the beginning of the twentieth century, the question of how to deal with the level of juvenile crime became a top priority. If children weren't stealing simply to feed themselves, the reasons for their criminal behaviour needed to be discovered. The emphasis shifted from punishment to finding out the root causes of juvenile offending. It was often suggested that it was the bad influence of the parents that contaminated the child, who would then simply continue a lawless lifestyle. Sometimes, drunken parental violence and neglect turned children into savages by forcing them to run away from home and live rough. Rather than punish these children, the legal system began to reclaim and reform them.

It was obvious to many people that children, even guilty ones, needed to be kept separate from hardened adult prisoners. Separate cells, children's courts and 'remand homes' where children were kept before sentence were all established. The Probation of Offenders' Act of 1907 and the Children's Act of 1908, the so-called Children's Charter, were the defining pieces of legislation. Children under the age of fourteen were no longer imprisoned. The Probation Act allowed magistrates, in proven yet trivial cases, to either dismiss the charge or discharge offenders on probation. This meant that children were under supervision and had to behave themselves for a certain period of time, not exceeding three years. In Liverpool, a special branch of the police was set up to act as Probation Officers. The Head Constable himself was one.

Holiday homes, such as the Liverpool Summer Camp for Destitute Girls, also took children from the squalor of the streets and showed them a world beyond their imagination. Nevertheless, it was difficult for some youngsters to free themselves from their dreadful experiences of home life. At one such camp at the beginning of the century, a visitor observed the slum children at play. She noticed an excited crowd gathered around some girls. One of them, known as 'Baby', had a black eye. After demanding an explanation for the injury, the visitor was told by an older girl that they were playing 'home'. One of them was pretending to be the father who came home drunk and gave the mother a beating.

For some commentators, it was felt that too much freedom from parental control was to blame for worsening juvenile crime.[6] It was as if poverty had nothing to do with it. In 1912, the first annual report of the licensing sessions for the Seaforth Division highlighted the problem of juvenile delinquency. In response to the report, the chairman of the committee asked what benefits were being gained from the vast amounts of money spent each year on education. Of the 142 young people appearing before Seaforth magistrates, only two could be described as ragamuffins. The rest came from families living in comfortable circumstances. The chairman concluded that it was an absence of moral teaching rather than poverty that was causing youngsters to turn to crime, particularly vandalism.

The influence of 'penny dreadful' comics was also cited as a cause of juvenile crime. It was commonly believed that these lurid and sensationally illustrated tales of highwaymen and vampires led children astray. In 1910, three young teenagers travelled from Bootle to Warrington in search of an aunt. Having failed to find her they were forced to tramp back on foot. Passing through Rainhill, they met some children going to school. One of the trio pointed a six-chambered revolver at the head of a girl while another ordered her to hand over a bag containing her dinner. The terrified children ran away while the armed robbers made off into the countryside with the food. Two constables were informed and chased after them through the fields. After a mile they managed to apprehend them. The gun was later found hidden in a tree. In court, the mother of one of them pleaded that she had never known her son do such a thing before. She admitted that he had lately been reading penny dreadful comics and often carried a pistol.

The problem of juvenile crime reached a crisis point during the Great War of 1914-18, when youth offending rose to a peak, sparking yet another debate about what to do with the city's young hooligans. In 1913 there were 1,565 prosecutions in Liverpool's juvenile courts. In 1916 the figure had risen to 2,508 and in 1917 to 2,774. Clearly something was going wrong. While many fathers were away fighting in the war – nearly 14,000 local men lost their lives – numerous gangs of unruly children were causing mayhem in the city. Unlike the crimes committed by boys in the nineteenth century, many of their robberies were not motivated by hunger. In 1917, a pack of youngsters were caught in Bootle after a pick-pocketing spree around Marsh Lane. To obtain change from a stolen ten-shilling note, one boy bought a loaf of bread and simply threw it away.

Some of the gangs were well organised, stealing to order from targeted premises, with a network of receivers ready to pay for the purloined goods. In 1919, a gang of eight boys was found guilty of a number of thefts from the south docks district. The property was passed on to a female lodging-house keeper in St James Street who kept what was referred to as a 'regular Fagin's kitchen'.

Vandalism also began to cause concern as children started to systematically destroy their surroundings. There were numerous complaints about wanton destruction, particularly of the countryside. In Allerton, boys trampled crops and smashed birds' eggs just for fun. In 1918, allotment holders complained that during the school holiday, young scamps would tear up their plots, not to steal the food but simply for the sake of it. Also in 1918, in fields in Prescot, a few miles outside Liverpool, over one-and-a-half acres of oats were either stolen or simply destroyed by four lads aged from ten to fourteen. When workmen on the farm tried to chase the gang, described in court as 'wild savages', they were pelted with bricks and were so afraid that afterwards they wouldn't go near the field. When the parents were informed of their children's behaviour, they merely screamed abuse.

In the late nineteenth century, it was argued that children needed parks and open spaces to play in and burn off surplus energy. Recreation was seen as a means of preventing crime. However, as the new century progressed, not even the parks were safe. In 1918, potatoes were ripped up in Newsham Park while in Stanley Park an epidemic of destruction led to a huge police operation and the arrest of thirty boys aged ten to fourteen. Trees and shrubs had been pulled down to build dens. Flowers were ripped up and bark stripped from trees. A small boy was asked what he was doing with a posy of orange blossoms. 'I was getting them to give to a girl in our street,' was his innocent reply.

Stanley Park seemed to attract the gangs. Throughout 1916 there were numerous prosecutions for rowdyism and insulting behaviour. The offences related to youths, both male and female, shouting, singing and throwing stones at park notices. A teenage girl was fined for flashing a torch in people's faces. Yet despite frequent arrests and fines, the gangs continued to gather. Lads would play pitch and toss or card games such as 'banker'. Street football in the Walton area was also a cause for concern. Fines were increased but it made no difference to the children who were simply entertaining themselves rather than committing serious crime.

Nevertheless, throughout the Great War various committees and conferences continued to debate the youth crime issue. Letters were sent to newspapers offering first-hand experience of the problems and suggesting solutions. Various reasons for the epidemic were put forward. Absentee fathers were the obvious explanation. The dearth of male teachers was also felt to have a negative effect on boys' behaviour. Street trading, together with irregular attendance at school, were seen as helping lead children astray. Comfortless homes, lack of religion, the absence of proper punishment and heavy-drinking parents were also seen as influential factors.

A great deal of criticism focused on parents. One newspaper correspondent felt that since mothers and fathers were mostly to blame for their offspring's bad behaviour, then they should be punished rather than the children. Some felt that parents should be forced to pay for the damage resulting from their children's crimes. It was suggested that some mothers were using the excuse that because the father was at war, the magistrates should therefore be lenient. They often were, although some magistrates feared that young delinquents were taking advantage of the policy of letting off first-time offenders. In 1916, a speaker at a conference on youth crime made the point that because food and clothing were being freely provided for poor children, some parents had given up all responsibility for them, including moral responsibility.

As with the debate over the youth gangs of the late nineteenth century, the arguments became polarised between those advocating stiffer punishments and those urging social reform. As regards solutions, more whipping was proposed. For some people, flogging worked and they had the figures to prove it. Over a five-year period, at the beginning of the twentieth century, 489 boys were whipped. Of these, 135 went on to commit more crimes. Forty of these were thrashed again. This time only ten were reconvicted. It was felt that the message was slowly getting through. Indeed, new powers were urged to allow teachers to beat children for misbehaving out of school hours.

In a letter to *The Daily Post*, published in 1916, one male correspondent was furious that whipping children was seen as the solution to crime.[7] He pointed out that although 'it is cheaper to flog boys than to educate them', some enlightened schools were actively trying to get rid of corporal punishment. The writer's own recommendations were to provide better housing, increase the school-leaving age, thereby keeping children occupied, and to encourage the provision of youth movements such as the Boy Scouts.

The scouting movement was seen as the great saviour of children. Lord Baden Powell created the organisation in 1907, largely in response to the problem of juvenile delinquency in Edwardian Britain. In teaching youths the values of leadership, comradeship and responsibility, the organisation played an important role in forging and maintaining a sense of self-discipline during a time of great social disorder. By 1913, there were 15,000 scouts in the UK. At the 1916 youth conference, a speaker proposed an early form of a mentoring scheme whereby a neglected child from the poorer districts would be allocated to a scout. The scout would become the child's 'pal or chum' and say to him, 'Come along with me; you don't understand life but I will show you the way to better things.' It was hoped that such a good example would lead children away from crime and that scouts would have more influence on deprived children than the police, since the 'guttersnipes' generally ran a mile from the law. In London, an experimental scheme started whereby each scout was encouraged to bring a hooligan along with him to meetings. In a three-month period, 2000 louts had been recruited. It is not clear whether the 'adopt a hooligan' scheme ever reached Liverpool.

In another conference on juvenile crime in the same year, Herbert Samuel, the Home Secretary, suggested that the root cause of the trouble was not wickedness in children but high spirits and misdirected energy. He suggested opening up the schools of an evening to organisations devoted to youth work, thus preventing youths hanging around the streets. He quoted Baden Powell:

> Now, then Mr Hooligan,
> Just send your boy to school again;
> Or 'pon my soul I'll let you know
> I am the School Board man.[8]

The value of the scouting movement in producing fine upright citizens was illustrated in an incident from 1910. Two men mugged a seaman in Manesty's Lane, off Hanover Street. William Carter and Joseph Manning, two eleven-year-old scouts, were nearby when one of the muggers rushed past, pursued by cries of, 'Stop him!' The public-spirited boys used their scout poles to halt him in his tracks. However, the man then attempted to bribe them in order to continue his escape. He offered Carter a halfpenny and Manning a penny. In court, Justice Grantham asked one of the tiny scouts whether he had accepted the backhander.

'Yes, sir', came the reply in a thin, piping voice.

'That was bribery and corruption', joked the judge.

However, the scouts were made of sterner moral stuff. After pocketing the money they continued the chase, eventually informing some stable boys that the man was a wanted thief. The judge asked the boy what they did when they caught him. 'We made him stand up against the wall,' replied the boy stoutly, amid loud laughter from the court.

However, the responsibilities of being a scout could sometimes result in trouble. In 1917, a Birkenhead scout saw a lad tormenting a smaller boy and went over to intervene. Losing his temper, he took out his knife and stuck it in the bully's ribs. As he sentenced the culprit to six strokes of the birch, the judge had some harsh words to say to him: 'If there is one thing abhorrent to the Anglo-Saxon race, it is the use of the knife. If you keep to the good old fists you are all right; but as soon as you introduce a foreign weapon – the knife – you cease to be an Englishman.'

That sense of Englishness was already under threat from another foreign source: movies about American cowboys and Indians. In addition to the absence of fatherly discipline, the cinema was seen as a further contributory factor in the rise of juvenile crime during the First World War. In the early twentieth century, the new technology of the cinema took over from penny dreadfuls as a likely cause of juvenile crime. By 1910, Liverpool's Head Constable, in his annual report, recognised the educational potential of the electric picture halls but nevertheless lamented that the petty crimes depicted on the big screen were being shown merely for amusement purposes.

The problems caused by cinemas were not restricted to Liverpool. Chief Constables from all over the country complained that children were stealing money to fund a Saturday morning movie habit. A meeting of the School Attendance Officers' National Association took place in Manchester in 1912. One of the speakers called for tighter controls of cinemas, which he felt were turning children to crime. He believed that youngsters who regularly watched films lost the mental effort to do well in school. Not only did the films corrupt their imaginations but the germ-laden atmosphere of the 'bug huts' or 'flea-pits' as they were called, helped spread infectious diseases. The speaker admitted that the cinema could be promoted for educational purposes but frowned on it being used merely to display the exploits of 'oily redskins'.

The speaker was probably right in his concern about Western films depicting cowboys and Indians. Around 1910, a gang called the Anderston Redskins would run amok through the streets of Glasgow, while in Manchester the Napoo gang used cutthroat razors to hack off girls' long plaits. After scalping the enemy, the hair was kept as a trophy. The lads, wearing trademark pink neckerchiefs, were a familiar sight around the dancehalls of Ancoats.

In 1918, a posse of three teenagers from Bootle lassoed two women in Stanley Road and dragged them screaming halfway down Rufford Road. One of the captives collapsed when she was released, while her friend fainted when she got back home. In court, one of the cowboys explained that they had meant no harm. They had tried the trick a few times on the girls from the smelting works and didn't realize that their latest victims were married ladies.

Also in 1918, four young members of the Red Star Gang in Widnes were arrested after a spate of shop breaking. After stealing oranges from one shop, the boys used the peel to wrap around a stone to deaden the noise of the sound of the plate glass window going in at the next shop. In court, a policeman claimed that visits to the pictures were at the bottom of the crime wave. The ringleader was subjected to an early form of an Anti Social Behaviour Order (ASBO). His two-year probation order included a ban on going to the cinema.

The movies were also blamed for the crimes of another Widnes gang calling themselves 'The Clutching Hand', also active in 1918. Led by ten-year-old Arthur Jackson, alias 'Chief Tomato', two of the boys broke into a shop through the fanlight while another two kept 'nicks'. They also raided a market and stole a huge slab of toffee. In court, the four mothers pleaded that cinema films had led their children astray. They had even visited the picture house managers and begged them to refuse the boys admittance. 'Chief Tomato' was sent to an industrial school for six years.

The Clutching Hand based themselves on an infamous gang that they had witnessed on the big screen in a film that left a lasting impression on many young people. *The Black Hand Gang*, released in 1906, tells the story of two members of a gang who write a letter to a butcher, demanding money. They threaten to harm the victim's family if he refuses. The film inspired many sequels over the years, including *The Last of the Black Hand Gang* (1912), *Detective Bonzo and the Black Hand Gang* (1924) and *The Black Hand*

Gang (1930). Throughout England, Scotland and even France, various Black Hand societies sprung up in imitation. In 1916, nine boys formed their own Black Hand Gang, featuring a captain, second-in-command, treasurer and other officials. They were found guilty of a spate of smash and grab raids on shops in Guildhall, London. The boys admitted to being inspired by the film. Also in 1916, fifteen lads formed a Middlesex branch of the Gang of the Clutching Hand. In some of the shops they burgled, they dipped their hands in some black stuff and left their mark. As they were sentenced, the magistrate reminded the boys of the bit at the end of the film when justice prevailed. 'That little act is now going to be acted in stern reality,' he promised as he sentenced the ringleader to three years' borstal.

In 1918, residents in the London suburb of Croydon received letters through the post. One read, 'Beware the Black Hand Gang will rob your house tonight.' Another stated, 'We shall have you yet. That dog has stopped us, but we are going to kill it. Look out for the Black Hand.' At the bottom of the note was a drawing of a stiletto knife and a mask. In Leicester, over a period of two weeks in 1932, more than twenty shops and businesses were burgled. In each case a typewritten note was left at the scene, bearing the message, 'With the compliments of the Black Hand Gang.' If the gang could not find any money or valuables, they would smash up the premises. Dogs were also enticed away, never to be seen again.

In 1936, at Wallsend in Northumberland, a ten-year-old boy was convicted of demanding money with menaces after an elderly widow found a note pushed under her door, signed, 'The Black Hand Gang.' It read, 'If you don't give us the money the windows of your house will go in.' At the bottom of the letter was a drawing of two crossed daggers. In the same year, Birmingham's own Black Hand Gang, consisting of ten schoolboys, broke into a factory and left behind a register containing the names of their members. Next to the signature of one fourteen-year-old was the word 'Boss'. Three of them also raided an office and broke into a safe, which they then hauled from room to room, wedging each door shut as they went, in a five-hour stand-off with the pursuing police. They were finally captured on the roof. Two other members broke into a house. When the householder returned late at night he found two of the boys sleeping in his bed, one of them wearing his wife's pyjamas! When three of the gang were finally sent to a reformatory, the 'Boss' struggled and yelled so much that he had to be carried from the court by a policeman.

Liverpool's own Black Hand Gang was relatively late on the scene and did not strike until 1941 (see Chapter 18). Nevertheless, there were plenty of other organised young tearaways operating on Merseyside in the lawless and often fatherless period during the Great War. In 1916, five boys, aged between twelve and fourteen, modelled themselves along military lines. Two held the rank of sergeant while the rest were privates. Promotion was possible for those who showed daring acts of bravery. On the other hand, if the sergeant failed in his leadership he was liable to be demoted. The gang succeeded in burgling one house but were caught red-handed the following night. In court, one of the sergeants risked losing his rank after displaying cowardice in the face of the enemy. He began to sob uncontrollably upon hearing that he was to be sent to a reformatory for five years. His underlings got off lightly with a flogging.

In 1917, it was reported that juvenile crime amongst Bootle children was showing no signs of decrease. The warning came during the trial of a gang of five boys found guilty of stealing one hundred pieces of oak flooring from a supply yard. The magistrate was astonished that the boys managed to take the wood, since an extremely high fence surrounded the premises. The sharp-witted lads had simply burrowed underneath.

If the artful dodgers could break into any premises, they could also break out of anywhere. A year later, a mother from Bootle grounded her young son after he was caught playing truant. She sent him to her bedroom but he absconded after stealing two pounds. He was caught in Marsh Lane and brought home. This time he was locked securely in the room while his mother went out. However, he again escaped after taking more money. His mother again rounded him up and decided more desperate measures needed to be taken. She stripped him naked, hid his clothes and tied him up. However, the young Houdini soon broke free and found his clothes. He then made his way to New Brighton with the rest of his boys. There, they were arrested after a policeman observed that they were spending so much money. In the cells, the lad had his boots confiscated after he made such a racket trying to kick down the door.

Nothing, it seems, could stop Liverpool's young tearaways.

7

No Surrender: Sectarian Gangs

IF STREET CORNER violence steadily declined after the demise of the High Rip, this does not mean to say that gang-based brutality disappeared entirely from Liverpool's streets. The early years of the twentieth century were often as bloodthirsty as the 1880s. All that changed was the focus of the violence. It must be remembered that thousands of Liverpudlians were born into one or other of the two biggest mobs in the city, 'I' or 'O', Irish or Orange. The lengthy thoroughfare of Great Homer Street became the boundary, a local no man's land, between Catholic and Protestant. Sporadic and explosive clashes between the factions became a traditional sport, with its own seasons and team colours.

By 1892, some people were concerned that sectarian violence was being underreported.[1] It was pointed out that a Sunday night riot had recently taken place, resulting in about 100 injured people being treated at the local dispensary. Weeks later, another Sunday night disturbance erupted not far from Rosehill Bridewell. Terrified neighbours stayed indoors as the factions fought it out. Several constables were injured as they made arrests, yet the authorities remained silent on the matter, leading to allegations that the police were deliberately suppressing or downplaying the news. It was as if such sectarian skirmishes had become so common that they were no longer newsworthy.

Sectarian fatalities, however, were always worth reporting. On 8 July 1901, Luke Crean, a coal heaver of Dryden Street, was killed in a senseless attack that may well have had sectarian motives but was also partly the result of a long-standing feud between two families, the Laceys and the Jenkins, who lived next door to each other in Adelaide Place, Back Roscommon Street. Crean was enjoying an afternoon drinking session with friends in the house of Pierce Lacey at number three. Crean and his pals had earlier tried to obtain work at the Canada Dock but had been turned away, so they visited a few pubs instead. The group was having a good time singing songs when a guest left the house briefly. As he got outside, Annie Turner jumped down the steps of the house next door, shouting, 'I am a true blue and no surrender.' The man tried to defuse the situation by asking, 'What is the good of fighting?' He then added hopefully, 'Have you got a few shillings?' A male voice from inside the house replied menacingly, 'I'll give you a few shillings.'

At this point the man returned to number three to inform his friends that the neighbours had just insulted him. Minutes later, three or four men, including the Jenkins brothers, burst the door of Lacey's house and invited the occupants out for a fight. Crean, William Brew, Thomas Maloney and a man called Singleton took up the challenge. The groups set about each other, with Annie Turner joining in. Emily Jenkins also involved herself by striking Crean on the head about a dozen times with the heel of her slipper. Turner then retired from the brawl to go indoors, only to return moments later with a hatchet, which she used to bury the blunt side in Crean's skull. As she did so, she shouted, 'You son of a bitch, you are beating my husband who was invalided home from the Front.' Crean and the man he was fighting, Thomas Jenkins, then fell into a cellar where they continued grappling until separated by the police. Crean managed to escape to a house in nearby Rachel Street where he collapsed unconscious.

Turner, who had hidden the weapon beneath her apron, later told a witness, 'Did you see the fight? I hit a man with a hatchet and if he comes back I will do the same to him.' She boasted to another witness, 'I have helped kill one Orangeman and I will help to kill another.' This is despite the fact that Turner was herself a Protestant. On being arrested, however, she stated, 'I never did it.' Crean died later the same day at the Northern Hospital. His skull was fractured and he had a large blood tumour above his left ear.

At the Assizes, Turner's defence argued that the blow was delivered in the heat of the moment and that there was no premeditation. However, his Lordship made the point that Turner, by returning to the house for the weapon, certainly knew what she was doing. It was also suggested that Crean injured his head when he fell down the cellar. The argument that Turner was only defending her husband was also dismissed since the man fighting with Crean was in fact her brother-in-law. The jury returned a verdict of manslaughter against Turner and she was jailed for fifteen years.

That same July saw a violent incident involving Orangemen coming back from a trip to Southport. Groups gathered outside Tithebarn Street Station awaiting the return of the marchers. However, some bystanders were there not to welcome but to attack the returnees. John Handley was one of a gang who rushed at a young Orangeman called William Parry, assaulting him and several of his relatives. In self-defence Parry made a running kick at Handley but missed and booted a policeman instead. When arrested, Handley admitted, 'I did it and they deserve it,' a claim he later denied in court. He was nevertheless jailed while Parry was discharged. During the fracas, Elizabeth McKenna assaulted Esther Bond, a relative of Parry, by grabbing her hair and dragging her to the ground. In court, McKenna claimed that her victim had provocatively thrust her orange lily in her face, although this was also denied. McKenna, a veteran of twenty-seven previous court appearances, was sentenced to seven days for being drunk and one month with hard labour for the assault.

The firebrand Protestant lecturer and crusader Pastor George Wise was a key figure in the tensions of the time. London-born Wise has been described as a 'short, stumpy, bespectacled, bachelor bear of a man, a monumental egotist, saint, demon rabble-rouser crafty politician – an elemental force uncontrollable even by himself'.[2] He arrived in Liverpool in 1888 and reinvigorated the Orange cause. His Bible class alone reached 1,600 members. When he was imprisoned for four months in August 1909, up to 100,000 supporters accompanied him on his way to gaol. Such was the breadth of support for the man and his cause. Wise campaigned vigorously against Popery and the threat of Rome. Not surprisingly, Catholics hated him.

On a late Saturday afternoon in April 1903, a huge crowd of Protestants wearing badges and flowers assembled at St Domingo Pit, Everton, to take part in a march to St George's Hall. The parade, accompanied by two bands and the sound of hymns, was organised by Mr Wise's Defence Committee. Half the marchers were youths aged thirteen to twenty, many of them young girls and women. The meeting proceeded without any bother or opposition from Catholics until a disturbance occurred in Commutation Row. The shout went up, 'The Catholics are coming', resulting in about 400 people breaking away from the meeting to dash across the plateau of St George's Hall in the direction of the disturbance.

It wasn't the Catholics but two Protestants who were responsible for the trouble. Frank and Thomas Patterson were scrapping and ended up assaulting a policeman as they resisted arrest. There were shouts of, 'They are Wiseites, let them go.' A group of fellow Protestants tried to rescue the men, bringing more policemen to the aid of their colleagues. This only inflamed the situation. As the prisoners were conveyed to the Dale Street Bridewell, the constables were violently attacked. Cries were heard, 'Go for them ... Stick together boys ... Now, boys, rally round and remember Derry Walls – no surrender.' As Sergeant Brown tried to pacify the angry crowd, he was thwacked on the nose, resulting in another arrest. David Dunne, the third prisoner, was particularly violent and put up a terrific struggle. The sergeant was now punched to the ground and kicked. His uniform was torn and he lost his helmet and stick. Superintendent Tomlinson came to the victim's aid and was duly smacked on the jaw.

Policeman after policeman flooded the scene to protect their superiors but the prisoner still managed to escape across the plateau to rejoin the main crowd. Here he was rearrested but not before he had thrown another policeman on his back, screaming, 'I will do you for getting me.' The authorities had anticipated trouble and had secretly stationed a fifty-strong reserve force of policemen inside St George's Hall the night before. These officers stormed into action, rushing the crowd, which now numbered about 2,000. Chief Superintendent Smith decided to use the reserves to draw a line across William Brown Street, thereby separating the arrested prisoners from the crowd. This inspired fresh opposition from the mob and the officers had to draw batons for protection. Some in the crowd were heard to shout, 'If the bobbies use weapons let us use them, boys.' Stones were then thrown at the line, injuring some officers. However, the line was held and steadily the crowd was pushed back down London Road to Islington, where they scattered. Frank and Thomas Patterson, together with David Dunne, were later sent to prison for their parts in the riot.

The year 1904 became a particularly explosive period for Catholic/Protestant relations. During the year, 639 disturbances were reported, with the police having to employ force on eighty occasions. Eighteen flashpoints were classed as riots.[3] On a Sunday afternoon in March, another George Wise crusade meeting in the south end was followed by a procession of about 2,000 Orange supporters. As the drum-and-fife bands turned into Mill Street, a crowd of Catholics waving green flags greeted them. One Catholic, armed with a knife, tried to make a name for himself by launching into the middle of the band in an attempt to burst the big bass drum. The action was either courageous or stupid depending on one's point of view. A riot inevitably followed.

Four men later appeared in court charged with attacking Tom Smith in Essex Street, Toxteth. Smith and a friend were minding their own business when a group of men on the other side of the street started shouting, 'Oh, here's one of the Leaghe,' before setting upon them. Smith was swiped with a belt and kicked while on the floor. He suffered three wounds to the head, a cut eye and broken fingers. His colleague managed to run away under a shower of stones. Of the four men arrested, only Charles Higgins would admit to the assault and he was therefore sentenced to one month's imprisonment with hard labour.

On 1 April 1904, some Protestants mistakenly beat up another Protestant youth. Later in the month, two Orange bands, the Sons of Derry and the Sons of William, led a procession of about 700 Protestants through Mill Street, an area inhabited by members of both factions. A man in the crowd, guilty of the heinous offence of wearing a green tie, was attacked by one of the Protestants. Again a riot ensued, quickly followed by revenge attacks. Protestants waylaid a Catholic band the next day.

On June 10, a Protestant procession entered Essex Street and loitered outside a house where three Catholic sisters were home alone. The girls' father was a Protestant but their mother was a Catholic. A gang smashed the windows while two men ran into the house and kicked one of the sisters in the head. The police apprehended the attackers but another man entered the back of the house and assaulted another sister in front of the police.

A month later, Robert Harrison was returning home from his work at the African Oil Mills in Parliament Street in the south end when three men attacked him. The accused were identified as William Thompson, James McCaffrey and James Hopkins. As Hopkins knifed the man in the back, somebody shouted, 'You belong to the Orange Lodge.' Two men went to the victim's assistance but were also assaulted. When arrested, McCaffrey and Thompson denied the charge and claimed they were somewhere else at the time. Hopkins admitted, 'I done it myself.' At the Police Court, the prosecution asked Thompson if he was a Catholic or Protestant. To the great amusement of the court, the bemused man replied, 'I don't know what I am.' The wise magistrate remarked, 'You are a very sensible man.' Only Hopkins was convicted and sentenced to five months with hard labour.

In August 1904, a Protestant band from Toxteth marched through the predominantly Catholic Pitt Street on its way to the Pier Head landing stage. It was claimed that the hot weather, and no doubt the accompanying bout of binge drinking, affected the marchers. There were frequent exhibitions of hilarity and bravado, accompanied by the violent hammering of the big bass drum. Catholic onlookers countered with hoots and groans, which provoked some of the marchers to break ranks and attack the crowd. Price Jones ran at a woman and threw a punch, which missed although the second blow thumped a child she was holding. Yet another disturbance followed but the police quickly gained control.

Later that month, at about eleven o'clock on a Monday evening, local residents of Toxteth Park were congratulating themselves on a trouble-free night. However, their hopes were short-lived. A 600-strong group of Orange marchers, aged fourteen to nineteen, appeared on the scene and chaos soon followed. The band and their ragged followers spread across Park Street forcing pedestrians to flee into side streets for their own safety. The marchers were decked in a uniform of corduroy, combined with the familiar peaked cap and muffler of the corner loafer. There was also a large contingent of basket girls in attendance. The loud beating of the drum awoke the neighbourhood and predictably brought out the opposition in strong numbers. Bricks, stones and missiles of every persuasion soon filled the air, resulting in several casualties. The skirmish was short-lived, however, as a large body of police soon flooded the area.

In November 1904, an open-air Protestant meeting in the north end of Liverpool led to serious trouble. At half past ten on a Saturday evening, a marching band playing hymns passed along Boundary Place at the top of London Road. As the procession reached Crown Street, William Waldron rushed at the marchers and attempted to stab the big drum. In the ensuing struggle he ended up slashing William Stewart across the head and stabbing John Tanner in the hand. In court, Waldron claimed that he was drunk and could not remember a thing but this did not prevent him from being sent to prison for three months with hard labour.

* * *

The year 1909 was a crisis point in Catholic/Protestant relations. This was the year of Liverpool's civil war. There were now about 173,000 Roman Catholics out of a Liverpool population of three-quarters of a million. In the spring, the congregation of Holy Cross Catholic Church in Great Crosshall Street decided to mark the sixtieth anniversary of the foundation of the Mission.

The subsequent procession on May 9 was bitterly opposed by the Orange community. They particularly objected to the parading of a life-sized statue of the Madonna and Child and other religious emblems. George Wise pointed out that this was in breach of the Catholic Emancipation Act, which forbade the parading of religious images in the street. The sectarian tension sparked by the march proved to be the catalyst for many other disturbances during the following month, as each procession and counter-procession provided a flashpoint for explosive violence.

In some parts of Liverpool, it was common practice for Catholic families to erect small altars in their windows. Throughout the middle of June 1909, houses in the streets and courts of St Joseph's parish were lit up with altars and candles while women and children sang hymns. On June 20, hordes of Protestants met in Juvenal Street East while rival gangs of Catholics massed in Juvenal Street West.

Confusion surrounds the events that followed. According to the Deputy Chief Constable, a fight amongst the Protestants escalated into a riot. It was alleged that swords, knives and iron pipes were used. One lady slapped another woman across the face with a wet fish. However, some bystanders claimed that the trouble was merely an isolated brawl involving drunken men. The police response was to clear Juvenal Street East. Seven hundred policemen, including a mounted division, swept through the street with violent results. The Catholic procession in Juvenal Street West, meanwhile, had to be cut short and the marchers escorted back to the church. The riot spilled into neighbouring Prince Edwin Street with bloody hand-to-hand clashes between Protestants and the police.

The hostilities then spread across to Netherfield Road, where an additional 300 police were involved. The aftermath of the riot was particularly damaging. Protestants couldn't believe that they would end up the victims of police brutality. The St Joseph's Catholics weren't too happy either, particularly as their procession had been curtailed. The disturbances continued into the early hours of the morning. House windows were broken and one property was set on fire. A mounted policeman was knocked down together with his horse, an officer had his jaw broken and another constable was stabbed in the back.

The animosity between the factions was at breaking point. Following the riot, a number of drink-fuelled disturbances broke out throughout the north end of the city. Particularly vulnerable were Protestant workers who had to pass through Catholic areas on their way to work. It was well known that carters were mainly Protestants and they were easily marked out for attack.

After the day of sectarian disturbances on June 20, Andrew Cathcart, of Pugin Street, off Walton Road, left early at five o'clock in the morning to go to the stables where he worked. Although he was a Protestant he was unconnected to any religious or political institutions. He worked with Catholics and there was

Molyneux Street, home of the High Ripper Bernard McCall, who was so vicious he even beat up his own parents.

A boy carrying jugs of ale for his parents. Drink was the fuel for many a violent confrontation in the rougher areas of the city.

A pickpocket at work in St John's Churchyard, in an illustration from 1891. Picking pockets was less risky than mugging and the gangs involved were known as 'bottling' teams.

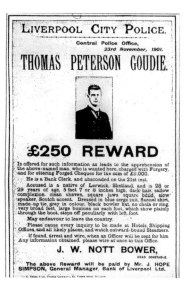

Wanted for the Great Liverpool Bank Fraud: a poster offering a reward for embezzler Thomas Goudie in 1901.

Dick Burge, the tough boxer who hatched a plot to fleece bank clerk Goudie.

Goudie being arrested in a *Crimewatch*-style reconstruction captured by the film-makers Mitchell and Kenyon. He was jailed for ten years with hard labour and died in HMP Parkhurst on the Isle of White.

Left: a young victim of domestic violence, which was all too common in Liverpool. Boys could also be flogged for minor offences such as, in the case pictured above right, for stealing two pigeons.

Street urchins in Scotland Road in 1895. Their poverty is all too obvious.

A cheery-looking juvenile gang outside 'Dandy' Pat Byrne's fountain in the notorious Scotland Road area in 1895.

LIVERPOOL INQUEST.

The mother and father of Daniel Ward (inset) leaving the coroner's court at Liverpool after the inquest on their son had been adjourned till December 15. Ward was shot during the Sinn Fein incendiarism on Saturday last when helping the police.

Above: Netherfield Road, the front line for many street clashes between rival Catholic and Protestant mobs.

Left: The parents of William Ward outside his inquest. The youthful William was shot dead while thwarting a suspected terrorist attack on the docks.

Opposite top: Bold Street in the city centre was rocked by three explosions in 1939 that were believed to be the work of the IRA.

Opposite bottom: Pitt Street in 1937, home to the city's Chinese community. It was once claimed that fifty per cent of Liverpool's Chinese were involved in opium production.

A wrecked shop after anti-German mobs ran riot in Liverpool following the sinking of the liner *Lusitania* in 1915.

A crude contemporary sketch of injured black seamen who appeared in court after the racial riots of 1919.

never any ill feeling between them. At seven in the evening he returned home with two workmates, Thomas Cookson and James Johnson. As they walked along Latimer Street a crowd, numbering a couple of hundred men, suddenly appeared behind them. A witness later claimed that she heard a girl shout, 'Here's three that were in the procession yesterday.' Cookson and Johnson ran for their lives, after one of them was assaulted, leaving Cathcart at the mercy of the mob. He was felled after being hit on the back of the head with either a length of wood or a rolling pin. Three or four men, armed with weapons, surrounded the poor man who tried in vain to protect his head with his hands. After a beating, a female Samaritan helped him up while a male witness looked on and did nothing. The man's excuse, revealed later in court, was that 'he had to look after his business'.

Cathcart managed to stagger but felt his sight leaving him with every step. He tried to take refuge in a bread shop, pleading, 'I am not an Orangeman.' However, the terrified shopkeeper turned him away and left him to his fate. The victim attempted to walk on but fell flat on his face and remembered being bludgeoned again on the back of the head. He regained consciousness in the ambulance.

When his sister visited him in hospital he was unconscious but muttering, 'Mean fellows, mean fellows.' He was later sent home. In a conversation with his friend Cookson, Cathcart explained that the Catholics might have mistaken him for a man called Aspinall, who was the leader of an Orange band. A few days later, Cathcart's condition worsened and he died of injuries to his brain. His last words as he put his hands to the back of his head, were, 'Oh this pain!' Two men were initially charged with causing his death but were discharged at the inquest due to unreliable evidence.

In a similar incident, another carter was attacked as he returned to his stables near Hopwood Street, off Vauxhall Road. After taking a few punches, the man abandoned his horse and ran. He had to hide in a loft until rescued by the police.

Protestant doors would sometimes be marked with paint in order to indicate that they deserved a visit from angry Catholics. On the night of June 21, a rumour spread that houses in Vescock Street, near Limekiln Lane, would be attacked. Appeals for police protection were dismissed by an overstretched police force. The house of a carter was stoned, leaving his wife injured. The family sought shelter in a neighbouring water closet until rescued by the police.

A Protestant family called Flynn, from Westmoreland Street, off Leeds Street, was warned in advance that they should flee their home because Catholics were going to attack. A thirty-strong mob arrived and proceeded to throw stones at the dwelling and smash the door down. Mrs Flynn's bed was dragged out into the street and set alight, along with her bedclothes. The next day the mob returned, leaving poor Mrs Flynn vainly searching for a policeman. The family was unable to return home.

Catholics living in predominantly Protestant areas were also at risk. The parish of Our Lady Immaculate in St Domingo was particularly vulnerable. The area had long been the scene of Protestant violence against Catholics. The parish priest, Father John Fitzgerald, outlined a catalogue of anti-Catholic incidents. In 1907, for example, a gang pursued two nuns, one of them flicking snot at them. The church had also been attacked. Vestments had been smeared with human faeces and thrown about the floor.

After the riots on 20 June 1909, a woman brandishing a poker attacked Father Fitzgerald as he tried to defend a group of children who were being taunted by a group of Protestant women. Throughout the summer, the Catholic community was under siege. A pregnant Catholic woman was also viciously assaulted. In St Anthony's parish, an area covering Scotland Road up to Netherfield Road, it was claimed that 157 Catholic families, a total of 833 individuals, had to flee from 'Protestant' streets. Letters were sent to some Catholic families ordering them to leave the area. The notes were signed, 'The Sons of Death.'

There were victims on both sides. In the predominantly Catholic parish of St Martin's-in-the-Fields, which included Vauxhall Road and Scotland Road, 110 Protestant families were driven out by sectarian hatred. A carter explained that his family had to flee from Oswald Street after 'several women threatened to tear the so-and-so bowels out of my missis'.[4] Nor were children immune from the hostility. A group of Protestant lads stood on a wall and urinated over some Catholic youngsters. On June 22, the pupils of St Anthony's Catholic School, Newsham Street, took on their counterparts at St Polycarp's Church of England School in Gordon Street. As news of the fight spread, aggrieved mothers rushed to the battleground to join in with their children. The affray was not an isolated incident. All Souls' Catholic School in Collingwood Street, a school in Sackville Street and a council school in Roscommon Street were all invaded by bands of armed women with scores to settle. Both children and teachers were assaulted.

In the heightened tension, a rumour circulated around Butler Street, off West Derby Road, that Catholics had burned down Heyworth Street School in Everton. It was feared that the mob was on its way to attack the junior school in Butler Street. Terrified mothers rushed to save their children, while a man with a gun also turned up to protect the pupils. On the other side of the religious divide, another rumour spread that a gang had travelled from Belfast to torch Catholic churches. After a meeting by the School Management Sub-committee, seventeen schools had to be closed in the north end in an effort to prevent an escalation of the terror.

* * *

The troubles continued the following year. On 19 and 20 June 1910, a house in China Street was attacked by a mob simply because the female tenant was believed to be a Catholic with a portrait of the despised Pope hanging on the wall. She wasn't even a Catholic. On July 10, there was more sectarian disorder in Islington. During an Orange parade, Thomas Charters assaulted Jack Minchella before knocking out Antonio Riozzi, two Italian Catholics. Charters, wearing a five-pointed star, claimed self-defence, believing that the men were about to attack him. There were about 500 people gathered in Clare Street, off Islington, when Mary Ann McGarry, with a stone in one hand and a file in the other, ran at the crowd screaming threats. Another woman took a large rock she had stashed under her shawl and threw it at the crowd, while a man ran around brandishing a poker.

On July 16, Mary Davies used a piece of wood to batter three young men in Hopwood Street. Two middle-aged women, one carrying a bottle, were also arrested in Soho Square. After being fined forty shillings for disorderly behaviour, one of the women turned gratefully to the magistrate and shouted, 'Thank you very much your worship. Long may you reign, and God love you, your worship.'

In the early hours of Monday, 24 April 1911 another senseless sectarian attack took place near Bibby's Mills in Formby Street, near the docks. The area was mainly Nationalist, although people of different religions worked happily together at the factory. The incident seems to have arisen owing to a case of mistaken identity. The previous day, about 3,000 people had marched to the south end. As they were returning home through the city centre at midnight, a chance meeting with groups of men going to work on the night shift sparked an ugly confrontation. As the workmen passed under a temporary bridge in Titchfield Street, near Scotland Road, they were ambushed. The marchers, both male and female, took the opportunity to throw bottles and missiles at the night men, perhaps believing that they were responsible for causing trouble during the march the previous day.

The workers attempted to run away but a whistle was blown, bringing reinforcements who eventually caught up with them in the area around Eldon Street. Weapons used included iron bars and pieces of lead swung around on lengths of string. A free-for-all fight ensued, leaving the pavement spattered with blood. One youth tripped and fell as he tried to escape. On getting to his feet he was immediately surrounded by a baying mob. Somebody shouted, 'Come on boys, we have one here. Drop him.' He was then beaten over the head and kicked. Another youth managed to reach Vauxhall Road where he was able to report the riot to a constable. Police reinforcements arrived to help the injured men, several of whom had to be taken to hospital to have their wounds dressed.

On Whit Monday, 1911, Joseph Owens and some relatives were returning home to a court off Prince Edwin Street, near Netherfield Road, after spending the day at Seaforth Shore. As the group approached home they heard voices singing, 'We are the sons of Billy and to hell with Popery.' A crowd then started verbally abusing them. Henry Hughes, who lived in the same court, rushed at Owens and knocked him down. Later that night, Joseph Owens grabbed Hughes while his brother, John Owens, cracked him over the head with a blunt instrument and stabbed him in the chest. Hughes was fortunate not to lose his life. A plea of self-defence was rejected and John was sentenced to twelve months and his brother to nine months, both sentences greeted with loud lamentations from a crowd of women in the court.

On 11 June 1911, a Catholic family named Carney were in bed when they heard a knock downstairs. The daughter opened the door only to be asked, 'What religion?' The girl innocently replied, 'Catholic.' There followed some sort of scuffle, which left the daughter lying on the floor. Although she appeared to have no injuries, she later died. Despite the inquest reaching a verdict of death by pneumonia, it was widely believed that she had been murdered. The family felt that they had been deliberately targeted. Earlier, somebody had marked the house 'Roman Catholic'. One of the attackers had apparently warned, 'There are Coggers [Catholics] here.'

That same month, Kew Street hosted the funeral of a Catholic youth. The lad had been injured in sectarian fighting in Bostock Street a year earlier. Members of the Catholic Defence League took part in the procession. A hostile crowd gathered on the other side of Great Homer Street, waving flags and shawls. The inevitable riot followed. On the same day, as Patrick O'Neill ran down Newsham Street he was tripped up by George Mortimer. Mortimer wrongly thought that the man was of the opposite religious persuasion. He discovered his mistake only after he had booted his victim six or seven times as he lay helpless on the floor.

'This was the most disgraceful assault I ever heard of,' remarked a disgusted stipendiary magistrate at Liverpool Police Court in July 1911. Henry Evans, a Protestant seaman, was walking along Netherfield Road North, innocently wearing a green muffler, the colour of Irish Catholics. The Orange district ran north of Netherfield Road. For an incensed Orangeman, a green item of clothing was like a red rag to a bull. Two concerned policemen pointed this out to Evans and advised him to take an alternative route through Edinburgh Street.

Evans took the advice but as he left the area a complete stranger called William Hilton rushed out of an alley and struck him so hard he was knocked into the middle of the street where he lay unconscious. Fortunately, the constables had followed Evans, witnessed the assault and were able to arrest the assailant. Hilton tried to claim that Evans had used provocative language but this was dismissed and he was sentenced to two months imprisonment. The magistrate found it unbelievable that a man could not walk down Netherfield Road without being attacked for apparently being of the wrong religion. 'It is impossible to think one lives in a civilised place,' he concluded.

Nevertheless, relations between Catholics and Protestants did improve as the years went by. In 1913, the Head Constable of Liverpool was able to state in his annual report: 'It is gratifying to be able to report that for the first time for many years the City was during the whole of the year entirely free from even the semblance of sectarian disorder.'[5]

However, as the Head Constable was writing his reassuring report, another threat was looming on the horizon. Sectarianism was soon to take on a disturbing new form.

8

The Troubles Escalate

AS HAND-TO-HAND street fighting between Catholics and Protestants gradually decreased in ferocity, no doubt helped by the distraction of the First World War, another sectarian threat descended on Liverpool. Throughout the Irish revolution of 1916-23, Liverpool played an important role in supplying volunteers and arms to the cause. Local families provided safe houses and escape routes for Irishmen on the run. In 1918, Sinn Fein won the Exchange seat. The so-called War of Independence, between 1919 and 1921, also saw the Irish Republican Army (IRA) wage guerrilla warfare against the British forces. The Liverpool IRA (Number 1 Company) numbered a few hundred members.

In January 1920, the Head Constable of Liverpool was forced to deny reports of Sinn Fein activity in the city. He called rumours of seizures of explosives and firearms 'gravely exaggerated' and 'misleading'. However, in a statement to the press, Councillor P.J. Kelly, head of Liverpool's Sinn Fein movement, declared, 'There is a Sinn Fein organisation in Liverpool, and it is extensive and growing. It is a branch of the parent society and we have at least a dozen branches in Liverpool.' Kelly was at pains to point out that there was no prospect of trouble at the moment and in any event, it wouldn't be Sinn Fein that would start it. Nevertheless, he did state, with an undertone of menace, that if trouble began, the difficulty would be not in rallying supporters in Liverpool but in restraining them.

Before the year was out, a massive outrage, believed to be the work of Sinn Fein members, rocked the waterfront area of Liverpool. Just before 9pm on 28 November 1920, the docks suffered seventeen separate arson attacks on cotton and timber warehouses. The high flammability of the stored materials gave the fire brigade massive problems and reinforcements had to be called from St Helens and Warrington. The fires were spread over the entire seven-mile length of the docks and were intended to cause maximum damage. By one o'clock in the morning, the sky was a blazing red colour.

Earlier in the evening, two men were seen acting suspiciously near a warehouse. An alert youth called William Ward ran for the police and gave the alarm. An officer arrived and questioned one of the men who explained that he was waiting for a girl. The constable became suspicious since the street was quite a distance away. As the officer went to examine the warehouse lock, one of the men whistled and the pair fled in opposite directions. The policeman sprinted after one of the men but when he got to Parliament Street, the other suspect fired a revolver at him. The bullet missed but hit William Ward, who had assisted in the pursuit. The nineteen-year-old, from Upper Harrington Street, was blasted just above the heart and died within minutes.

The gunman escaped but the policeman continued to chase after the first man. Suddenly, the fugitive threw his heavy bolt cutters over his shoulder to try to slow down his pursuer. He then ran into the crowd but was knocked down by a spectator and quickly arrested. Back at the police station, a search of the prisoner revealed a plan of the docks. It was later alleged that various marks on the plan indicated where the fires were to be started.

When he appeared in court the next day, with his head bandaged and sporting two black eyes, the mystery man refused to give his name and was known only as 'number eighty-seven'. The only information that he would offer was that he was a twenty-eight-year-old Irishman from Dublin and a member of Sinn Fein. He denied being a member of the IRA. He was in fact Matthew Fowler, who lodged in Birkenhead and worked at the docks.

During later questioning, he was asked, 'What do you think you are you doing over here?'

He replied, 'We are doing what your people are doing over there.'

Fowler denied that he threw the bolt cutters at the police and made clear that he deplored violence, although he didn't think that setting fire to warehouses was a violent act since it didn't involve the loss of life. Unfortunately, on this occasion this was not the case.

Three weeks later, a policeman identified nineteen-year-old plasterer Francis McPartlin as being the other man who fired the shot and ran away. At the Assizes, both men were charged with the murder of William Ward. However, McPartlin was discharged due to lack of evidence. The young man was not a member of Sinn Fein or any other organisation and had witnesses to show that he was at a dance on the night in question. Although Fowler denied that he helped to start the fires, he was found guilty and put away for two years.

In a separate incident on the same night, at Bankhall near Bootle, two plain-clothed officers chased five arson suspects, one carrying a bolt cutter. During the chase, one of the men turned on the officers and fired a revolver, the bullet passing through his intended victim's coat.

In 1921, terrorists executed a well-organised series of outrages across Merseyside. Just after eight o'clock on March 9, thirteen fires broke out simultaneously on farms in both Lancashire and Cheshire. On the outskirts of Liverpool there were six arson attacks, hitting Childwall, West Derby, Woolton and Wavertree. At Wallasey, four hayricks were set ablaze while in Leasowe three others also went up in flames. The fires caused no casualties but a fireman returning to the city was killed when his wagon overturned. Thousands of pounds' worth of damage was done. Five men were later arrested at Crosby, not far from the railway station. It was reported that one of the men was carrying a revolver. All were believed to be members of Sinn Fein. In April 1921, a glass-cutting tool was used to damage 400 shop windows in the city centre. In June, a detachment tried to cut telephone wires in Gateacre. When challenged by the police they exchanged revolver shots.

The following month saw a terrifying new phase of terrorism in Liverpool. One evening, about fifty masked raiders, carrying revolvers and bottles of paraffin, scoured the city in a fleet of motorcars. Divided into a number of smaller groups of between six to fifteen members, the men carried out a carefully planned series of raids on six premises in various districts. The victims were all relatives of members of the Royal Irish Constabulary and the auxiliary forces in Ireland. The raiders drove from property to property, lighting paraffin fires as they went. One house was completely destroyed and a family made homeless at another address. The men entered a home in Toxteth and, after grappling with the occupier, left behind nine tins of paraffin.

A seventy-seven-year-old farmer was also attacked. Faced with a gun, the old man picked up a poker in a futile effort to defend himself. He nevertheless succeeded in wrestling one of his assailants to the ground and only released his strangle hold when another man pointed a pistol at his temple and warned, 'I'll blow your brains out if you don't let this man go.' When the pensioner was bound and gagged, his Airedale terrier took over the battle. As the dog went for the men they simply shot it. Yet the heavily bleeding animal put up enough fight to drive the men from the property before they could set fire to the paraffin-soaked carpet. The dog was found 400 yards from the house at the point where it finally gave up the chase.

Another old man was targeted. A seventy-year-old of Tuebrook was faced with nine men. They had gained entry by pretending that they had a letter from his son in the R.I.C. The man and his wife were then bound and gagged at gunpoint and left to their fate as the house was set on fire. Fortunately, the man managed to escape and alert the police who put out the blaze. A woman from Fishguard Street, off Breck Road, was also tricked into opening the door on the pretext of receiving a letter from her brother, another R.I.C. member. The men seized her by the throat but quickly fled when the woman's screams began to attract the attention of the neighbours.

Two houses in Dingle were hit simultaneously. 'What do you want?' asked somebody in the first property. 'We want your lives,' came the menacing reply from the masked figure. Next door, the occupants were not so easily scared. The men ordered the family to put up their hands but an old seadog called Frank Brailsford had other ideas. The man's wartime heroics had left him with only one leg and a paralysed arm. Yet faced with a number of pointed revolvers, the old salt grabbed a sewing machine and hurled it one-handed across the room. The men fled.

The troubles continued. In 1923, police raided a house in the Irish quarter of Liverpool and found 10,000 rounds of ball revolver ammunition, a German Mauser pistol, a Thomson machine gun, various revolvers and ammunition pouches. It was believed that the weapons were intended for the irregulars in Ireland.

Meanwhile, old-fashioned sectarian rivalry on Liverpool's streets occasionally resurfaced with predictably violent results. In July 1927, during an Orange march through Pall Mall, it was alleged that one man left the procession on several occasions in order to prod the crowd with his ceremonial sword. As a result, Richard Greer was stabbed in the arm and chest. In Lime Street, another sword bearer, whose job was to act as an escort to the child marchers, claimed that he had been clipped on the chin by a stone. Suitably incensed, the man began to whirl his sword above his head like a madman while shouting and swearing. Unfortunately, he lost his balance and fell on his own sword, a mishap that caused great amusement in court. When the procession passed through Victoria Street, a Catholic called James Culshaw felt obliged to wave a green handkerchief, a foolish act that resulted in him being attacked by a bunch of angry Orangemen who broke away from the main group. He had to be rescued by the police.

Sectarian animosity became less intense as the years rolled by, restricted mainly to stone throwing and the shouting of abuse. However, from time to time terrorist incidents erupted which reminded everyone of the troubles still being played out. In April 1939, three explosions shook Liverpool's fashionable shopping district. At midnight, an optician's in Bold Street had its windows blown out. The metal grill was also propelled across the street and through the window of the store opposite. While police were investigating the blast, a further explosion rocked the street. A police superintendent then found a small parcel lodged in the shutter of the window of another store. As he picked up the package, it began to sizzle. He managed to throw it away before it exploded. Placed outside the window of Owen Owen's store in Clayton Square, a policeman found a cigarette packet with a wire running from it, connected to a stick of gelignite. The officer managed to put the bomb in a bucket of water. Fortunately nobody was injured in the explosions, which were believed to be the work of the IRA.

Balloons were often used in bomb making. In August 1939, Liverpool suffered a number of scares after unexploded devices were discovered in Lloyds Bank in Victoria Street and an office block in nearby Stanley Street. Sticks of gelignite had been parcelled with acid-filled balloons. However, the detonators to fire the explosives had not been included, leading police to conclude that the culprits were inexperienced terrorists.

A few days later, Dubliner George Whittaker, with his face bandaged, appeared at Liverpool Police Court accused of causing an explosion in Renshaw Street in the town centre. At just after eleven in the evening, Whittaker was seen with flames and smoke coming out of his pocket. He quickly discarded his coat, which then blew up in the street. Whittaker, a member of the IRA, explained, 'I did not expect the bomb to go off until 2am but one of the balloons must have been a weak one.' Over the next few days, pillar-boxes were blown up in Prescot Road, Mill Lane and Green Lane.

However, at the end of the week an innocent Irishman went into a shop in Toxteth to buy a balloon for a child who lived at the same lodgings. In the climate of fear, he was immediately suspected of being an IRA terrorist and was set upon by hundreds of angry men, who had gathered outside the shop. Windows were smashed and a few policemen injured during a running battle with the mob. It took half an hour and several baton charges for the police to rescue the man and restore order.

Also in 1939, a sixteen-year-old Dublin lad called Brendan Behan, later to become an acclaimed writer, was caught in Liverpool in possession of explosives intended to cause bloodshed and mayhem in some of the city's biggest stores. He also planned to blow up a battleship at the docks. In December, a policeman went to a house in Aubrey Street where he found the lad in the front bedroom standing by an open suitcase containing a bottle of acid. Behan also had a part of a fountain pen in his hand. A search then revealed a quantity of potassium chlorate, sugar and some balloons. The acid was to be injected into the balloons, hence the fountain pen filler. After eating through the rubber and coming into contact with the other ingredients, the chemical mix would cause an almighty explosion.

Giving the name of Peter Russell, the youth claimed that he was a painter working at Cammell Laird shipyard. He explained that the white powder was for his ears and produced a doctor's note in support. However, he then admitted that he was a member of the IRA and declared that given the chance he would blow up the place. He allegedly admitted, 'I have been sent over to take the place of Chris Kenneally, Nick Lynch and the others, who have been arrested. I was to reorganise further operations in Liverpool. I intended to put bombs in big stores, Lewis's and Hughes's, I think they call it.'

However, when the statement was later read out in court, Behan interrupted, 'That's a lot of damned lies.' A detective continued reading the disclosure, which went on to claim that the lad intended putting some of the bombs through letterboxes on the very night he was arrested. The statement went on, 'I would have put one in Cammell Laird's if I had the chance. I am only sixteen and they can't do much with me.' Behan proceeded to deny that he had made such 'ridiculous assertions', before launching into a political speech about regaining every inch of Irish national territory. It was also stated in court that he belonged to a family of Republicans and had joined the Fianna only to be later recruited into the IRA. He was trained in the use of delayed action bombs and had already been sent on a mission to London to make explosives.

The judge wished to know if there was proof that Behan was only sixteen, since the maximum penalty for the same offence committed by an adult was fourteen years' imprisonment. It was suspected that Behan was aware of this and took advantage of the leniency afforded to juvenile offenders. After being sentenced to three years' borstal detention, Behan shouted, 'God save Ireland.' His experiences of being incarcerated were later recounted in the autobiographical *Borstal Boy*. After deportation, Behan went on to serve five years of a fourteen-year sentence for shooting a policeman during an IRA ceremony.

The threat of terrorist activity never went away. In November 1954, the port of Liverpool was put on a war footing after the authorities received threats that the IRA was planning to seize weapons and armaments to aid them in their war effort. For the second time in a fortnight, the police strongly suspected that the IRA was intending to raid arsenals in the thirty Territorial Army centres spread across the city. Soldiers with fixed bayonets and sub-machine guns surrounded key targets. Plain-clothed military policemen patrolled in pairs, while every constable remained on high alert. At TA centres throughout the city, weapons not being used were chained together as a precaution. The doors of the centres were locked and behind every door stood a soldier with a rifle at the ready.

While tensions between Liverpool's Catholic and Orange communities simmered constantly throughout the late nineteenth and early twentieth centuries, there were also spasmodic outbreaks of disorder involving other religious, ethnic and national groups, including the Chinese, West Indians, West Africans, Germans, Japanese, Jews and even Muslims. Liverpool's tearaways would have a go at anyone.

9

Racial Unrest and Racist Gangs

'ENGLAND IS A free country where any man may pursue his peculiar tastes and fancies with impunity so long as they do not bring him into conflict with the law.'[1] Thus was the message of *The Liverpool Review* in 1891, which then concluded, 'But there is a limit to all things, even in England.'

What had stirred the journal was the tentative emergence of Islam in Liverpool. In 1889, Britain's first mosque had been established, albeit a small one in a three-storey house in Brougham Terrace, off West Derby Road. The religion had been brought to Liverpool largely through the efforts of William Henry Quilliam, a former solicitor and Wesleyan Methodist who converted to Islam in 1884 after a trip to Morocco. In 1892, the mosque had fifty-two members.

A service was held on a Sunday evening, open to both Muslims and Christians but a later service was directed at the 'faithful' only. Here, the Muezzin would shout the call to prayer from the balcony of the house. This at first brought abuse and ridicule from the curious crowd who had gathered but it also angered some people, who began to throw fireworks and other missiles, including on one occasion a snowball containing a rock. Women also had mud thrown at them as they left the mosque. *The Liverpool Review* had little sympathy for the Muslims. The journal didn't care what the faithful got up to inside the privacy of their own homes but for them to make public demonstrations of an 'un-English religion' was almost inciting violence.

At the dawn of the new century other groups came under attack. In 1906, the *Daily Courier* featured a hate-filled, racist report criticising the presence of the Chinese in Liverpool.[2] Before the Aliens Act of 1905 there were no precise means of regulating migration. The Act focused people's fears about foreigners, particularly those with a different coloured skin. In

1906, thirty-two Chinese men, with no guarantees of employment, arrived in Liverpool from London. This act of 'dumping' foreigners provoked a backlash, with particular concerns about employment.

In fact, Liverpool's Chinese community is the oldest in Europe and dates from the mid-nineteenth century. By 1885, the Chinese had started to settle around Pitt Street, Cleveland Square and Frederick Street, near to the south end docks. Until German bombers partly destroyed the area during the blitz, this district contained the hub of the Chinese settlers. By 1911, there were 502 Chinese in Liverpool. The area known as Chinatown was also home to Lascar seamen, Scandinavians and West Africans. Yet despite the fact that the city, as a major port, had always played host to different races and cultures, the presence of the Chinese in Liverpool unleashed a great deal of bigotry, prejudice and fear of a loss of imagined racial purity.

When ethnic groups kept themselves to themselves there wasn't much of a problem. *The Liverpool Courier* got to the heart of the dilemma when it warned that, as a result of Liverpool women going out with Chinese men, the English race was in danger of being tainted with Chinese blood. As proof, the newspaper pointed out that it was not uncommon to see women with hybrid names such as Mary Cheung! Since there were no Chinese women in Liverpool, the men had to look for partners amongst the local community. In his annual report for 1910, Liverpool's Head Constable felt that the 'lure of the Chinaman was also developing amongst working-class young women to their utter demoralisation'.[3] It was felt that young girls were attracted to Chinese men because they did not drink or beat their women. Unfortunately, the same could not be said of many Liverpool men. 'Harem life, or being kept in idleness and luxury', were an understandably better proposition than being kept as a household drudge and rewarded with black eyes.

The 1906 backlash against the Chinese continued with allegations that they even ate dead cats. A journalist's attempt to take photographs in Chinatown was met by angry resistance and the man was hustled out of the place. It had come to the point where an Englishman could not even walk in parts of his own country. A flurry of anti-Chinese letters soon followed in the local press. One man urged the authorities to 'root out these Asiatics, who cannot be reformed and who are the natural perpetrators of every species of wickedness'. Someone called Chin Chin wrote in defence of his countrymen, 'You never see a Chinaman the worse for liquor, staggering about the pavement on a Saturday night, shouting and brawling, fighting the police, and knocking a defenceless woman about.'

One eccentric correspondent saw Chinese immigration as part of a plot to fill the country with foreigners in order to make Britain part of the Chinese empire, without a single shot being fired. Others criticised the Chinese for working for lower wages, thereby depriving Englishmen of jobs. One writer felt that the Chinese were taking laundry work from Liverpool women, often widows with small children to support.

It must be said that apart from the twin vices of gambling and opium smoking (see Chapter 10) the Chinese were mostly law-abiding. They were certainly peaceful, although the odd violent incident was reported. In September 1910, about twenty Chinese armed with pokers and iron bars attacked a boarding house in Birkenhead. It seems that one of the men had demanded some money from the proprietor. Because he refused, they smashed his windows before leaving.

It was also in Birkenhead that one of the worst anti-Chinese clashes occurred. In April 1911, just before midnight, a Chinese man innocently changed his shirt in an upper room above a row of shops in Price Street, at the junction with Park Street. A small community of Chinese used the premises as boarding houses and general stores. The man was unaware that his silhouette was visible through the bare window. Rumours soon circulated that a man had appeared naked at the window and had insulted two English women who were passing. Within minutes a large crowd of angry men, motivated by misguided chivalry for their womenfolk, had gathered outside armed with bricks and sticks, which they used to batter down the doors, shutters and windows. The Chinese men inside resisted the invitation to come outside and fight and wisely barricaded themselves inside. Police soon intervened and calm was restored.

However, the next night the same premises were attacked by a hostile mob, numbering 3,000 men. The demonstrators were armed with bricks, which they used to smash the upper windows of the properties. The lower windows had already been broken the night before. One Chinese boarder was badly injured in the face by flying glass. The situation was so bad that about forty police were called to restore order. They formed a line and with truncheons drawn they charged the mob. The crowd was so incensed at this action that they turned their attentions to attacking the police. A dozen officers were subsequently wounded, one kicked unconscious as he tried to make an arrest.

Afterwards, the Chinese explained the hostility by claiming that it was caused by their refusal to give money to St Laurence's in Park Street. It seems that nuns were always pestering them for charitable contributions. Their refusal to donate provoked the anger of the mainly Catholic community.

Anti-Chinese feeling soon spread. Close to the Birkenhead Chinese quarter, a local man threatened to kill a Chinese man and had to be dragged away by the police, still begging for an opportunity to have a crack at his intended victim. Another Chinaman was attacked in Hamilton Square. A policeman observed a figure follow the man before knocking him to the floor and kicking him. Upon the blast of the officer's whistle, the assailant ran away but was caught by another constable. The man responsible for the racist attack was called O'Holleran, as Irish a name as any.

By 1915, the Germans had become the latest target for aggrieved Liverpudlians, after a German submarine attacked the *Lusitania*, an unarmed British transatlantic liner carrying armaments to England. On May 7, she was torpedoed off the coast of Ireland and within eighteen minutes she had sunk, with the loss of 1,198 lives, including quite a few Liverpudlians. Feelings against Germans ran high and during three days of rioting, 200 shops were wrecked for no better reason than that the mob thought that Germans owned them. In an orgy of xenophobia, front windows were kicked in or bricked as the rabble moved en masse through the streets. From Ben Jonson Street and Sawney Pope Street in the north end down to Great George Street in the south end, crowds spontaneously erupted to scour the districts for traces of the Hun.

For Liverpudlians, Germans and pork butchers were synonymous. One shop situated at the corner of Smithdown Road and Arundel Avenue was almost demolished and the stock either looted or destroyed. Women pelted each other with strings of sausages while one lady felt the need to scrub the pavement with a joint of pork. After destroying the ground floor shop, the crowd then moved upstairs to sack the living quarters. A piano was turned into matchwood and a large mirror reduced to tiny fragments of glass.

Messrs Franz and Co. owned a sweet shop in Chapel Gardens, off Scotland Road, known as the 'German Confectionary'. On May 9, shortly before ten o' clock, a crowd of men, women and children travelled from Scotland Road with the intention of smashing up the shop. Armed with sticks, iron bars and hatchets, they broke into the premises and almost destroyed the place. The sweets were carried away before the shop was finally set on fire. A crowd also attacked a German pork butchers shop in Bootle. The tenant fled, leaving men to arm themselves with knives taken from the premises. They tried to storm the attic where the butcher's wife and eight children were cowering. Once upstairs, the mob threw what they could out of the window and chucked filth around the rooms. After looting the bedrooms and cellars they set fire to the property.

Once shops were dealt with, the crowds moved on to target the private dwellings of anyone with a remote or vague connection to Germany. When the crowds ran out of Germans they turned their attention to the properties of other foreigners, including Chinese laundries. Indeed, anybody with a foreign-sounding name was particularly vulnerable. With Liverpool historically experiencing a constant flow of foreign sailors and visitors, it would be easy to think that the different nationalities rubbed along nicely in one huge cultural melting pot. However, there have always been tensions and outbreaks of hostility towards non-white faces.

In 1917, a Japanese officer from a steamship docked in Liverpool complained about racism towards his crew. Although Japan was Britain's ally in the Great War, one group of Japanese sailors was insulted and spat at in the face as they passed some women in the street. Packs of boys would also throw stones at them, shouting in mocking tones, 'Harrow! Jap! Come on!' The Japanese officer could only contrast the polite behaviour of his countrymen with the uncivilised antics of some Liverpudlians.

In June 1919, Liverpool suffered a wave of racial unrest that anticipated the Toxteth riots of 1981. During the previous four years, the black population of Liverpool had grown steadily. The labour shortage during the First World War led to an influx of West Africans and West Indians. Black people fought in the war and contributed to the war economy. Located in the lodging houses and hostels near the south end docks, the number of registered black people had grown to about 5,000. The area became Liverpool's own Harlem. The blacks formed two distinct groups: seamen and dockers. The seamen were mostly from the Gold Coast and Sierra Leone and worked on Elder Dempster liners. They lived mainly in the streets lying behind Park Road near Northumberland Street. Of course, being seamen, most of these were only temporary residents. A much smaller figure of about 500-600 lived and raised families in the vicinity of Pitt Street.

However, once the war ended there was great competition for employment and houses. Many white people believed that the blacks had helped to glut the labour market, once the local soldiers and sailors had returned from military service. At the end of the First World War there was also a growing assertion of British national identity and popular patriotism. Black people were seen as a problem and became scapegoats for the city's socio-economic decline. A month before the riot, there were even calls to repatriate the blacks since they were seen as preventing white men from gaining employment. Indeed, some poverty-stricken blacks dearly wished to return home. They argued that they were being prevented from working due to the colour of their skin. However, despite the hardships and racism they faced, they stayed on.

Competition for jobs was only partly responsible for the racial tension. The origin of the trouble was also likely to be the relationship between black men and white women. Some white women were boasting that black men were better lovers than the whites. 'Black men were best,' was the verdict of one Liverpool lass at the time. There had also been some long-standing animosity between the blacks and Europeans, including Danes, Russian Poles and Scandinavians (famous for their 'lobscouse' dish from which the term 'scouse' derives). On 5 June 1919, there was a serious affray between West Indians and some Swedish sailors in the area around Great George Square. The previous evening, a Scandinavian had stabbed a West African.

Tensions ran high between the two groups when they met in The Liverpool Arms, at the corner of Bailey Street and Grenville Street. The West Africans had banded together to gain their revenge and later that night the opportunity arose to attack seven Scandinavians. The men pulled out knives and razors and cut up a few Swedes. The Scandinavian Home in Great George Square was also ransacked before the disturbances spread to Upper Pitt Street, where several local men joined in. 'Come on you English dogs. I'll do for you,' was the shout from one black man.

As a policeman tried to restore order he was slashed about the face and back. Police assistance was summoned and the blacks, one of them wearing a naval uniform, fled to their quarters in Upper Pitt Street. From various houses, guns were fired at the police. One constable was shot through the mouth, the bullet passing through his chin, tongue and neck before penetrating another officer. A colleague was also blasted in the face. In response, the police raided a boarding house in Upper Pitt Street. At this point there are conflicting versions of events. It was alleged that a white mob had already attacked the house, smashing the windows before storming the property. One of the lodgers, a black Bermudan called Charles Wootton, tried to stop the angry crowd by swinging an axe. In a bold act of self-defence, eight men were injured, two seriously. Wootton was then arrested. However, the police version of events states that he was detained on suspicion of firing the revolver.

Whatever happened first, several black men armed with razors, pokers and knives, confronted the police when they entered the property. In the struggle, twenty-four-year-old Wootton escaped towards the docks. The police, together with a furious crowd of up to 300 men, pursued him. Wootton was helped on his way by volleys of missiles. He was eventually arrested near the wall of the Queen's Dock. As the officers simultaneously tried to detain him and protect him from the mob, the terrified man was forcibly wrenched from the arms of the police. Again, there is some confusion as to what happened next. Wootton then either broke free of the crowd and voluntarily jumped into the River Mersey to escape or, more likely, was thrown in by the rabble.

Wootton swam for a short time before sinking. Amidst chants from the crowd of 'Let him drown', a brave detective climbed down a ship's rope and was about to rescue the man when a stone struck Wootton on the head, causing him to sink. His body was later recovered with a grappling iron. No arrests were made. Charles Wootton had a pauper's burial in an unmarked grave in Smithdown Road Cemetery but his name lives on after a cultural and educational centre in Toxteth was named after him.

The riots continued for some nights, with up to 10,000 local white residents joining in the disturbances. On Sunday, June 8, three West Africans were stabbed in the street. The following day, blacks were attacked in Upper Stanhope Street. As locals surrounded a black man called Joseph Ankra, he whirled a piece of iron above his head and shouted, 'Down with the white race! I will kill the first white man who touches me.' Newspapers were keen to report anti-white slogans shouted by black men but omitted what white men must have shouted back. Although acting in self-defence, Ankra was arrested and fined. Another crowd of about sixty white men surrounded George Lawson, a black fireman. The terrified Lawson opened a pocket knife with his teeth and threatened the mob. Unfortunately he also tried to stab a policeman and was arrested. Nothing happened to the white men who were about to attack him.

On June 9, David Clare was amongst a crowd of about 2,000 white men who assembled outside a boarding house in Jackson Street used by 400 black seamen. Gangs of men, aged between eighteen and thirty, wrecked the building, smashing windows and furniture. A detective claimed that he saw Clare in the bedroom using a table leg to wallop a black man. In revenge, another black man threw Clare head first down the stairs where he was arrested. One white female rioter was heard shouting, 'Now's the time to finish the nigger's wives'. It was alleged that James Bray and Edward Murphy were also part of a gang that climbed on the roof of the building to strip slates to throw at the black people below.

The rabble tried to torch a house in Stanhope Street the following night. A property in Mill Street, occupied by black men, was also broken into. The furniture was taken outside and set alight. One mob chased a black man down the street before swatting him on the head with the buckle end of a belt. The Mill Street attacks were largely directed against West Africans despite the fact that the original trouble involved West Indians. However, the victims were black and that was all that mattered to their white attackers. Mounted police patrolled the south end of the city while a special reserve of constables was drafted in to maintain calm. Liverpool's Head Constable had to ask the local military authorities for help in finding accommodation for the 700 black men who were lodged for their own protection in the Great George Street Bridewell and fire stations. Seventy black men also took refuge in the Ethiopian Hall, off Brownlow Hill.

By Friday June 13, the disturbances had died down. Batches of prisoners, both male and female, later appeared before the courts. Many of them claimed that they were victims of mistaken identity. One of the accused offered an amusing plea of innocence. He claimed to have been drunk from June 9 to 15 and could remember nothing except that he was nowhere near the scene of the trouble.

Parallel to the disturbances in Liverpool, there were also outbreaks of racial violence in other ports, including Glasgow, Hull and London. Indeed, many dockland communities suffered from working-class racism. In Cardiff, the cause of the trouble was again the relationship between black men and white women. Blacks armed with revolvers and razors clashed with white men armed with sticks and stones. A man called Harold Smart died after having his throat cut open. Police were shot at and properties housing blacks were wrecked. At the South Wales town of Barry, which was home to hundreds of black Brazilians, a white man was knifed to death. In response, a 1,000-strong mob, including many women, took to the streets to raid the black quarter of town.

Not all racially motivated violence involved blacks versus whites. During the Second World War there were occasional dancehall feuds between rival groups of West Indians and West Africans. There were also skirmishes between members of the black and Chinese communities. Again, the cause of the tension was women, particularly white women.

Over a few days in October 1943, there were various outbreaks of violence, resulting in five black men being taken to hospital with head wounds. In one incident about fifty Chinese, armed with knives and iron bars, gathered outside a hostel for black seamen in Grove Street. Earlier in the day an armed gang of Chinese was arrested in Catherine Street. They were waiting for some black men to appear. When a policeman confiscated a foot-long knife from one of the Chinese, he explained, 'For black man. He took five pounds from me.' His friend was also found to be carrying a hammer. However, upon being charged, the man explained that he had the knife to cut some bread. His colleague claimed that he was on his way to a friend's house to knock in some nails.

A black man, with his head heavily bandaged, was arrested after chasing a Chinese man along Upper Canning Street. He brandished a revolver, which he pointed at a pursuing officer before he was disarmed. His excuse when charged was that, 'Yesterday Chinaman hit me with a knife. I kill him.' Members of both factions later appeared in court and were each fined £1. An optimistic magistrate hoped that their differences would soon be settled.

After the war, the focus of racial violence switched once again. In 1947, the murder of two British soldiers by Palestinian terrorists led to an anti-Jewish backlash from aggrieved Liverpudlians. In August, in Birkenhead, fifty slaughtermen refused to kill cattle for the Jewish community. Notices were pinned at the entrance of the Canada Dock reading, 'Death to all Jews.' Shops and property belonging to Jews were ransacked and looted over several nights of violence. Police engaged in hand-to-hand combat with the rioters, leaving several officers injured.

Police tried to arrest a group of youths who were standing next to a collection of bricks and stones, piled high ready for throwing. A volley of missiles greeted them. A stone cracked an officer on the side of the head and the lads ran away pursued by the police. A sergeant cornered a fifteen-year-old on the landing of a tenement. The lad resisted arrest with a struggle. As his mates appeared, he shouted, 'Come on, push him over here,' meaning to throw the officer over the landing. Nevertheless, the policeman was able to make the arrest. On being asked why he was carrying a stone in his pocket, the boy replied, 'It's to see you off with. You're all in with the Jews.'

In another incident, the leader of a crowd of about 300 demonstrators yelled, 'Let them have it,' and, 'We don't want the swines here.' After arrests were made, the crowd descended on Lawrence Street Bridewell, off Scotland Road, where they shouted, 'You lot of ___. Lock the ___ Jews up. Let's go and get them out.' Attempts to storm the lock-up were thwarted by the police.

Anti-Jewish disturbances were renewed during the afternoon in Myrtle Street, in the south end. Cooper's tailor's shop had been trashed the night before and a crowd, several hundred strong, gathered to see what they could pillage. Women and children entered the shop and scattered accounts books and papers around the street. One looter outside a clothes shop boasted, 'This is a Jew's shop. I am making him suffer. I have done this and will do it again.' He admitted that if he hadn't been arrested he would have continued to smash Jewish shops. Patrol cars were then called to Smithdown Road where there were more disturbances. A crowd of youths smashed the windows of a licensed broker. The Jewish owner, who had served in the First World War and acted as a warden in the last war, couldn't understand why he had been targeted. In Lodge Lane, a mob tried to prevent a Jewish shopkeeper boarding up his premises.

As evening fell and the light faded the disorder was renewed. This was met by an increased police presence. In all there were over 100 incidents of wilful damage, mostly in the south end of the city. A paint shop in Myrtle Street was torched along with premises in Crown Street. Fire engines were also stoned on their way to deal with the fires. A small wooden synagogue in Lower Lane cemetery in Fazakerley was burned down and the caretaker beaten up by a group of men. Shortly before midnight, police in Paddington decided to baton charge a crowd who were looting damaged premises.

Quite a few juveniles were arrested, much to the disgust of their parents. In court, one aggrieved mother told an arresting officer, 'You couldn't put your hands on the big people, so you got hold of these boys.' The children were mostly arrested for smashing windows and looting. An eleven-year-old dived into a shop and emerged seconds later proudly clutching two bars of soap. A sixteen-year-old explained to a policeman, 'It's the Jews' shops we're after.'

A few days later, during a boxing match at Liverpool Stadium, the shout went up, 'What about getting the Jews out.' After leaving the event, two men, fired up with hatred, entered a public house in Earle Street where a man was having a quiet drink. One of the men took out a cosh and clobbered him over the head before kicking and punching him to the floor. A chair was then thrown at the victim, as he lay helpless. Fortunately it missed. In court, one of the attackers claimed that it was only a bit of rough and tumble. Both men received two months' imprisonment.

After the war, feuds were renewed between rival gangs of West Indian and West African seamen. The West Indians objected to drinking in the same bar as the Africans in a hostel that both groups frequented. On a dance night in May 1947, a West Indian shot at a West African after the African had stabbed a Jamaican colleague the previous day. A police raid on the premises netted a knuckleduster, iron bar, knives and a revolver.

In July 1948, the south end of Liverpool was again the scene of race riots. As in 1919, the disturbances took place over a hot bank holiday weekend, partly fuelled by alcohol. There was also the familiar background of competition for employment, complicated by xenophobia, racism, bigotry and fear. The same old arguments were bandied about that the black seamen and dockers who had contributed so much to the war effort were now taking white men's jobs.

The source of the disturbances was an attack by white men on an Anglo-Indian restaurant in Park Lane on Saturday, July 31. The establishment was full of black diners at the time. At about 10pm, doors and windows were smashed. What sparked this initial attack remains a mystery. In a subsequent incident, at 10.20pm, a policeman heard screams and shouting coming from a large crowd in Jordan Street. A West African seaman was in the middle of a mob brandishing a knife. He repeatedly stabbed a white man in the face. A constable dragged the knifeman away but he soon broke free and jabbed another man in the face. After being restrained once again, the assailant escaped and ran away. He was seen entering Colsea House, a hostel for black seamen in Upper Stanhope Street. The officer followed and once again arrested him. The prisoner protested by pleading, 'I've got no knife.'

On the same night, on the corner of Upper Parliament Street and Park Way, a policeman saw two white girls surrounded by a ring of black men. The young women were screaming, although the men were doing nothing to them. In fact, the girls did not complain to the police. Nevertheless, the officer dispersed the crowd but five minutes later the same men, armed with weapons, were seen chasing a white man. The men were tracked down to a house and arrested after a running battle.

The disturbances continued near the Rialto Cinema. Crowds of men, divided along racial lines, hurled bricks and bottles at each other. A black man was arrested for carrying a pistol in Upper Parliament Street while another was detained for wielding a carving knife. It was alleged that he was shouting at his opponents, 'Do not come over to this side of the street.' There were also reports of a gunshot outside the Rialto. Another version has it that a man pointed an automatic pistol at the police but it failed to fire. Twenty patrol cars scoured the area but failed to find the gunman. Some blacks shouted, 'Dirty whites,' and, 'Down with the whites.' As some white men walked along, a group of armed blacks followed them, chanting, 'We kill white men.' The whites, being outnumbered, wisely ran for their lives. The racist slogans echo those of the 1919 riots. As in the earlier disturbances, newspapers did not report what white men must have shouted back.

The Monday bank holiday saw more trouble. A large crowd of white men stood staring at fifty blacks congregated outside Wilkie's Club, in Upper Parliament Street, suspected of being the headquarters of the black faction. The blacks thought that they were going to come under attack. When the police arrived, they retreated inside the club and locked themselves in. Bottles were thrown from the windows as officers tried to disperse the crowd.

After battling for hours, the police managed to storm the building but were faced with a wall of empty beer bottles intended for use as ammunition. Police patrol cars were smashed and eight men taken to hospital with head injuries and stab wounds. What originally started as an attack by white men on blacks became a conflict between blacks and the police. The local white men seem to disappear from the picture when the police arrive.

Fifty to sixty people, most of them black, ended up in court accused of carrying the following weapons: bottles, swords, razors, screwdrivers, daggers, iron bars, coshes, axes, and even a banister rail. Mr Livermore, defending the black men, claimed that the trouble was caused by 'irresponsible elements' within the community. He denied that the blacks were solely responsible for the disturbances and claimed that the police had assaulted the prisoners. Most of the men were acquitted but the West African knifeman was jailed for fifteen months.[4]

Liverpool continued to suffer periodic outbreaks of racial tension. In 1954, Liverpool University sociologist John Barron Mays could still write of the Congo Gang, which consisted of mixed raced youngsters from Toxteth who banded together to beat up white children, thereby imitating the racial feuds of their elders.[5] The Sixties also saw south end clashes between black and white teenage gangs called the Shiners and the John Bulls (see Chapter 22).

There are many possible reasons for the racial hostilities. Competition for jobs and local women certainly played their part. Also, at the heart of the mistrust of foreigners, particularly those of a different colour, is a fear of the corrupting influence of alien customs. The local culture, if not the British way of life, is often seen as under threat from perverse and un-English practices. In the nineteenth century, blame was laid on the Irish, particularly the importation of their heavy drinking and brawling lifestyles, which ultimately gave rise to the Cornermen gangs and the High Rip. For the authorities, the Chinese and the Blacks were responsible for bringing with them something equally deplorable: drugs.

10

Dope Fiends

DRUGS WERE NOT illegal at the beginning of the twentieth century but their use would lay the foundations for later criminal gang activity. It wasn't until 1916 that anti-drug laws were introduced into the United Kingdom. The Defence of the Realm Act prohibited the possession of cocaine and opium without a prescription. The Dangerous Drugs Act followed in 1920. People's addiction to drugs created a demand that had to be met somehow. In America the Prohibition era of the 1920s generated a gangster-led market in illicit alcohol. Similarly, when drug use became prohibited in Britain, the opportunity was created for illegally supplying the demand. Liverpool's status as a major port meant that it was ideally situated to meet the challenge.

The drug trade would later provide scores of post-war Liverpool gangsters with a lucrative living. It was from the following tentative beginnings that the modern barons would learn the methods and economics of drug smuggling. Young street entrepreneurs would also develop and sharpen their dealing skills. It will be seen how proximity to the docks helped define the territorial boundaries of Liverpool's drug trade, along with its largely ethnic customer base. Over many years, the chains of command were slowly forged and the network of supply created that would establish the city as a drugs capital.

Opium smoking has been going on in Liverpool since the beginning of the twentieth century, when the Chinese began to settle near to the south docks. It has been claimed that fifty-per-cent of the Chinese population in Liverpool were involved in opium production. The drug was smuggled into Liverpool on board ships from Hong Kong and Shanghai. The opium would be carefully concealed inside small wooden logs, which were given a special marking to aid their discovery once the ship reached port. By 1916, a vast trade in the drug had sprung up in Liverpool, despite the fact that opium smuggling carried serious risks. Chinese traffickers faced deportation and the strong possibility of being beheaded back home. On the other hand, the rewards were great. One Liverpool-Chinese dealer boasted that in six months he had disposed of £1,000-worth of the drug.

The problem of opium use was highlighted in 1912. Some Chinese grocers sold the drug in any quantity. Even children could buy it over the counter. Many countries, including China itself, had strict regulations regarding its sale but Britain had no such controls. It was alleged that local white girls had been drugged after being sold opium-laced sweetmeats. A petition was organised urging the Government to bring in legislation to restrict the sale of the drug. When the 1916 Act was passed, a police clampdown followed. However, opium smoking continued, only to be interrupted by the occasional police raids.

In 1917 there were dramatic scenes in Frederick Street. A strong police presence surrounded a marked premises and made short work of the doors. Many of the inmates were in a drugged stupor and offered little resistance. However, when the police visited an adjacent property they had a real battle on their hands. Several Chinese ran upstairs and clambered onto the roof where they pelted the police with their boots and any other missiles they could find. As the officers advanced, the men leapt from building to building like cats. With the aid of ladders and a fire escape the police finally rounded up the suspects who joined their drugged countrymen in the Argyle Street Bridewell. Thirty-three arrests were made. Drug-making apparatus was confiscated along with needles, pipes and several pounds of opium ready for use. The district remained in uproar for some time afterwards.

In 1918, a journalist and his female companion visited a Chinese drugs den. The pair entered an ordinary-looking house in a dingy street and proceeded up a flight of stairs where they met an old Chinese man. 'A new chum,' the lady announced as she laid some money on the table. A few moments later they entered another room decorated in an oriental style. Youths lay reclining on cushions arranged in a circular pattern on the floor. In the middle of the room was the opium 'lay out', as it was called – a flat brass tray with a long glistening needle and a pipe. On a piece of cardboard was the drug itself, a thick black sticky wax. A young man began the proceedings by using the needle to pick up a lump of opium and hold it to the flame of the lamp. The drug bubbled as it cooked, changing colour to a golden brown. After rolling the mixture into a pill shape, the youth balanced the opium on the pipe. One pipe served the whole group who patiently took turns to inhale the fumes before collapsing into a contented haze.

The journalist simply watched the strange proceedings into the early hours before taking his leave. As he passed along the landing he peered into another room where a living skeleton of a man lay on a divan mumbling incoherently as he reached his bony hand for the pipe. As he was shown out of the building, the journalist asked about the skeleton. 'Killing himself, sir,' he was told. 'He can't help it now, can't stop if it he tried. He'd go right off it. He can't stop – none of them can once they get the habit.'

It was felt that the Chinese were deliberately keeping their opium dens in a filthy, stinking condition to put off English users. Rather than sit in squalor to take the drug, wealthy addicts from London's West End would instead pay the Chinese a fee of £5 to visit their own houses. As well as bringing the drug and smoking apparatus, the dealer would cook it up on the spot in a sort of 'deals on wheels' service. In this way the clever dealers avoided the risk of having their own premises raided.

In 1919, Liverpool police staged the biggest ever drugs raid in Chinatown. At half past eight one evening, about 120 plain-clothed officers descended on twenty properties scattered throughout the Pitt Street and Paradise Street area. The targets were the innocent-looking shops selling tobacco and sweets that littered the district. It was rightly suspected that behind the shop fronts lay opium-smoking establishments. When the police entered the various rooms, some of the occupants were reclining on the floor quietly puffing away while others were so out of it that officers had to carry them to the nearby Bridewell. The occupants were so taken by surprise that most could do nothing but surrender, although one crafty man, upon seeing the police burst in, quickly passed his pipe to the person lying next to him. Others simply dropped their pipes on the bed or threw them out of the window. One man claimed he had only gone into the room for a cup of tea.

Seventy arrests were made. In every house visited, opium was seized along with the implements for its use, including pipes, bowls, and scales. It was not uncommon for users to conceal their pipes on a length of string inside the hollow stem of a brass bedstead. The knob would then be screwed back. In one property, almost a hundredweight of the drug was found hidden beneath the floorboards. When questioned, the householder claimed that it was pepper to be used in the boiling of pigs' feet. During the raid, a large crowd gathered to cheer the police as they escorted the prisoners away. All those convicted were fined various amounts.

Although it was mostly the Chinese who smoked the opium, the trade in the drug also involved English people, both male and female. In 1923, police in a taxi shadowed a car travelling from the Limehouse district of London to the West End. Limehouse was the capital's own Chinatown district. At the end of the journey, May Roberts was seen receiving a parcel containing raw black opium worth £100 from Charles Ellis. A search of Ellis's luggage uncovered a cloakroom ticket issued at London Bridge Station where a further search revealed more opium weighing five pounds together with a pair of scales. It seems that Roberts had been cohabitating with a Chinese man for six years and frequently travelled backwards and forwards between London and Liverpool where she was a known trafficker.

By 1929, it was felt that Liverpool was out of bounds for opium smugglers due to the extra vigilance of the authorities. However, there was then feared to be a revival of the trade in the port after a woman in Liverpool was sent to prison for trafficking in the drug. Detectives kept the docks under close observation after being told to expect another consignment. It was revealed that there was a secret opium smuggling headquarters in London from which wealthy traders conducted worldwide operations. The drug was ordered from China and sent to South America from where it was shipped back to England, sometimes arriving in Liverpool.

In 1934, opium traffickers discovered an original way of smuggling the drug. Jou Ling Sam was a former laundryman from Liverpool and London. In 1921, he went to Cardiff where he opened a restaurant and grocer's shop. Although he did not use drugs, for some time he was suspected of being the man behind a small amount of drug trafficking in South Wales. A number of carrier pigeons were found at the rear of his premises and it was believed that the birds were sent to Liverpool and London, only to return carrying small quantities of the drug. At his home, police found a Bible and other books containing hollowed out pages, ideal for hiding illicit goods. The man was found guilty and given a fine of a £100 or three months' imprisonment.

In 1939, after a three-day surveillance operation, two detectives staged a midnight raid on a Chinese laundry in Kensington. After forcing open the front door, they confronted a large dog and for the next twenty minutes struggled to entice the beast into the street. They then entered an upstairs bedroom where they had to grope their way through a haze of opium fumes. A Chinese man, lying in bed clutching a pipe as long as a walking stick, declared, 'Me know nothing.' He was nevertheless arrested and fined for possessing prepared opium. His English wife admitted that she was the occupier of the premises and was also fined.

Cocaine was another popular drug. All firms dealing in cocaine had to have a permit from the Home Secretary. Chemists could only supply the drug with the aid of a doctor's prescription. To meet the demand from users, cocaine therefore had to be smuggled into the country. The blame for this was laid on the Chinese.

The year 1918 saw numerous cocaine scares. With thousands of colonial and American soldiers passing through London at the end of the Great War, there were plenty of easy victims of the cocaine scam. It seems that some troops were returning to their units in a dazed condition, totally penniless. They were not drunk but suffering from the effects of cocaine. The soldiers were befriended in cafes, cinemas or music halls where they would be offered a cigarette laced with the drug. They would remember nothing more till they woke up with empty pockets. Local newspapers covered the story but it is not clear whether the practice was also common in Liverpool.

Cocaine was certainly used in the city. In 1923, seven men appeared in court accused of smuggling cocaine. A Liverpool seaman called Frederick Walker pleaded guilty and explained to the court that while in Hamburg a foreigner approached him and asked him if he could find a market in England for the white stuff.

Back in Liverpool, Walker met two men called Taylor and Lazarus and promised to get them some cocaine. Lazarus revealed that he had a prospective customer in London. On his next trip to Hamburg, Walker received a package from the foreigner. It contained six large and several smaller bottles of cocaine. Taylor paid £15 for the deal with another £10 going to the foreigner. Some of the men involved in the operation were caught with the cocaine and a subsequent raid on Walker's house uncovered four large bottles and seventy-two smaller bottles of the drug hidden in a chocolate box in the cupboard.

The 'dopo circles', or 'sniffing brigade' as they were called, used the terms 'C' and 'H' to refer to cocaine and heroin. In London, it was reported that ninety per cent of drug addicts took cocaine and nothing else. With heroin, the novice user usually suffered such a severe fright that he abandoned the drug forever. Only experienced cocaine users turned to heroin for the occasional extra buzz. Cocaine was normally sniffed although veterans would inject the drug, mixed with water, into the arm just above the elbow. American police would squeeze the arm of those under arrest. The ensuing cry of pain would indicate a 'dope fiend'.

In 1918, cocaine was selling in London for £10 an ounce, although it was reported that a bottle containing two and a half ounces went for £100. The buyer was a recent wealthy convert to the drug, having discovered its pleasures only a fortnight earlier. In 1944, a black Londoner was caught in Liverpool in the act of buying cocaine from a wholesale chemist. He had travelled north with plenty of cash aiming to secure large quantities of the drug to take back to the capital. It was believed that he was part of a gang that supplied cocaine to addicts.

Morphine was another highly sought-after drug. Many patients were prescribed it for medical conditions and found it hard to come off it. Some men became hooked while serving in the Great War. Morphine and cocaine kits, including a syringe and needles, could be purchased at Harrods store in London. The advert on the box boasted: 'A useful present for friends at the Front.'

In 1924, Joseph Metcalfe was charged under the Dangerous Drugs Act for being in unlawful possession of two boxes of morphine and two syringes. Acting on information, a detective met Metcalfe in Brownlow Hill. Pretending to be a civilian, the officer asked, 'Have you got the stuff?' Metcalfe replied, 'It depends on what you mean. I don't like to show the stuff in the street.' Nevertheless, he then handed over the morphine and was immediately arrested. Despite claiming that the drug was for his own use, he was imprisoned for six months.

Drug taking was not restricted to men. In 1918, a respectable lady was reduced to stealing a bottle of cocaine from a dentist's surgery in Lord Street. She claimed that she needed the drug to help her escape her personal problems. Women from the lower classes, however, had their own means of escaping the terrible reality of their lives. A year later, a meeting of the City Justices highlighted the misuse of methylated spirits. In the poorer districts of Liverpool some women had turned to drinking the spirit, which was between six and ten times as strong as whisky. The addition of paraffin was supposed to make the liquid undrinkable but this did not deter hardened drinkers in the city's worst slums. Women bought the spirit from chemists and paint shops by pretending it was needed for painting furniture. One seller of the spirit reported sales of about twenty applications a day, which he suspected were used for drinking rather than household tasks. He decided to stop selling it.

In 1919, a policeman described how, at half past nine in the morning, he found four women drunk from swigging the spirit:

> They had got past the fighting stage when I arrived at the scene but their faces were matted with blood, and their clothes torn. Writhing like snakes, and with terror-stricken, wide-open eyes, they lay on the floor, and fought for breath like a person when the death rattle enters the throat ... eventually their struggles ceased, and after a state of coma they recovered, but the wreck that each looked can better be imagined than described.[1]

The Justices planned to send a petition to the Home Office requesting a tightening up of the laws regarding the sale of the spirit. Yet, in 1921 there were still sixty-seven cases of drinking methylated spirits in Liverpool, fifty-five of them involving women.[2] In 1929, fifty-seven-year-old Mary Walsh was found dead in a Bootle park. Her only possession was a bottle of meths. Since 1903, she had been arrested ninety times. On the last three occasions she was under the influence of meths, a drink to which she had only recently become addicted.

Methylated spirits remained the drink of choice for hardened alcoholics. In 1930, a male meths drinker was arrested in Southport. He told the police, 'I take it because I get fed up and I have to have something to make me enjoy life. It is food and drink to me. With two pennyworth I am happy for the day.'

* * *

By 1947, the German bombs had scattered the Chinese community over a large area. There was no longer any particular district that could be referred to as Chinatown. Herbert Winstanley, Liverpool's Chief Constable, admitted that opium smoking went on within the Chinese community but boasted that no European had ever been caught taking the drug. However, the scene was about to change and the local white population was to become increasingly involved in the use of drugs. Local crime reporter Richard Whittington-Egan points out that in 1947, of the fifty-one arrests for drug possession in Liverpool, fifty cases involved opium. Six years later, of the fifty-three prosecutions relating to drugs, only eleven involved opium.[3]

Marijuana was the new drug on the block. Also called hashish, cannabis, Indian hemp, ganga and weed, the drug was largely brought into Liverpool by black seamen. However, it was also possible to buy the seeds of the hemp plant in canary food mix at the local pet shop. Sharp-eyed policemen sometimes spotted the plant being cultivated on derelict ground in the Parliament Street area. The occasional window box would also provide a nice display of yellow flowers. The main dope dealing area was within the boundaries of Warwick Street, Park Road, Parliament Street and Crown Street in the south end district.

Most people will perhaps view the taking of cannabis as a modern trend. However, some Victorians also dabbled in its use. In 1891, a local journal carried a curious headline: 'Drug eating in

Liverpool.'[4] The accompanying article told the story of one man's experience of taking hashish, which was also known as 'bang' or 'bhang'. A well-known trader in the Victoria Street area of the city centre attended an evening party at a friend's house. The host, who experimented in chemistry, brought up the subject of the drug. He invited his guests to visit his laboratory and sample some hashish. The company was told that the drug would make them feel jolly all evening. Everybody declined the offer except for the businessmen, who at nine o'clock took one grain mixed in a spoonful of jam.

For the first few hours the man could feel nothing unusual. However, on finishing a hearty supper his head began to swim and a delirious sensation came over him. He told his host he was feeling funny and was escorted to the study and placed in front of a roaring fire. 'Now give way to your feelings and enjoy yourself,' the man was told. He was transported thousands of miles into the air where he saw the most beautiful gardens with nymphs frolicking about. In a flash, the scene suddenly changed and he witnessed every person he had ever known standing in a row and then every house and street he had ever visited. He was able to travel the entire earth, seeing things so strange he couldn't even describe them.

The host entered the room, much to the man's disgust as his dreams were interrupted. His pulse had been raised to 120 beats per minute and his face was glowing. The visionary experiences continued. The guests were alarmed but the man told them to leave him alone. At one o'clock the next morning, the man's friends were anxious to get him home. However, he was fixed rigid to the spot and told them he was happy to remain. It was then decided to administer vinegar as an antidote. In a few minutes the trance wore off and he was persuaded to leave. That night he dreamed of weird scenes and even the next day could not shake off the strange sensations. His business friends thought that he was possessed. The man wisely decided never to partake in drugs again.

In 1935, hashish was again making headlines in the local newspapers. A young Liverpool man had read about the wonders of Indian hemp and decided to separate the seeds found in parrot food and plant them in his garden. When they reached five feet high he plucked the leaves and tops of the plant and mixed them with tobacco to make a cigarette. The lad enjoyed the experience so much that he told his girlfriend who was eager to share a joint. Unfortunately, the young woman became so ill and mentally disoriented that she had to be rushed to the Southern Hospital. Although the Dangerous Drugs Act controlled the purchase of the extract and tincture of Indian hemp, it was not yet illegal to possess and smoke the plant.

The issue of drug smuggling was being debated even before the Second World War. In 1937, the *Liverpool Weekly Post* pointed out the ingenuity of foreign drug traffickers.[5] Owing to their compactness, combined with a high profit margin, drugs were the most sought-after form of contraband. Customs officers quickly latched on to the obvious hiding places such as double-bottomed trunks, suitcases with false linings and hollow-heeled shoes. Because of this extra vigilance, the traffickers were forced to become ever more creative and cunning. In Egypt, a consignment of prunes had their stones removed and replaced with hashish. A Sudanese corporal noticed that a caravan of camels, being taken across the border for sale, had not had their thick coats cropped. Running his hand along the silky hair he felt something hard. The smugglers had shaved away a strip of hair on both sides of the hump, glued slabs of hashish on the camel's skin and then stuck the hair back on top.

Along the African coast, the Loubetis Gang found an ingenious method of smuggling. The drugs would be sent by passenger liner and taken ashore under the noses of customs officers. When the ship berthed, several young men and women would go on board on the pretext of having a look around. The girls would pick up the drugs and hide them intimately. Although the men would be searched on leaving the ship, the women were never subjected to the same thorough examination.

However, as well as the big drugs rings, amateurs could also dabble in trafficking. Cars would have hollow running boards, double-bottomed toolboxes and false oil tanks. Spare tyres would be stuffed with heroin and cocaine. Indeed, heroin was even found in the bell of a bike and the hollow wooden leg of a cripple. British criminals would later devise their own methods of drug smuggling. Liverpool, being a major seaport, was at the forefront of the trade. Once a vessel had reached dock, opium or hashish, attached to a log of wood, would be thrown overboard into the Mersey. The seven-knot currents of the river would float the package into the waiting arms of a gang in a small boat. Hashish was also smuggled into the country by being sewn into the hems and linings of the zoot suits of West Indian seamen. Customs officers claimed that Liverpool was an international clearing-house for hashish, the drug eventually ending up in America.

Black seamen sold Indian hemp to local men on shore who then toured the pubs of the south end selling packages for five shillings each. In 1947, a Nigerian stowaway, lodging in Grove Street, was caught in possession of the drug and jailed after the prosecutor claimed that users often went on to commit violent offences. A detective related how he had seen girls under the influence banging their heads against a wall. In court, a witness also reported that smoking a reefer was the equivalent of drinking half a bottle of rum and was capable of making the user go 'sexually mad'.

By the end of 1947, the press had become aware of the new threat facing Liverpool's youth. 'Girls Smoke Drug Cigarettes' was the headline in a local newspaper.[6] The story revealed that teenagers, aged fourteen and fifteen, were buying cigarettes laced with Indian hemp, a drug that induced 'pleasant sensations'. The scare stories increased. In 1948, Professor James Webster, a Home Office pathologist, warned that for a mere three shillings people could buy enough cannabis to incite them to commit murder. The warning came after the conviction in Birmingham of a tall Jamaican dealer, known appropriately as 'Lofty the drug man'. When arrested, he had not only packs of cannabis but also letters addressed to Liverpool requesting more supplies. It seems that the city was attracting weekend visitors from the rest of the country desperate to score some 'dope'. The cheapness of the drug was seen as a sign of how plentiful it was. Black seamen and their white girlfriends were said to be the biggest users, often becoming addicts.

In 1948, in the area between the Anglican Cathedral and the River Mersey, cannabis could be obtained as easily as tobacco. For ten shillings it was possible to buy four hashish cigarettes, called 'wraps'. Black men would openly smoke the drug in the street, a measure of how little they feared the police. West Indians, together with a few West Africans, were blamed for turning the south end maze of streets and alleys around Washington Street, Rathbone Street and Nile Street into 'Britain's vice capital'.[7] Prostitutes would buy a single wrap and smoke it as they lounged on the street corners around Great George Place.

The drug was suspected of driving women sexually wild. For this reason, it was claimed that West Indians offered it to white girls in the seedy nightclubs that littered the area. While acknowledging that most West Indians were decent law-abiding citizens, an undercover journalist identified a hardcore of 'riff raff' who were intent on living lives of idleness and lawlessness. They were said to plot crime, deal in drugs and organise prostitution, and all this while drawing benefits. The reporter went on to admit that there was also an opium problem with the Chinese but added that this race was generally well behaved. The real issue was that black people were seen as more of a threat. The Chinese conducted their drug taking and gambling in the privacy of their own homes. The West Indians, on the other hand, were a more visible presence on the streets and generally less subservient to the authority of the policeman on his beat who tried to move them on.

By 1952, the issue of reefer madness had still not gone away. Newspapers again turned their attention to the topic of 'love weed', as cannabis was now being called, as a result of its power to make users lose their inhibitions. Liverpool was identified as the county's main source of supply. A local gang was ready to buy every pound of the stuff that was smuggled ashore. A telegram containing a disguised message would periodically be sent to an address in London, resulting in two young women travelling northwards to collect a consignment. The drug was then selling in Liverpool for £25 per pound. An offshoot of the trade was the selling of harmless herb cigarettes as genuine reefers, thereby swindling users. It was felt that the scam would not fool streetwise Liverpool lasses.

Pre-war drug taking was a relatively minor pastime in Liverpool, indulged in by a select few and confined mainly to various ethnic groups. It was only when young white women started taking substances that were normally associated with black seamen that the press and public became worried about drug abuse. Even then, the moral panic centred largely on the threat of sexual promiscuity and was no doubt also linked to racial prejudice. Black men were seen as corrupting white girls. It was a good few years before the larger social menace of drugs became a national problem. The concern then would focus not so much on loose morals but on issues of criminality associated with organised trafficking and drug-related thieving.

Yet all this was in the future. Meanwhile, Liverpool had its own social problems to contend with. Drugs and alcohol are certainly popular ways of overcoming destitution and squalor. By entering oblivion, the dispossessed are able to mentally escape their dismal surroundings, if only for a few short hours. Another way of escaping penury is through crime. Some people attempt to steal their way out of material hardship.

However, for a growing band of Liverpudlians at the beginning of the twentieth century, the best means of tackling poverty was through social action and protest. Against a background of simmering racial and sectarian tension, Liverpool also played host to periodic outbursts of civil unrest and riots. Poverty, unemployment and politics often led to anarchistic and violent clashes between Liverpudlians and the authorities. Liverpool's tearaways had yet another opportunity to take up arms.

11

A Nightmare of Civilisation

AT THE BEGINNING of the twentieth century, those workers fortunate to have a job suffered low and irregular wages. There was no job security. Periods of work alternated with debilitating stints of unemployment. Tough management practices and harsh work discipline were a constant source of grievance. The working classes had to fight every inch of the way for better conditions and a reasonable standard of living.

The great transport strike of 1911 involved a summer-long series of disputes, kick-started by the seamen coming out on June 14. The source of the trouble was the refusal of ship owners to employ workers who belonged to a trade union. The dispute soon escalated to include carters, railwaymen and dockers, the most militant groups of workers. By mid-August, thousands of striking workers brought Liverpool to a standstill.

For nearly three months nothing moved in the city. The hot weather only exacerbated the problem of food rotting in the streets, left there by striking road sweeps. The city was indeed close to revolution. During the strike, Lord Derby's doom-laden message to Winston Churchill was, 'The city is in a state of siege – the hospitals have but two days supply – in forty-eight hours all poor people will be face to face with starvation and God alone knows what happens when that moment arrives.'

The climax of the strike came on Sunday August 13, the so-called 'Bloody Sunday'. Between 80,000 to 90,000 people gathered around the plateau of St. Georges Hall for a demonstration in support of the railwaymen. There are conflicting accounts about how the trouble was ignited. Either a policeman assaulted some spectators innocently perched on window ledges or a crowd overturned a cart believing that the driver was a blackleg. Whatever happened, a small disturbance in Lord Nelson Street led to the police baton charging the crowd. The officers had been hiding in the Hall, awaiting trouble. Two hundred people were injured in the fierce exchanges that followed.

Sections of the crowd attempted to storm Lime Street station by tearing down the iron gates at the Lord Nelson Street entrance. Stones, iron nuts and pieces of timber were thrown at the police. Metal advertisements were torn from the walls and used as razor-sharp missiles. Station staff got out hosepipes and tried to drown the men's rage. Helped on their way by a police baton charge, the drenched rioters were driven back into London Road, only to return with incensed colleagues who turned on the police with even greater ferocity. It was the turn of the police to be driven back.

In the short-lived yet bloody hand-to-hand fighting that followed, several heads were broken. A stream of injured and unconscious men, including twenty police officers and fifty civilians, were shepherded into the station waiting rooms to be given first aid. Staff from the Lime Street Hotel provided sheets and tablecloths, which were torn up and used as makeshift bandages for smashed and bloodied skulls. The staff also offered the casualties drinking water but many said that they preferred beer. The Riot Act was read but did nothing to stop the night of looting that followed, together with numerous bloody confrontations between the police and the public. As protection from the disturbances, warehousemen and merchants armed themselves and shopkeepers barricaded their premises.

Three days of insurrection followed. In the network of squalid streets in the Everton district, street-fighting men swapped the usual sectarian brawls for disorder of a different kind. The guerrilla tactics and fighting skills honed and perfected during previous religious skirmishes were put to good use by the insurgents. Anticipating further trouble, the police phoned the Territorial Barracks in Islington to request reinforcements. Over 260 troops from the Second Yorkshire Regiment were sent to Lower Everton at the double. Bottles, slates and bricks welcomed them, resulting in six soldiers being wounded about the head and face. At one point the troops were ordered to fix bayonets to clear the raving mob. In pitch darkness, men relocated onto the roofs to rain down missiles. Two soldiers were told to fire at the invisible targets above them. After ten rounds, no injuries were reported but the actions of the troops served to further incense the rioters.

Although in one sense the strike brought together the religious rivalries, with Protestant carters and Catholic dockers uniting in solidarity, there were nevertheless scattered outbreaks of sectarian disorder around Great Homer Street later the same night. Groups of aggrieved Catholics and Orange supporters took the opportunity to settle some old scores. Backyard walls were ripped down to provide ammunition and iron railings turned into weapons. In Edinburgh Street, a man fired four shots with a revolver, fortunately missing his target. The arrival of the police had the ironic effect of reuniting the Catholics and Protestants, as they temporarily put aside their differences to turn on the officers with stones and bottles. The street became the scene of vicious hand-to-hand battles that had little to do with the strike itself.

Similarly, the inevitable looting that followed the rioting was more the work of local hard cases and criminals than the strikers themselves. Pawnshops were stripped, bakers broken into and public houses attacked. As the troops and police arrived, men and women retreated indoors and onto the roofs to shout curses and insults while throwing whatever came to hand at the darkness below.

The following morning, the police removed cartloads of missiles and ammunition in order to prevent a repeat performance. Troops were also marched through the dangerous areas in a bold show of strength. They were watched by thousands of angry men standing in small groups on street corners.

The disturbances resulted in three deaths. On August 14, a policeman died after being kicked by Thomas Kelly. PC Davies was in St Anne Street when the drunken Kelly approached swinging his arms and jostling people off the pavement. The officer tried to arrest the man but Kelly violently resisted. At this point, PC Balance attempted to assist his colleague but he was also assaulted and knocked to the floor. While the constable lay helpless, Kelly delivered an almighty kick to his stomach. A large, hostile crowd joined in by throwing bottles and stones at the policemen. About forty officers from the Bradford force then arrived to drive the crowd away.

Kelly was eventually escorted to Rose Hill Bridewell where he was charged and subsequently sentenced to five months' imprisonment. At the bridewell, PC Balance complained of feeling unwell. He started vomiting blood and was admitted to hospital. After two operations on his intestines, he died of pneumonia. However, the doctors thought that the kicking was not the cause of his demise. A verdict of death by natural causes was passed and the charge against Kelly of doing grievous bodily harm was withdrawn.

On Tuesday August 15, thirty-four soldiers from the Hussars and Scots Greys, together with some policemen, escorted a convoy of five prison vans along the dock road on the way to Walton Gaol. In Vauxhall Road, at the corner of Hopwood Street, they were attacked by a 3,000-strong mob throwing stones. The horses supplied by the War Office were not suitably shod for the cobbled streets of Liverpool and about six animals slipped or were knocked down by missiles. A sergeant claimed that he saw one man in the crowd lying flat on the ground shooting a revolver at the troops. It was not known whether the weapon was firing blanks or ball cartridges.

As some of the crowd made attempts to free the prisoners, the Hussars fired six shots, killing two carters. Michael Prendergast was shot dead instantly while John Sutcliffe was blasted in the head and died later in hospital. The young woman he was due to marry identified his body. Andrew Doolan was also shot through the thigh and a policeman badly injured in the affray. The prison vans eventually reached their destination but afterwards the Warwickshires, assisted by a body of mounted police, were called to Vauxhall Road where they engaged for an hour in fierce fighting with the crowds.

A mixture of Catholics and Protestants later attended the funerals of both men, a promising sign of conciliation between the groups. As time went on, the intensity of the sectarian disorder decreased. Tensions still existed but they were more likely to flare up into punch-ups rather than full-scale riots.

Throughout the evening, guerrilla warfare took place around Scotland Road. In Everton Valley, a crowd held up tramcars and for a while there was a tense stand off between stone throwers and the Warwickshire troops who stood with fixed bayonets at the ready. A large mob erected a barbed wire barricade, fortified with dustbins, in Netherfield Road, at the border of the Orange quarter. The streetlights had also been put out of action, leaving the area in a dangerous state of pitch darkness. The climax came when a body of policemen broke through the barricade to escort a squad of lamplighters, who restored the lights.

Over 2,300 troops, from six regiments, patrolled Liverpool's streets as the city ground to a halt. The Royal Navy cruiser *Antrim* moored in the River Mersey to provide support for the gunboats as the Government waited anxiously to see if the riots could be brought under control. Shops and pubs kept their shutters up. Walton Gaol was bursting at the seams.

For some people, the strikers had no justifiable grievance. An army officer claimed that rioting Liverpudlians were simply hooligans out to destroy anything in their path without the slightest provocation. He might have had a point. For these sons and daughters of the Cornermen gangs of the 1880s, the rioting probably had nothing to do with social justice, but was merely an opportunity to indulge in a bit of looting and violence. Liverpool was 'a nightmare of civilization', according to one journal, which added, 'Liverpool is the most criminal, the most drunken, the most lawless city in the United Kingdom.'[1]

By the end of August, the strike was over and the citizens of Liverpool were left to reflect on the causes and consequences of the terrible violence. A clergyman who lived and worked in what he termed 'the danger zone' offered three of his own solutions to prevent further trouble.[2] He demanded the early closing of the public houses to prevent men and women getting drunk. He felt that the women were worse than the men for drinking and accused them of breeding hooligans. Secondly, he urged more flogging of schoolchildren to make them better behaved. Thirdly, he supported the whipping of prisoners.

The clergyman was not the first, nor would he be the last, to praise nostalgically the efforts of Justice Day in stamping out previous bouts of hooliganism. Kindness, reformatories and borstals were all seen as wasted on the city's blackguards. However, the clergyman's words went unheeded and eight years later, during the Police Strike, the gunboats were back as Liverpool once again teetered on the brink of anarchy. During the dispute, which began on 31 July 1919, tanks, warships and 2,500 troops were sent to maintain order as the streets of the city became 'bobbyless'. The main grievance was over pay and hours of work, along with the right to belong to a recognised union. In Liverpool, 954 police officers downed truncheons, together with 114 in Birkenhead, sixty-three in Bootle and one in Wallasey.

At the beginning of August, 900 soldiers from the Nottingham and Derby and South Staffordshire regiments were drafted into the city from their camp at Great Crosby. Billeted in tents in St John's Gardens, behind St George's Hall, the soldiers were initially kept out of sight. They were there to aid the non-striking policemen who would have been powerless against the mobs of looters. Troops were also taken in lorries to guard Birkenhead docks. As they boarded their vehicles they were issued with live cartridges. Meanwhile, the authorities placed adverts in the local newspapers appealing for new police recruits.

On the Saturday night of August 2, the crowds kicked off when a lad threw a brick through a jeweller's window in London Road. Within minutes the destruction spread as drunken men staggered out of the pubs and continued to smash windows in search of jewellery, tobacco, boots and clothes. The area between Scotland Road and London Road quickly became a war zone with sixty arrests made in one night of violence.

Just after midnight, an armoured car, heavily escorted by soldiers with fixed bayonets, arrived on the scene. Inside the vehicle was a magistrate who proceeded to read the Riot Act for the last time on mainland Britain. Even though the words were shouted through a megaphone it is doubtful whether the turbulent crowd either heard them or took any notice. Troops formed a cordon at the point where London Road meets Lime Street. After firing warning shots as they left St George's Plateau, a squad of soldiers in steel helmets clubbed their rifles and made a charge with fixed bayonets. The crowd scattered, escaping up the rabbit warren of side streets adjoining London Road. Members of the CID, armed with heavy batons, assisted the soldiers by making their own charge, four abreast, down the road. Once the thoroughfare was cleared, some impatient looters, eager to return to the shops, were sandwiched between the advancing troops and the police on their way back. In the confusion, a detective sergeant was severely injured when he was smashed in the face by the butt end of a rifle, a blow intended for a looter. With audacious recklessness, the looters quickly returned with iron bars and heavy rocks to systematically smash every plate glass window in their path. Tired of helping themselves, some looters started to throw goods out of the windows to those unable to gain admission. Several people were injured in the scramble to catch a windfall.

The military and new police recruits faced an impossible task. An Australian soldier with more courage than sense battled his way to the front of a crowd of looters. In an authoritarian tone he called out, 'Now stop this nonsense.' He was promptly felled by a blow on the head from a broken window sash wielded by a hooligan. Nevertheless the 'flying column', as the new recruits were called, did their best to maintain order on the streets. These were men who had already been 'over the top' in France during the Great War and were afraid of nobody. 'Pity help the looters when these boys get at them,' was the comment from one experienced policeman. Many of the recruits returned to their headquarters with broken truncheons, which they eagerly exchanged for new ones ready for the next advance on the gangs of Liverpool.

Yet the riots continued. Hordes of rough-looking women accompanied the men, pointing out the best bargains to be had. In the chaos not everybody struck gold. One man was caught and later fined for being in possession of a single boot and a coat hanger. Nevertheless, unafraid of falling glass, lads continued to jump in and out of huge jagged holes in the shop windows to make lightning sweeps of anything valuable. Facing total darkness once inside, some looters even found time to put on the lights to aid their searches. Others, in their haste, dropped as much as they carried.

When the crowds dispersed, a huge, silver candelabra lay in the middle of London Road. Indeed, the gutters were littered with jewellery and watches, even costume dummies lay like dead bodies in the street. The scene of carnage was said to resemble the war zone of Ypres in Belgium, through which Liverpool lasses proudly paraded in their stolen furs. For years afterwards, the riot was known as 'The Loot'.

The Royal Marines arrived at the Pier Head to assist the soldiers and police in house-to-house raids in the back-street slums, in an attempt to recover the spoils of war. Facing a desperate situation, the Government decided to send in reinforcements. An infantry battalion, originally intended for duty in India, was sent as backup. A troop of tanks was parked menacingly outside St George's Hall.

On the Sunday afternoon, raiders turned their attention to the premises of J.P. O'Brien and Co, export bottlers of Tariff Street, off Vauxhall Road. The promise of unlimited alcohol swelled the number of looters to hundreds who began to force their way into what must have seemed like heaven on earth. Handcarts aided the relief effort and shortly afterwards sons and daughters of the looters were scouring the district selling stout at a penny a bottle. Later that day, some of their fathers lay insensible in the street, overcome by too much of a good thing.

During a third raid on the bottling factory, a lorry full of soldiers caught twenty-five thieves red-handed. Another lorry carrying additional military support arrived at the same time. The first lorry was used to take the prisoners back to Rose Hill Bridewell. The second lorry followed some distance behind. In Love Lane, an angry mob stoned the vehicles and the troops responded by firing a volley of warning shots. Meanwhile, in the chaos, the prisoners tried to escape by cutting the canvas covers. The gunfire having little effect, a second round was ordered.

A drunken hard case called Cuthbert Howlett, of Skirvington Street, ran after the second lorry shouting defiance at the troops. He waved a claw hammer as he tried to climb onto the running board of the lorry. At first he was disarmed and beaten back but on a second attempt to storm the vehicle he was shot in the thigh. Howlett staggered across the street before collapsing to the ground. He was rushed to the Northern Hospital where he later died.

The rioters were either incredibly brave or mad. As soldiers pushed and clubbed the throng down the length of Scotland Road, one man defiantly bared his chest and screamed, 'Shoot me. Shoot me.' He then urged the mob to charge the troops. Later, during a tense standoff, a tough policeman used his truncheon to draw a line in the road. He then warned the crowd that the first man to cross the boundary would be severely dealt with. Inevitably one man tried his luck and was cudgelled to the ground.

On Sunday night, the trouble resumed in London Road, although the sight of the bayonets had a deterrent effect on the crowd. After a few feeble attempts at looting they dispersed. For some however, attacking the troops and police was better sport than pillaging the shops. In Christian Street, Islington, youths banded together to stone the special constables. Several officers were injured in the running battle but after a few bayonet and baton charges the mob was overcome. After soldiers fired in the air, a stray bullet ricocheted and hit a looter in the neck. 'They fought like young lions,' was one soldier's view of the police on duty.

This violent response from the military did nothing to quell the looters' passions. Crane's musical instrument shop in Scotland Road was raided and several pianos dragged into the street. A defiant cacophony of free-style jazz filled the midnight air. Only a determined baton charge from the police put an end to the free concert, although sporadic fighting continued through the night in the pitch-black alleys and side streets.

As dawn broke on the Monday, persistent rain dampened the spirits of the remaining insurgents and they returned home with their bloodstained clothes being washed as they walked. The police and troops had finally regained control and the rest of the day was quiet, except for the hospital wards and police cells, which were full to bursting with casualties and assailants. The warship *Valiant* and two escorting destroyers, which had set off from Scapa Flow two days earlier, now steamed up the Mersey to protect the docks. It was all over.

During the strike a total of 377 arrests were made for looting. There were comical scenes in court. One woman, called Fitzgerald, objected to being remanded for stealing some boots. She explained, 'I didn't steal any boots. I hadn't time to find a pair to fit me.' One man asked for bail on the grounds that he had a nasty bayonet wound in his back. The concerned magistrate enquired whether he had sustained the injury in the trenches. 'No,

London Road,' came the reply. The average sentence was three months' imprisonment. Shops and pubs were looted of £150,000-worth of goods and the total damage was estimated to be over £200,000. The strike itself failed. The police union was never recognised and the striking officers were sacked with the loss of their pension. None of them was ever reinstated.

Seven years later, during the General Strike, the police found themselves on the other side, pitted against the strikers on the orders of the Government. The industrial action, which lasted from 4-12 May 1926, was organised by the TUC in support of the coal miners' campaign to resist wage cuts. During the nine days of the national strike, the Liverpool police had learned the lessons of the past and were better prepared to meet the emergencies. There were, however, isolated incidents of disorder. In May, a striking carter tipped up a colleague's load. Five newspaper sellers in Park Road joined in with thirty other youths to shout abuse at tramcar drivers, 'You dirty scabs. Come out you blacklegs.' A man was convicted after interfering with a lorry load of beer leaving Higson's Brewery in Stanhope Street and shouting, 'Come out you ____ scab. Rush him boys.' Fifty men out of a crowd of 2000 then attacked the lorry.

The disorder was mainly on the other side of the Mersey. As a late night omnibus was returning to the tramway depot in Birkenhead, a voluntary patrol motorcyclist was pushed over and kicked by a member of a crowd that had gathered outside. A policeman arrested the assailant but was also assaulted when someone threw a roadside lamp at him. A party of special constables marching along Cleveland Street in Birkenhead were set upon by a mob throwing bricks. Four officers and three voluntary drivers were injured. In Wallasey, six strikers were arrested after attempting to stop the buses driven by volunteer drivers. As a precaution, the vehicles were guarded by police officers. Bricks were thrown at the windows and in the ensuing battle two policemen were bitten, one on the neck and the other on the hand. Yet compared to the earlier transport and police strikes, all this was pretty tame.

The Wirral was the scene of another disturbance six years later. In September 1932 there was a meeting of about 1,200 unemployed in a Birkenhead Park. After listening to speeches by Communist Party leaders, the crowd, jeering and singing the 'Red Flag', marched over to the Public Assistances Office in Conway Street where many people were already gathered. Alleged ringleader Joseph Rawlings led a deputation into the office. The crowd outside waited impatiently for them to reappear.

After ten minutes a shout come from the back, ordering the women near the doors to get clear as an attempt was to be made to storm the building. Richard Murphy was handed a pole with a Communist banner attached, which he wielded like a bayonet against a policeman. Sections of the crowd began spitting at the police. Rawlings then emerged to address the people. It seems that he had barged in on a meeting, resulting in two members of the committee walking out of the room. Rawlings announced that he was not happy with the way they had been treated. He wanted Mr Baker, the chairman of the Public Assistances Office, to apologise for some remarks he was supposed to have made about the unemployed in Birkenhead. Somebody in the crowd shouted, 'Let's go to Baker's house and wreck it. There are no bobbies there.' Another man revealed that Baker had already escaped by the back door.

A procession led by a band of pipers and men carrying red flags then marched to Mr Baker's house. In Grange Road, the crowd threw stones and smashed two shop windows. When they reached their destination in Bryaston Road, Mr Baker's son opened the door and informed the waiting deputation that his father was not at home. To cries from a megaphone of, 'We want Baker', the crowd began to break up the coping stones of a wall and hurl the fragments at the police. An open clasp knife was also thrown. Somebody shouted, 'Come on lads. Get the ____ out. We have no homes and he won't have one when we have finished with him.' Murphy, still brandishing his pole screamed, 'Come on lads. I will run this through Baker's guts, or any ____ bobby who tries to stop me.'

After the deputation left the house, the police cautiously locked the gates against the crowd. However, two attempts were made to storm the house. Five policemen prevented the first rush by putting their weight against the gates but the second attack burst the gates open and the crowd spilled into Mr Baker's garden. Threats were made to loot the house. In the meantime, Mr Baker's son had telephoned for police reinforcements. As the officers passed along Woodchurch Road, the crowd, now numbering 2,000, stopped them from joining their colleagues in the garden. Under a barrage of missiles and faced with cries of 'Let the swines have it', the fourteen extra constables had to draw their batons to fight their way through.

Eight men were later found guilty of rioting. Joseph Rawlings was sentenced to twenty months with hard labour. Upon hearing that he was being sent down for three years, Richard Murphy shouted to the judge, 'Thank you my lord. Wait till I get out. I'll ____ well shoot you.'

Despite these isolated incidents on the Wirral, Liverpool saw no repeat of the communal bloodlust of previous disturbances. In October 1936, there were numerous scuffles and some relatively minor disorder in response to a march through the city centre by a group of fascists, led by leader Oswald Mosley. Crowds gathered along the route to shout, 'Down with Fascism,' 'Smash them,' and, 'Stand up to them lads.' Some sang the *Internationale*, the revolutionary hymn of the Socialists. Three hundred police were on duty to maintain order but could not prevent the inevitable missiles being thrown at the marchers or eighty-four windows being smashed along the way. Two fascists were walking through Ranelagh Place when a crowd of 100 men rushed at them and punched them to the floor. One demonstrator shouted, 'There's Mosley, the white-livered bastard. Out with the razors and cut the swines to pieces.' In a separate incident, a sixty-one-year-old demonstrator was arrested for carrying a sword.

The usual sequel to such disturbances was a bit of looting. Yet only one shop was attacked. A man smashed the window of a confectioners' in St John's Lane and stole a packet of chocolate and four bars of rock. As he was being arrested he shouted, 'Help me lads! I'm getting pinched!' The crowd then turned on the police, throwing bottles and stones. A brick knocked off detective Balmer's hat. Meanwhile, the rest of the goods in the shop window disappeared. However, the fact that only one shop was affected is perhaps a measure of how much the situation had improved since the anarchic days of the transport and police strikes.

Spontaneous displays of mass violence gradually became a rare spectacle on Liverpool's streets. Apart from sporadic and localized attacks on the police making arrests, and a dwindling number of religious disturbances, the next major riot occurred eleven years later when, ironically, the mob turned on the Jews. Either the police had become more efficient in maintaining control of Liverpool's streets or Liverpudlians were now better behaved.

At the Liverpool Assizes in January 1924, the judge remarked that in the last thirty years serious crime had greatly decreased. He pointed out that in November 1894 there had been 103 prisoners dealt with by the grand jury. At the present assizes there were only forty-six prisoners, eleven of whom were Chinese men caught in a single gambling house raid. Indeed, in the July assize of the previous year, there had been only thirty prisoners standing for trial. Clearly the situation was getting better, particularly when taking into account that during the same period the population of South West Lancashire had increased by at least a quarter of a million.

Various reasons were given for the improvement in people's behaviour. The major ones included more professional policing, the spread of education and better housing conditions. Perhaps a more comfortable environment at home helped deter men from spending all their time in the alehouse or hanging around street corners. Drink-related violence was also decreasing. People were less likely to be beaten up by drunken Cornermen standing outside the pubs. During the First World War, the strength of beer was reduced and the price increased through taxation. Pub opening hours were also shortened. People were offered new sources of entertainment such as dancehalls and social clubs. In 1913, there were thirty-two cinemas in Liverpool and the number of establishments continued to grow. Sport became increasingly important, with men becoming passionate about their local football teams.

The 1930s saw the authorities demolish large areas of the city centre. New corporation housing programmes later saw thousands of people move into the spacious suburbs such as Norris Green, Dovecot and Huyton. Over ten years, more than 35,000 new houses and flats were constructed across the city. Four large-scale re-development schemes were also implemented. The result was that many hard cases and criminal families from the town centre were dispersed. This may have led to improvements in the overcrowded slum areas but for some, the problems were simply displaced.

By 1935, newspapers were complaining that the improvements in social conditions were doing nothing to curb the hooliganism and vandalism in the new estates. There were reports that young women were afraid to walk out of an evening past the rows of shops where the gangs gathered. As modern houses were being built, windows and street lamps were constantly smashed. 'Today the youth of the city is out of hand,' was the conclusion of one newspaper.[3] The alarming headline, 'This City of Lawless Youth', could well have been written fifty years earlier at the height of the High Rip reign of terror.

What had happened? Despite the social improvements and the growth of the entertainment and sporting industries, a period of economic depression had left thousands of people with little money to enjoy the diversions. Grinding poverty drove Liverpool's tearaways to desperation and lawlessness.

12

The Depression:
Who Controls the Streets?

AFTER THE TRIUMPH of winning the Great War, and a temporary economic boom, the 1920s continued with mass unemployment and hunger. Liverpool went into a slow and steady decline as a major port. The promise of a 'land fit for heroes' became a sick joke. Soup kitchens abounded while pawnshops were the only thriving businesses. The Great Depression, from 1929 to 1934, was part of a worldwide slump in output and prices. The result was a massive rise in unemployment.

In Liverpool, about 60,000 people were out of work. Half-starved, ragged men would queue at the Labour Exchanges or loiter on street corners to share a woodbine and mutter their resentment. The poverty, means-testing and benefit reductions for the unemployed had perhaps sapped the very strength of the working classes. For despite the awful hardship caused by the economic depression there seems to have been little organised gang activity, certainly nothing to match the days of the High Rip. Crimes were committed, of course, but individuals and small teams were largely responsible.

The 1920s and 1930s produced some notorious street fighting hardmen, much feared in their own areas. These characters were not simply young hooligans. Some had served their country with distinction in the First World War. The fearlessness and courage of Liverpool's military men was well known. During the war, a Liverpool Regiment was dubbed the 'Scruffy Fifth'. At the end of the war they became the 'Glorious Fifth'. However, during the years of economic depression that followed, some of these poverty-stricken ex-servicemen became desperate and lawless.

In 1925, a gang attacked and robbed William Farrington in Seaforth. Members included Charles Halliday, Edward Lynch and their leader, local hard case William Inman. Described as a man of tremendous strength, Inman was particularly dangerous when drunk. Unfortunately, he turned to drink after suffering a horrific ordeal during the war. He had served on a ship that had been torpedoed and sunk in 1917. His best friend lost his life. Inman afterwards worked as a dock labourer and marine fireman. In 1919, during the police strike, he joined the city fire brigade until he resigned in 1920. Although his record at sea was good, back on land he was a much-feared figure around the Bootle and Seaforth areas.

The men accosted Farrington as he walked down the street. They knocked him insensible, broke his nose and robbed him of everything he was carrying. When a female witness screamed, the men turned upon her and knocked her unconscious to keep quiet. Inman went on the run for two months and when the police arrested him a crowd interfered and rescued him. However, in February 1926, the three men eventually faced justice. Justice Swift gave both Halliday and Lynch six months' imprisonment and eighteen strokes of the cat, sentences that recalled the ruthless justice of 'Judgement Day'. Sentencing Inman to three years and twenty strokes, the judge promised, 'You shall trouble the banks of the Mersey no more for a considerable time.'

However, the sentence had little effect on Inman, for upon release he was soon in trouble again. In 1930 he killed Edward Molloy on Christmas Eve after a robbery went tragically wrong. As Molloy was getting off a tram, Inman stole a bottle of rum that was sticking out of his pocket. Molloy turned round and remonstrated with the thief but was seized by the throat and savagely punched to the floor. He died days later. Inman was convicted of manslaughter and jailed for seven years.

In 1940, Inman was back in court. A policeman was walking down Pell Road in Bootle, just after midnight, when he saw someone flashing a torch. He asked Inman to point the beam downwards but was immediately blinded by the full glare in his face. With the officer unable to see, Inman smashed him in the face with the torch, damaging his nose and breaking his teeth. In the struggle, the policeman fell to the floor and was kicked in the legs. Inman's defence was that he thought the constable was a man who had been causing trouble at his sister's house and was about to attack him. He didn't realise that he was assaulting a police officer and was extremely sorry. He received another prison sentence.

As Inman was putting fear into the residents of the north end of Liverpool, two men were terrorising the south end district of Garston. In 1926, John Doogan and Andrew Doolan, both in their mid-forties, appeared in court accused of demanding money with menaces from disabled and vulnerable old people. Doolan may well have been the same man who was shot in the thigh during the 1911 Transport Strike. Described by the prosecution, as 'a couple of big, blustering, bullying hooligans', they were as ruthless as any High Ripper.

In one incident, a severely ill woman, who could barely walk, was about to enter a public house when the men accosted her. Doogan, an ex-Irish Guardsman, demanded the price of a cup of tea. She replied that a kindly neighbour had given her sixpence for a glass of wine to buck her up and warned the men that they would be taking money from a dying woman. They took it regardless, after further threats.

Later, a Mrs Mossop and another woman were walking in Banks Road when the pair approached and asked, 'How are you fixed? Are you going to mug us?' The women pleaded they had nothing but Doogan caught one of them by the shoulder while Doolan threatened, 'Knock it out of them.' The women ran away.

A week later, one of the women was with her young niece when she met the men in Church Road. Doogan demanded the price of two pints. When told that the poor woman had only her husband's dole money, he growled, 'We are out for it. We will knock it out of somebody.' The woman was then thumped in the face several times. Despite being blind in one eye, she received a cut to her other eye and was left dazed.

Hours later, a disabled ex-serviceman met the pair in King Street. Doogan asked, 'How are you fixed? You mug other people and you can mug us.' The man replied that they were better able to work for their money than he was. As he turned to walk away, Doogan added, 'Not so fast. You get ten shillings dole and you are going to mug a couple of pints for Andy and me or you are going through it.' The man continued to walk away when Doogan smashed him in the mouth, knocking out two of his teeth. The victim collapsed on the floor, dislocating his elbow and while on the ground he was kicked in the legs. He ended up hospitalised for a fortnight.

Both men were arrested and appeared in court. In his defence, Doogan tried to justify his attack on Mrs Mossop by explaining that she had provoked him by saying that his wife was living with a black man. During the argument she had raised her hand as if to strike him and he merely gave her a few 'taps' on the forehead. As for the attack on the disabled man, Doogan explained that the ex-serviceman, after having a row with Doolan, approached him in an aggressive manner. In self-defence Doogan was forced to give the man a 'slight tap' on the forehead. Alarmed at the defendant's frivolous misuse of language, the judge felt compelled to point out to the jury that a Garston 'love tap' was a very unpleasant thing. Doogan received five years. He had already been put away for five years in 1920 for violence and wounding. Doolan was imprisoned for three years.

The 1920s also saw younger gangs beginning to make their mark in Liverpool. Fearless and cocky youths, now known as 'bucks', took over from the old Cornermen and were the forerunners of the modern day 'scally'. A retired policeman recalls dealing with them:

'Bucks' was the ordinary police talk for the working man or yobbo – the unruly kind of person who hung around street corners. Young fellers about fourteen to twenty – hanging round the corners, making a noise, and upsetting the people in the houses. There was Razor McGloshan's gangs of bucks in Crown Street. All the young men were bucks – a young buck in the old days used to be a gentleman.[1]

The question of who owned the streets was constantly being put to the test. The police would come along and move lads on, only for them to later regroup. This absurd ritual was played out all day and night. Frustrations led some policemen to take it upon themselves to personally wipe out the young bucks on their beat, using whatever means necessary. Many a personal feud was resolved on the city's cobbled streets and back alleys. One grudge involved a constable called Basil Rose and a local hard man called Patrick Sweeney. Sweeney was a member of a notorious family who were feared around the Scotland Road area.[2] Rose, however, was afraid of nobody. Their relationship was destined to end in tears.

In 1932, Rose popped his head into a public house at the corner of Hunter Street and beckoned Sweeney to come outside. After a short conversation, the policeman grabbed Sweeney by the scarf and violently prodded him in the stomach with his truncheon. As the winded man fell face downwards to the ground, Rose whacked him on the head. Two other officers arrived and pulled the bloodied and dazed victim upright, only for his trousers to fall to his ankles. Rose again hit him on the head.

A concerned woman came to speak to the policeman but he replied, 'You ____ off or I will do the same to you.' Tramcars were held up as Sweeney was dragged 'like a dog' across Byrom Street. The angry crowd thought that Sweeney was dead. However, as he moved his head there were relieved shouts of 'He is alive.' Unfortunately for Rose, a police inspector was a passenger on one of the trams and witnessed Sweeney's beating. The inspector later gave evidence against Rose, who maintained that Sweeney had attacked him first by butting him and kneeing him in the groin. Rose was found guilty, fined and dismissed from the force. He later joined the army and turned his aggression on Rommel but lost his life at El Alamein.

Yet the police were just as likely to be beaten up by the groups of bucks that littered their beat. Constables were on the front line of what must have seemed at times to be a warzone. Unlike other cities such as Manchester, where factions from rival districts would often fight each other for street supremacy, in pre-war Liverpool the main enemy was always the police. In some rough districts, violent and unruly crowds would appear spontaneously whenever an arrest was being made. In this sense, every member of the public was potentially a member of a gang, ready to strike when the signal came. The following examples of street commotions in both the north and south ends demonstrate that the mob was an ever-present danger.

On a Saturday night in May 1929, a mob attacked two constables as they tried to arrest a man in Marsh Lane. The district was later referred to in court as 'the Scotland Road of Bootle'. Asked whether Marsh Lane was a 'terrible place', a policeman replied from the witness box, 'It is not the place, but some of the people in it.' The affray resulted in 3-400 people gathering to watch the arrest. Bricks and cans were then thrown at the police in the attempt to rescue the prisoner. After violent scenes that verged on a riot, the Chief Constable was nevertheless left with a glimmer of hope. He boasted, 'There is one little bright spot in the whole affair. A certain section of the crowd showed sympathy to the constables.'

Such thoughtfulness, however, did not stretch as far as the south end of the city. In May 1933, a policeman tried to arrest the Harper brothers for fighting each other. As the drunken men were being escorted through Northumberland Street and Mill Street on their way to the police station, the angry crowd grew in numbers. One brother resisted arrest by first punching the officer and then knocking off his helmet, which was then used by the crowd for a game of football. Hostile sections of the mob, which now numbered about 700 people, made several attempts to release the prisoners. Bottles, stones, bricks and tin cans were used as missiles before thirty policemen, with batons drawn, moved in to restore order. The brothers were each gaoled for three months.

* * *

Street betting was another activity that pitted the police against young men. Gambling was a major source of entertainment and income for the working classes and a headache for the police responsible for raiding the betting schools. In 1924, senior officers drew attention to a common bookmakers' practice of employing teenagers as runners. Thanks to the leniency of the Probation Act, those who were caught would get off relatively lightly. If adults were found guilty, on the other hand, they would receive a hefty fine. The practice anticipates the methods of modern-day drug dealers who employ children to deliver the deals knowing that they will not be punished if caught.

The scam came under the spotlight after a sixteen-year-old admitted loitering in Eldon Place for the purpose of betting. It was believed that he was one of a gang working for a well-known bookmaker. Police had kept watch on him for ten minutes, during which time he had accepted slips and money from fourteen men, twenty women and seven children. In his possession were a payout sheet, a football sweepstake and over nine pounds in cash. Unwilling to name any names, he was adamant that he was working on his own, a claim that the magistrate thought incredible.

In 1926, a Sunday afternoon raid on a gambling school in Christmas Street, off Stanley Road, netted up to forty lads playing pitch and toss. The Clerk of the Court asked one youth, 'Can't you find something better to do on a Sunday afternoon?' The lad replied, 'Well, we went to play football but we lost the ball.'

A particularly successful raid was carried out in Speke on a Sunday afternoon in 1933. A team of eighteen plain-clothed policemen descended on some waste ground near the Mersey foreshore where they found up to 300 people split into two groups sitting twenty yards apart. Both parties were playing banker. Somebody shouted 'raid' and the gamblers and spectators fled in all directions, some even jumping into the river to escape. However, seventeen men from Garston were arrested and fined. A similar raid on a gambling school in Upper Frederick Street, in 1934, was less successful. As the police tried to make arrests, a crowd of fifty men attacked them. A policeman spoke of the difficulty in carrying out such raids. The neighbourhood was so clued up that the same constables couldn't be used twice. Plain-clothed officers had to undertake surveillance heavily disguised.

The streets remained a battleground for young people and the police. As far back as 1911, letters were being sent to the local press complaining about lads playing street football in Anfield. In 1929, Bootle shopkeepers were still expressing concern that footballs were constantly being kicked into their shops and street lamps regularly broken by rowdy footballers. Yet the activity of these youths is a measure of how things had progressed. Years earlier, the complaints would have been about vicious street brawls and stabbings. It was as if the hooligans were now more interested in sport. Some enlightened commentators certainly felt that while lads were kicking footballs, they were not kicking policemen.

Whereas in the past, the police were often criticised for not doing enough to stamp out disorder in the street, they were now being taken to task for their heavy-handedness in dealing with young people, particularly after the tragic case involving seventeen-year-old Joseph Spring. In 1927, a constable claimed that he saw a group of lads and girls messing about on the corner of Pontac Lane, in the Scotland Road district. They were laughing, pushing each other and kicking a football. Their behaviour seems pretty tame but was enough to get Spring and two teenage girls arrested. Spring allegedly had his arm twisted up his back as he was escorted to the bridewell. It seems that the lad was not the ruffian type and was so upset and ashamed about having to appear in court that he hanged himself. The magistrate appealed to the police to be a little more lenient when dealing with young people in the street. It was to be remembered that these youths lived in overcrowded conditions with no leisure facilities. The street was their natural playground. The case against the two girls was duly dismissed.

Nevertheless, the idea that young people were out of control continued to cause concern. The phenomenon was being highlighted without fail every few years. In 1927, in Ellesmere Port, the current craze involved setting off explosives. In the days before high-powered fireworks, kids had to make their own entertainment. The 'bombing' craze, as it was known, saw youths filling up empty beer bottles with a small quantity of carbide, followed by sand and then water. The bottle was sealed and the lads would retire to a safe distance to allow time for the water to seep through the sand to reach the carbide, at which point the container would explode. Unfortunately, a fourteen-year-old lost the sight of one eye after the bottle blew up in his face.

Various solutions to juvenile crime were offered. At a Child Welfare Convention in 1927, the Director of the Borstal Association felt that the answer to the crime wave was religion.

Other speakers expressed the view that cinemas, poor parenting and young women drinking cocktails in public bars were all corrosive influences. The view was expressed that sending young offenders to prison was useless. It was felt that the first time a lad was imprisoned, he would cry; the second time he would laugh.

As the social debate raged on, Liverpool's thieves continued to search for lucrative rewards. While desperate men such as the Garston muggers, Doolan and Doogan, felt driven to pick on penniless pensioners, the better organised and more aspiring robbers preferred to target individuals known to be carrying plenty of cash. In 1924, two pay clerks were delivering money to a school in Wellington Street, off Scotland Road, when three men attacked them. The team was waiting on the corner pretending to look into a shop window. The clerks were then ambushed as they entered a back street at the rear of the school. One of the men was clubbed twice on the head with a stick while his accomplice was smacked in the face with a heavy instrument. The gang escaped on bicycles with the cashbox containing over £200, carelessly leaving a revolver at the scene.

Five years later, a nineteen-year-old bank messenger was robbed of £1,000, a huge sum. The youth was on his way to the bank when he was knocked unconscious in James Street Station. At eleven thirty in the morning a porter heard noises coming from a room at the bottom of a flight of stairs leading from the booking offices to the platform. The lad's mouth had been gagged with a handkerchief and his hands tied with string. An hour earlier he had been walking down the stairs when a man or gang came up behind him and bashed him on the head. The messenger had probably been followed from the bank into the station. As most people used the lift, the stairs were very quiet, the ideal place to commit a robbery unnoticed. The attacker was then free either to jump into the lift to ascend to street level or escape by train. It was a well-executed crime.

For some villains, robbing businesses was more lucrative than mugging individuals, particularly for those with the time, audacity and expertise to tackle safes. Yet cracking open strong boxes was time consuming, dangerous and sometimes not worth the effort. In 1922, after breaking into the offices of Tranmere Rovers

Football Club, a gang of Birkenhead men spent the entire night sawing the hinges off the safe. As day broke they still hadn't opened the door. They left the club exhausted after stealing a few biscuits to replenish their wasted energy.

In 1929, some men broke into a china store in London Road. After spending hours attacking the safe with jemmies, they were just about to open the door when they were disturbed. Painters, working all night in the T.J. Hughes store opposite, telephoned police after seeing silhouettes of figures with electric lamps acting suspiciously on the premises. As officers arrived, the burglars decamped, leaving £400 in the four-foot-high safe, which weighed half a ton. The thieves came well prepared for a lengthy job for they left behind bits of their sandwiches and bottles of beer.

When burglars used explosives to blow a Liverpool safe in 1930, they ended up with threepence. Some safes were deliberately kept empty with a little note in saying something along the lines of 'Ha! Ha! there's nothing here.' Raiders also left their own notes. When thieves broke into Pegrams store in Breck Road, Anfield, in 1932, they managed to steal a quantity of tinned food but were unable to find any money. The disappointed robbers left a message on a scrap of paper: 'Leave a better light over the safe next time.'

In 1931, nine youths pleaded guilty to twenty-eight cases of breaking and entering, mostly in the Allerton area. The gang split into various groups to do different jobs. They were highly successful but not very professional. Bits of jewellery were thrown into the gutters and down the sewers, although one lad sewed his stash of valuables into his mattress for safekeeping. Some of the crimes were committed while the lads were on bail. After a discussion, they decided that since they were sure to be sent to borstal for three years they might as well have a final spree before being sent down.

It was claimed in court that some of the gang were well-behaved lads from respectable families who had fallen in with a bad crowd. One individual was seemingly driven to crime through suffering a lengthy period of unemployment. However, in the opinion of the prosecutor, three youths were particularly 'dangerous'. In addition to the burglaries, the lads were involved in some violent handbag snatches from old women.

In 1936, a 'hole in the wall gang' almost pulled off a lucrative robbery. One evening, the Nichol brothers, together with another man, broke into the Co-Op shop in Linacre Road, off Stanley Road. A passing policeman heard noises and decided to investigate. In the unoccupied premises next door, a window had been broken and the back door was open. After searching each room in turn, he entered the top bedroom and was confronted with a man's legs protruding from a hole that had been cut in the ceiling. The officer pulled on the man's limbs until his shoe came off. The legs then disappeared through the hole. The constable shone his torch and saw the raiders huddled together in the loft. Suddenly a brick was thrown through the hole at the officer. The men then jumped down, almost bringing the ceiling with them. Blinded by flying plaster and dust, the officer still managed to grab one of the brothers while the others escaped. Another constable in the street saw the brother running away. Borrowing a bicycle, the officer pursued and arrested him. On their way to the police station they met up with the third man who was also detained. One of the Nichols moaned, 'Well that's finished it – another few minutes and we'd have had the ____ safe.'

As these accounts demonstrate, the police were often successful in thwarting the street corner bucks and professional burglars. In order to escape the long arm of the law, criminals responded by creating new forms of crime that gave them some freedom from police interference. As the twentieth century progressed, the successful controls of beat policing meant that the disorder and delinquency shifted from the street corners to the new centres of entertainment, such as the dancehalls, nightclubs and racecourses.

The random mugging of strangers evolved into the menacing intimidation of known individuals. On an organised basis, such behaviour in turn became the basis of protection rackets involving targeted businesses. The cunning skills and expertise of the old-style burglars, pickpockets and cracksmen started to give way to the more crude exploits of the smash-and-grab raiders. With little money, young people also looked for new and inexpensive means of entertainment and excitement. This was the age of the joyrider and motor bandit and the emergence of the popular figure of the gangster.

13

From Bucks to Gangsters

AN INCREASING NUMBER of well-off people were able to afford motorcars in the aftermath of the Great War. 'Horseless carriages' had been around since the late nineteenth century when they were seen as a passing fad of the rich. However, by 1915 there were 139,000 passenger cars in Britain. The fashion for cheaper vehicles began in 1923 with the production of the compact Austin Seven.

Youths responded by stealing the vehicles for pleasure. In 1926, Harold Hurd and Reginald Jones met two girls in the King's Arms public house, near St George's Hall. The lads invited the ladies for a spin in a four-seater saloon, taken earlier from outside the Adelphi Hotel. They travelled towards Manchester and then turned back. After receiving information about the theft, two policemen tried to intercept the car but had to jump out of the way as the vehicle accelerated to forty miles per hour. However, a constable managed to jump onto the car's running board and bravely hang on as it sped towards Old Swan. Hurd pleaded with his mate, 'We are caught now; let's give up,' to which Jones replied, 'Kick the ____ off.' The door was then pushed open and the officer fell heavily in the road, injuring his head.

Further on, a group of optimistic policemen formed a line across the road in an attempt to bring the villains to a screeching halt. However, to hearty cries of, 'Don't stop. Kill the lot of the ____', the vehicle simply ploughed through the cordon, forcing the officers to jump clear. The car then turned into a side street where the joyriders decamped, although they were captured shortly afterwards. Jones explained, 'I took the car but with no intention of stealing it. I took it merely for a joy ride after I had had a few drinks.' The admission reveals that taking a car was seen simply as borrowing rather than stealing.

Also in 1926, three Liverpool youths were brought to justice after taking thirty-two motors from the south end of the city. The gang, motivated by a love of adventure, would normally abandon a car after a few hours but one favourite vehicle was kept for a month. In all but a couple of cases, the motors were returned to their rightful owners undamaged and with nothing stolen, except for petrol. Some of the vehicles were in fact taken merely to keep the 'special' car supplied with fuel. The lads enjoyed trips to Lancaster and North Wales. They would travel until the petrol ran out and simply steal another car for the return journey. The lads were all from good middle-class families and perhaps because of this were treated quite leniently with probation orders and fines. What concerned the magistrate was the effect such crimes could have on lower-class offenders: 'Can you wonder that the example set by lads of your advantage and social position is followed by your poorer brethren in this city.'

It wasn't only cars that were involved in joyriding. In 1929, a group of Liverpudlians went joyriding in a boat. The Liverpool/Eastham ferry steamer *Ruby* was berthed on the other side of the river when some young men jumped aboard and rushed to the bridge to telegraph 'full steam ahead'. As the boat raced across the Mersey the gang smashed up the furniture, damaged vending machines and threw the lifebelts overboard. On reaching Liverpool the rogue seamen ran for it.

Joyriding was a nuisance for car owners but a relatively harmless pursuit. Smash and grab raids using motorcars were an altogether more serious concern for the police. In 1927, a car containing three men pulled up outside Pryor's jewellers in Greek Street. In front of hundreds of shoppers, one man jumped out, raced to the window and smashed it with a mallet. He then pulled a tray of rings out of the gaping hole, put it under his arm and used both hands to push his way through the crowd of amazed onlookers. He was in the car and speeding down London Road before anybody could take stock of what had happened. One of his accomplices stayed in the car brandishing a revolver in case of complications. In 1932, a Scotland Road pawnbroker's shop was also hit in a lightning raid. A team ripped off the metal grill from the window and took a quantity of jewellery before jumping into a motor and escaping. When the Grassendale sub-post office in Aigburth Road was burgled, the thieves carried away the safe in a motorcar.

The use of getaway vehicles became a common feature of organised crimes. Not only could motors help criminals escape, they also broadened the geographical opportunities for committing crime. By 1932, newspapers were warning of a nationwide epidemic of crimes committed by modern highwaymen in cars. These 'motor bandits', as they were called, were always looking for new dodges. One man driving late from Sheffield to Doncaster saw a distressed woman trying to push a vehicle. He gallantly stopped to help but was then held up and robbed by two men who jumped into the 'broken' car and sped away. Another man on a late night journey from Leeds to Sheffield pulled over when he saw a torch being flashed at him. He was approached by what he thought were two policemen. Unfortunately they turned out to be armed robbers who took his wallet, disabled his vehicle and roared off on a motorbike.

Liverpool hoodlums also used motors to stage daring out-of-town robberies. In 1936, John Barratt of Liverpool teamed up with Edward McNally of Preston to stage an armed raid on the Heald Green branch of the Manchester District Bank. As Mr Thornley, the manager, was about to transport £220 to another bank, Barratt confronted him and shouted the classic gangster line, 'Put them up!' As the men fought, McNally repeatedly pistol-whipped the manager.

A woman then arrived to witness the raid. McNally ran for it leaving Barratt and Thornley locked in a violent struggle. McNally leaped into the car but a shopkeeper, who realised what was going on, jumped onto the running board and attempted to switch off the engine. McNally knocked the man off and sped away. Barratt had now escaped from the bank manager and he ran after the car shouting for his colleague to stop. McNally was taking no chances and left his accomplice to his fate. Another shopkeeper made a citizen's arrest while McNally was later captured in Manchester.

Back at the police station, Barratt was magnanimous about Mr Thornley: 'If all bank managers were like him there would be no robberies.' McNally was also full of praise: 'I could tell he had been in the army ... he fought like a tiger.' Barratt received fifteen months in prison and fifteen lashes of the cat while McNally got off with twelve months and twelve lashes.

The use of vehicles to escape from the police led to the invention of a novel gadget. In 1936, Sir Malcolm Campbell, at the time the world's fastest motorist, created what he called 'the claw of the law'. A telescopic steel arm fronted with claws a foot wide was to be fitted to the front of police cars. On making contact with the rear bumpers of the bandit's vehicle, the claw would become firmly locked. The police could then put on their brakes and bring the getaway car to a halt. When not in use, the claw was hidden, but could stretch out over five feet and move upwards and downwards when operated by a lever on the dashboard. The device underwent tests at Hendon Police College.

Yet not even the 'claw of the law' could hold back the bandits. Once in the driver's seat, and roaring down country lanes far from the city centre, the tearaways were a law unto themselves. In this sense, the motorcar provided villains with a personal space and freedom from the prying eyes of the city beat constables.

* * *

In the nineteenth century a great deal of disorder centred on the streets and street corners, particularly outside public houses where young men usually congregated. As the twentieth century progressed, the disturbances shifted to the new centres of entertainment, the dancehalls and nightclubs. The cheap dancehalls became a source of great concern to the police who were often called to break up fights between drunken revellers. Vandalism was also common, as windows and furniture were smashed during mini riots.

In 1926, a practical joke at a dance in the Royal Assembly Rooms in Great George Street in the south end, turned nasty. The hall was a great favourite with foreign seamen. Hugh Gorry, together with his brother and James McDonough were due to rejoin their ships the following morning. In high spirits on their last night of freedom, and partly celebrating the end of the General Strike, they thought that it would be good fun to have a mock fight on the dance floor at the end of which Gorry would pull out a toy pistol and fire a shot. The prank was intended to 'give the girls a thrill'. Unfortunately the gun fired a cork that hit McDonough in face, scorching his eyeball. Everybody carried on dancing until somebody shouted, 'He's shot.' Not surprisingly this changed the mood and panic set in. However, the situation was soon calmed with the arrival of the police.

With more privacy than the public dancehalls, the nightclubs provided the city's tearaways with a measure of sanctuary from the law. The creation of shebeens, or illegal drinking dens, laid the foundation for nightclubs. Such establishments have always been closely linked with gangland activity, particularly through protection rackets, prostitution and gambling. In 1936, the chairman of Liverpool Licensing Committee voiced concern over the growth of clubs of an 'undesirable nature'. He did not mean well-organised social, athletic and political clubs but those that existed solely for drinking and gambling. These were little more than open betting establishments since patrons did not need to be members. Indeed, it was bookmakers who chiefly ran such clubs. The chairman was particularly angry at the way these organisations seemed to enjoy immunity from police inspection. To hinder officers from staging raids, spy holes, padlocks, electric bells and barbed wire were often employed.

In the battle against gambling, the police were always going to lose the war. When raids on betting establishments were taking place back in the 1890s, the point was made that such action was futile. Gamblers accepted the fines with the same grace that they accepted the occasional loss on the horses. Indeed, some hardened gamblers were actually taking bets on when the next police raid would take place. The press publicity surrounding the raids actually became a form of advertising, the result being that even more people went on to join the clubs.

Nightclubs became the natural headquarters of gangsters and bucks that would meet to discuss future criminal plans. One particular establishment in Farnworth Street, Kensington, run by Alfred Brierley, came in for strong criticism at the Liverpool Police Court in 1929. It was claimed that the club was the meeting place of the most undesirable characters in the city. Disgusting and shocking scenes took place there in the early hours of the morning.

The club had been under police observation from November to December 1928. Detectives posing as customers witnessed drinking after hours, sometimes until 5.30am. Brierley also acted as banker during card games and other gambling pursuits. Fights were common and on one occasion a detective was asked if he wanted to take part in a 'burst' (burglary) on a jeweller's shop. A pickpocket, who claimed to have the finest fingers in the Midlands, once gave an open demonstration of his skills to other customers. It was pointed out in court that women would often enter the club in the early hours, the implication being that there was something seedy going on. However, Brierley explained the presence of the females by claiming that they were the wives of members who, on their way home from dances, would call in to pick up their husbands. A likely story.

Brierley eventually became suspicious of the presence of the police officers and asked a customer to lend him a revolver so that he could 'bump them off'. Little did he know that he was talking to another detective. The club was struck off the register of licensed premises and the establishment suspended for twelve months. Various fines were also issued to the management and some customers who were caught drinking late.

However, new clubs constantly sprang up to replace those that were closed down. In 1935, forty-two new clubs were registered in Liverpool but forty-one were struck off. However, this was far from a victory for the licensing authorities. When a club started attracting the attention of the police, it would close down only to open up again under a different name further up the road. Sometimes the club would stay where it was with another name pinned up outside. The management, of course, would remain the same.

The nightclubs helped create a new type of criminal. In the 1920s newspapers started to refer to crooks and dancehall rowdies as 'gangsters', rather than hooligans. The term, of course, has American origins. When the various migrants settled in America in the late nineteenth century they brought with them the organised street gangs of French and Italian cities, the violent political activists of Ireland and the Mafiosi of Sicily. This influx laid the foundations for the sinister criminal societies of the 1920s.

The Sicilian, Irish and Jewish gangsters of the 1920s were the sons of the immigrants of the 1880s. The criminal landscape of America changed after the First World War when demobbed soldiers came home to face unemployment and social unrest. Some turned to civil disobedience or trade union agitation as a means of protest against the injustices of poverty and deprivation. Others turned to crime.

It was into this explosive mix that the Government in 1920 introduced an unworkable piece of legislation – Prohibition. The bootlegging of alcohol became a major criminal industry. From the ranks of unemployed ex-soldiers, the gangs found no trouble attracting men who had little respect for a government that had denied them social justice. Chicago boasted the ideal social and geographical conditions to become the capital of the criminal underworld. After the repeal of Prohibition in 1933, the mobsters moved into prostitution, gambling and even politics.

By the mid Twenties, certain individuals, such as Al Capone, were becoming prominent. In addition to the big organised crime syndicates of the major cities, there were many individual bandits who acted independently, striking at isolated banks and filling stations before roaring off in their stolen vehicles. John Dillinger, 'Baby Face' Nelson and Bonnie and Clyde were amongst the most infamous. On a much smaller scale, Liverpool's own gangsters used intimidation and ruthless violence to forge their reputations. Yet, there was a certain swagger and coolness about the new breed of local hoodlums that differed from the brute violence of an earlier age.

In 1931, a dance at the Edge Hill branch of the Independent Labour Party, in Upper Parliament Street, was invaded by a group of five youths. The gang, led by Michael Kelly, had terrorised the club, along with various dancehalls, for some time. They would cause disturbances and then assault anybody who dared remonstrate with them. Although they were not members, the lads rushed past the doorman and started causing trouble with the officials. Eighteen chairs and a glass panel were smashed in the fracas. A constable was called but on entering the club he was attacked with a chair. The MC was also knocked to the floor and beaten.

In court, it was alleged that in December 1930, Kelly and his mates had staged a similar raid on a Labour Club in Lodge Lane. It was also claimed that to avoid trouble and to keep the peace, clubs usually tolerated the disgraceful behaviour of the young toughs. They each received a fine. The sturdily built Kelly, from the Edge Hill district, was a persistent troublemaker. He began his criminal career aged twelve and progressed to leading his associates in bullying, assaulting people and defying law and order at every opportunity. He had convictions for shop breaking, wilful damage, theft of a motor vehicle and assaulting the police.

On a quiet afternoon in August 1936, four men raided the Shenstone FC and Supporters Club. While two stood guard, Michael Kelly and Thomas Bird entered the club through a back room but were challenged by the chairman who realised that they were not members. It seems that the men were after some winnings supposedly due to Bird. The chairman, however, disputed that a bet had been made. Kelly warned the man, 'We want a pound. It will be better for you to let us have it.' The men then punched the chairman in the face and as he lay unconscious they rifled his pockets and took a wallet containing £17. A club member tried to intervene but was told it was private business. As the men were leaving, Kelly turned to the member and warned, 'See nothing, hear nothing, say nothing.'

The men were found guilty, despite witnesses being threatened by colleagues of the accused. The judge gave Kelly eighteen months while Bird was sent away for three years, perhaps because he had the worst record of the two. His criminal past was also atrocious. He had convictions for shop-breaking, warehouse breaking, wounding and assaulting the police. A detective inspector admitted that he had nothing good to say about the man who was a terror to the neighbourhood. He was also described by the police as 'addicted to thieving and beyond control'.

Bird had been to Borstal once and prison on numerous occasions without ever learning his lesson. In June 1930, together with an accomplice he was caught in the act of burgling Sturla's outfitters in Wavertree Road. He was carrying a jemmy and a knuckleduster and wearing clothes that had been stolen in earlier raids on the shop. The knuckleduster was unusual in that it fitted over two fingers rather than four. In court, Bird claimed that it was simply the handle of a chain. The Recorder agreed only for a juror to suggest that nevertheless the object 'might serve its purpose'. An angry Bird put the juror straight: 'A knuckle duster fits over four fingers.' The Recorder interjected, 'You are evidently an expert.' The iron bar that was found in Bird's possession was then produced. The Recorder remarked that at least it wasn't a toothpick. Despite claiming that the police knocked the confession out of him, Bird was sent to borstal for three years.

In 1939, Kelly was back in the news. Again described in court as the ringleader of a dangerous gang, he had been convicted six times since 1931 for offences involving violence. Kelly, whom a detective called 'a menace to the community', pleaded guilty to assaulting three men in two separate incidents. Jailing him for five years, the judge promised that, 'the Kelly gang will now be in a state of suspended animation.'

As well as the nightclubs, the gangsters also began to move into other areas where fear and intimidation could net a hefty profit. This was also the great age of the racecourse protection rackets. A bitter feud of the time concerned the famous Liverpool detective, Bert Balmer and a mysterious gangland boss known as 'the Colonel'. Balmer retired as Deputy Chief Constable in 1967, after serving over forty years in the Liverpool police force. In the 1930s, protection rackets at the races were a cause for concern throughout the country. Intimidation was replacing outright violence as a means of obtaining money. In his serialised memoirs,[3] Balmer recalled the time when he was a member of the Flying Squad investigating the activities of a notorious racecourse gang led by the London-based Colonel. On Grand National day in 1937 the men, who travelled throughout the country, were due in Liverpool. The gangster's menacing catchphrase was, 'I always pay my debts', which meant that if anybody crossed him he would wreak his revenge.

The battle-scarred bunch of five toughs, which included two Australians, would demand money off a bookmaker on the pretext of protecting him from some imaginary and invented rival mob that were out to get him. If the bookmaker refused to pay up, he would be shown an open cutthroat razor and threatened with a beating. This was the year before Graham Greene published his account of the same sort of racket in his novel *Brighton Rock*, later turned into a film featuring Richard Attenborough as the vicious young hoodlum 'Pinkie'. The book was in fact based on another real-life racecourse battle between London's Sabini mob and Alf White's King's Cross Gang.

Balmer and a colleague wandered through the racecourse and spotted the Colonel and his associates walking separately through the crowds. The men's modus operandi was to stay apart until the moment when they decided to strike. After the big race had finished, people began to leave the course. At this point the detective's attention was drawn to an altercation on some waste ground outside a pub near to one of the exits. Two men lay on the ground having been slashed across the face. It was no surprise to learn that the victims were a bookmaker and his clerk. One man needed eighteen stitches and his colleague fifteen. On being interviewed, the men kept quiet except to say, 'If we talk we will get it again. We should have paid.'

Balmer made another tour of the racecourse with an informant, known as 'Salty', a former hoodlum with vast experience of racecourse criminal practice. The pair had a secret code by which they communicated. At one point, Salty gave the signal not to approach but to follow him. He then boarded a tram to Liverpool town centre where he visited a public house, with Balmer following behind. On safe ground, Salty informed the detective that the bookmaker had been attacked because he had double-crossed the Colonel. The informer also gave Balmer the location of the gangster's new drinking place. It seems that he had recently changed pubs because he suspected that the police were on to him.

Balmer visited the victims in Walton Hospital. He warned them that the feud was not over and that someone was going to end up dead, either on a mortuary slab or at the end of the hangman's noose. He left it up to them to decide who it was going to be. Balmer then toured the public houses looking for any witness brave enough to talk. Time was of the essence since it was known that the men were due to leave Liverpool the following morning. Balmer knew that if there were any bloodstains on the gangsters' clothes, such evidence would soon be destroyed.

Salty then came up with the name of a witness who seemed reliable. The man saw the attack and could identify the culprit by sight although not by name. After taking a statement, Balmer and his squad went after the Colonel, who was holed up in a lodging house away from the rest of his boys. The householder opened the door and after a few enquiries directed Balmer up to the guest's bedroom. The Colonel must have heard what was going on, for when Balmer walked into the room, he was hiding behind the door. The detective turned and grabbed the man's arm but as he did so the Colonel reached for a razor and slashed at him, narrowly missing his face but slicing his coat. The pair fought on with Balmer trying desperately to grab the razor. In the struggle, the gangster's arm was broken and he gave up.

On the way to the bridewell the Colonel suggested, 'I'll take a lie down for a carpet or half a stretch.' In other words, he would plead guilty if he could be dealt with at the lower court where he would receive a lenient sentence of about six months' imprisonment. However, he ended up doing four years and Balmer was proud to announce the gift of a new coat.

The presence of two Australian outlaws on Liverpool's streets was symptomatic of a wider scare about foreign gangs infiltrating the country. As if Liverpool didn't have enough of its own gangsters, the city was also playing host to imported villains. In 1938, it was estimated that each year 20,000 illegal immigrants were entering Britain. They included confidence tricksters, bogus marriage traffickers and other assorted criminals. 'Almost all the aliens who come over here under cover are crooks of one kind or another,' was the verdict of one local newspaper.[4]

It was believed that a powerful and organised outfit from Antwerp and six other gangs based in Paris were responsible for much of the people smuggling. These criminals were also involved in drugs and the white slave traffic whereby young women were obliged to take part in dodgy marriages to unscrupulous Englishmen. Such women sometimes had to turn to prostitution in order to pay an ongoing levy imposed by racketeers. There were various other ways of entering the country. Fake passports could easily be bought on the Continent. Foreigners could travel as bogus seamen and simply disappear once they reached an English port.

Yet the scaremongering over foreign gangs was soon to be
eclipsed by an even greater foreign threat. In 1939, Britain was at
war with Germany. In the chaos and disorder of international
hostilities, Liverpool's own mobs would regain the centre stage,
with a level of violence and bloodshed unseen since the days of the
High Rip.

14

The Second World War

DURING THE SECOND World War, Liverpool suffered attacks from two fronts. As a major port for the Atlantic convoys delivering supplies, the city became a prime target for the Luftwaffe. With ninety bombing raids between 1940 and 1942, including the devastating blitz of May 1941, the Germans did their best to physically destroy the city from the air. Ten thousand homes were destroyed and 120,000 buildings damaged.

Down on the ground, amongst the bombed-out buildings and blacked-out streets, there was another war taking place, between the police and the tearaways. In 1938, the Chief Constable of Liverpool had boasted that adult crime was falling. The number of offences committed in 1937 was the lowest since 1932. However, the situation was about to change. The outbreak of war presented considerable problems for the authorities but plenty of opportunities for the criminal gangs and young tearaways. The heavy workload of the rescue services during air raids left the police overstretched and unable to deal with their normal crime-fighting duties.

Wartime deprivation and austerity created the ideal conditions for the growth of spivs who could get their hands on anything. The ships and docks remained a convenient source of illicit treasures. Also, in 1941, the Americans were brought into the war. Many disembarked at Liverpool and brought with them much sought after goods. Those housed at the Burtonwood air force base, near Warrington, were able to provide highly desired items such as cigarettes, nylons and chewing gum. The visitors were bled dry. 'I've never seen such a collection of bums, stiffs, and hangers-on anywhere as I've seen in Liverpool,' was the view of one American officer.

As well as racketeering and the black market, there was the problem of deserters committing crime. At the end of the war it was estimated that there were 10,000 deserters roaming the country, 1,000 of them foreigners. Many of these men had to survive without identity cards or ration cards and often turned to crime, particularly burglary, to survive. The dark, deserted streets of the wartime blackout were an ideal environment for hold-ups and other villainy. The looting of damaged stores after air raids was rife.

Villains from other parts of the country also flocked to Liverpool to take advantage of the lax security and wartime distractions. In 1941, a gang of well-known thieves from London visited the city to raid a jeweller's shop in Mount Pleasant. In a well-planned crime, they took lodgings over the adjoining premises and spent the night smashing a hole through the twenty-four inch thick brick wall. It was daybreak when the men finally reached the safe, so they decided to wait until mid morning when the noise of the trams would disguise the sound of the metal doors being hacked open. However, police disturbed the raiders who fled through the streets of the town centre throwing away jewellery as they ran. A policeman was cracked on the head by a brick as he tried to make an arrest.

Wartime conditions threw up all kinds of new problems for the police. People sleeping in public air raid shelters were sometimes inconvenienced by the behaviour of drunken hooligans who gambled and fought while others were trying to sleep. The lads were not the only problem. Just before midnight during a blackout in 1939, a policeman in Dovecot, on the outskirts of the city, approached three young women who were singing and shouting at the top of their voices. When told to be quiet, one of them enquired, 'Who the ____ are you talking to?' The constable asked the girls for their names but the nineteen-year-old ringleader ordered her friends to keep silent, adding, 'I'll fix this swine, he'll get no ____ name from me.' When told that she was under arrest, the teenager smacked the constable in the face and bit his finger. She threatened, 'My father would kill the likes of you.'

A fifteen-year-old then jumped on the officer's back and throttled him before punching him in the face. The third girl ran away. The valiant officer got the two young women to the police telephone box only to lose the younger prisoner in the struggle.

When questioned back at the station, the elder girl claimed that they were singing only so that people would not bump into them during the blackout. She also complained of police brutality, despite suffering only a scratch on her wrist. All three girls were put on probation.

In 1940, there was a new moral outrage. Teenage girls were spending the nights with undesirable men in public air raid shelters, effectively using the places as love nests. One Liverpool gang was known as the 'Shelter Girls'. They took advantage of the air raids as an excuse not to go home and instead spent their time singing, dancing and keeping people awake. The situation was so bad that respectable people were shunning the big shelters.

Members of the armed forces, back in Liverpool on home leave, became easy targets for local thieves and hard cases. In 1940, there was a spate of crimes against servicemen who had been lured into having a drink with strangers in pubs. They would later find that their money had been stolen from their pockets. One man was found guilty of befriending and robbing torpedoed sailors recuperating at Liverpool Sailors' Home.

In June 1941, a soldier on home leave was walking up Breck Road when three girls stopped him at the junction of Richmond Park. The man was asked for a light but as he reached for his lighter he heard a voice behind him shout, 'If you give her a light you will get cut.' He then noticed a group of six youths across the road. The soldier shouted back, 'We'll see,' and proceeded to light the girl's cigarette. As he turned around, a man called Cuthbert McHale rushed at him shouting, 'You asked for it.' The victim was then stabbed twice in the stomach. The injured man responded with a blow to McHale's jaw but was rewarded with a slash across his wrist. Although he was taken to hospital to be stitched, his wounds were not serious. He denied being 'fighting drunk' and calling McHale 'yellow'. At Manchester Assizes, a detective sergeant claimed that McHale was the ringleader of a gang, adding that he was 'out of control'. McHale, who was already out on licence from an approved school, was found guilty of occasioning actual bodily harm and sent back to the institution.

In 1941, five lads, described by the prosecution as 'a young gang', were accused of various wartime offences. According to the prosecutor, the lads specialized in raiding bomb-damaged buildings to steal all they could while the police were fighting the flames from surrounding properties. They would also visit various hostels and ply soldiers and sailors with drink before stealing their property. Some seamen were left penniless in a strange city. Two of the thieves were charged with filching boots, intended for torpedoed sailors, from the Gordon Smith Institute for Seamen in Paradise Street. They had also taken sherry from a bombed out public house and robbed a suitcase from a sailor in Lime Street. Other associates had stolen the wallet from a drunken sailor and attempted to open the safe after breaking into the Overseas League. Four of the youths were sent to borstal.

The lack of experienced constables on the streets inspired some young tearaways to push their luck with the war reserve officers on duty. In 1942, five youths from Paddington attacked a 'special' policeman called Dunn. Just after 10pm the constable heard some lads singing, shouting and swearing in Mason Street. He asked them to behave themselves but one replied, 'Fuck you. I am telling you to move.' His mate then punched the officer, breaking his false teeth. The rest of the gang closed in, punching Dunn, jumping on his back and pulling him to the ground where they gave him a good kicking. The policeman managed to stagger away and find two other officers on patrol, including Acting Sergeant Clarke.

The lads ran away but the spokesman was caught. He shouted, 'He is only a ____ special.' As he spoke, he felled Clarke and kicked him while he lay on the floor. 'Get the gang,' he shouted as the others reappeared and closed in for the kill. Reserve Constable Dunn managed to draw his baton but found it snatched from him and used to club the sergeant on the head. Other officers arrived on the scene and the pack fled but were later traced and arrested.

Amidst the devastation, the Blitz provided Liverpudlians with some heaven-sent opportunities. In May 1941, during one of the heaviest air raids in the district, a pub in Bootle was wrecked. A team of policemen on night patrol were therefore amazed when they went to inspect the premises. What was left of the bomb-damaged pub was packed with about forty customers drinking free beer. In a true wartime spirit of cooperation, four men had selflessly volunteered to act as barmen. The crowd was so engrossed in having a good night out that they didn't even notice the officers. The entire stock of the bar, including all the beer and whisky, had disappeared. One of those arrested claimed that he had only had a mouthful.

The war years also saw the creation of many inventive scams. In 1941, a group of five youths, aged fifteen and sixteen, visited a Liverpool firm's pay office and called out the tally numbers of men they knew to be off sick, thereby obtaining wages by false pretences. Five tins, stamped with the corresponding tally numbers, were duly handed over, each containing £4. The gang also burgled houses in the Edge Hill area while the occupants were huddled in air raid shelters.

In 1945, a sixteen-year-old absconder from an approved school went to a hospital swathed in bandages asking to borrow a pair of crutches. He claimed that he was a wounded soldier. He limped off with his crutches only to return two days later. He was so grateful that he asked the institution for a charity box so that he could collect some money in appreciation of their kindness. He collected cash in London Road then pocketed the money. When he appeared in court he was felt to be such an unruly character that only a remand in prison could guarantee the public some measure of safety.

The war also provided great opportunities for women thieves. While the men were away, teams of female shoplifters would scour the department stores, using children as a distraction and prams as wagons to carry out the booty. The crime itself was nothing new. As far back as the First World War, female crews were active in the big city centre stores. In 1918, eight women were arrested on a single day in Blacklers. The women, who were married and in comfortable circumstances, included a few mother and daughter teams. Stockings, curtains and jackets were the favoured items. One woman claimed that her young children must have picked up the picture books found in her possession.

In 1936, the growing practice of displaying goods openly in stores, copying the American system, was seen as a major reason for the increase in pilfering. Temptation was too great for some people. The shortage of goods during the war was a further incentive for some to grab what they could. Since women did the shopping, they were best placed to take advantage of lax security. Not only did they target the goods in the stores but also fellow women shoppers. Female dippers were as skilled as male pickpockets. Liverpool detective Bert Balmer recalls one thief who carried a razor to split open the bottom of other ladies' handbags. The contents would then fall neatly into her large shopping bag.

In 1940, two women used a fifteen-year-old boy as an accomplice in their shoplifting expeditions. The women raided the big department stores, including T.J. Hughes, Owen Owens and Marks and Spencers. After they had selected and stockpiled various items, the lad would secrete them under the big rubber cape he was wearing. He would then go outside and drop the goods into a pram. The team would carry out the procedure several times until they had enough swag. In T.J. Hughes a female supervisor saw what was going on and approached the youth. 'You have nothing on me, baby,' he cheekily declared. However, a detective was called and found a stash of contraband in the pram. The women received one month's imprisonment while the boy was put on probation.

Also in 1940, detectives observed forty-eight-year-old Mrs Kelly and her daughter loitering suspiciously in the city centre. The women spent their time mingling with passengers boarding tramcars at the corner of Church Street and Paradise Street. The older woman was seen putting her hand in the coat pocket of a passenger. When stopped and searched, a stranger's purse was found in her possession. On being told that she was being arrested, Mrs Kelly threw herself to the ground and bit the officer on the leg. It took another four policemen to carry her into the patrol van. At the bridewell, she asked for a glass of water and promptly threw it over two detectives. Kelly was imprisoned for two months while her daughter received a fine.

A year earlier, Kelly, who had twenty-one previous convictions, had appeared in the dock with her arm in a sling in a futile attempt to persuade the court that it was impossible for her to have been dipping women's pockets in Lewis's store a few days earlier. She was, according to one detective, the worst bag snatcher and pickpocket in the North of England.

In 1948 the *Liverpool Echo* reported a disturbing new trend in robbery. 'Shoplifters in Trousers' was the headline, announcing that it wasn't only women that were involved in store thefts. It seems that men were increasingly turning their hand to a bit of lifting in the big department stores.

* * *

Women pilfering from shops and commuters was small scale compared to what was on offer to men working at the docks. 'Where there are docks there is crime should be one of the easiest maxims for a sociologist to memorize,' says crime writer James Morton.[1] If Liverpool villains were famous for one particular type of crime it was robbery from the docks. While such theft was a particular problem during the war, it was certainly not a new phenomenon. In 1891, an industrious serial offender called Cornelius Cullen was again found guilty of pilfering from the docks. Cullen, who specialised in the theft of rope and cotton, had amassed fifty-seven convictions in over four years.

While Cullen was a prolific thief, some pilferers were petty offenders. In 1903, Thomas Riley, a dock labourer, was charged with stealing eight green tomatoes belonging to the Mersey Docks and Harbour Board. Asked what he had to say for himself, Riley explained to the court that another man had given him the tomatoes. In his defence, he helpfully pointed out to the magistrate, 'Giving's not stealing.'

The magistrate attempted to put Riley straight on that matter. He explained, 'Suppose you are working at the docks and take off your coat, leaving it hanging up somewhere, and as I pass, I say, "That's a very nice coat," and suppose a man tells me to take it, do you think I would be justified in doing so?' Riley thought about it for a moment before replying that he wasn't quite sure that anybody would want the tattered garment he was presently wearing. In reply to the magistrate, the famished Riley admitted that he had eaten two of the unripe tomatoes. The magistrate decided that his punishment ought to be to eat the rest of the fruit, with a doctor in attendance.

By the time of the Second World War, dock theft had become a more serious concern. The docks were not only a seven-mile treasure trove for adult thieves, but also a huge adventure playground for kids. Boys known as 'lorry skippers' would hitch rides before jumping off and running away, almost causing accidents. Kids would also target lorry drivers and carters travelling along the Dock Road. The juvenile raiders would slash the ropes securing cases to the wagons or rip open sacks of sugar. The infamous Peanut Gang began their criminal careers by tearing open bags of peanuts stored at the docks (see Chapter 17).

Dock theft was commonplace throughout the war years. There were two main types of pilfering. The first was small scale and opportunistic. Dockers sometimes robbed useful items for their own individual use. It was not uncommon for men to break open a package of food or drink and consume it as they worked. Of the many cases reported daily in the press, the ones that stand out are those that tested the thief's ingenuity and powers of invention, both verbal and practical, to the limit.

In September 1940, a passing policeman spotted a couple of dockers sitting awkwardly on some packages as they waited for the bus home. Pairs of overalls suspiciously covered the improvised seats. Upon inspection, the packages turned out to be drums of paint. The men explained, in vain it might be added, that they had found the paint on board a ship and were taking it home for safekeeping. They were adamant that they intended to return it the next day. Around the same time, a docker was arrested at the gates after trying to smuggle out contraband. He had cunningly tied the legs of his underpants and filled them with tea. Two years later, a Bootle docker was caught waddling through the gates with a leg of lamb down each trouser leg and a kidney in each sock.

The second type of stealing was large scale, more organised and professional. Goods stolen might include a few thousand cigarettes or cases of whisky. Peroxide was particularly in demand. This was more the remit of the gangs, for in order for the goods to reach the public there had to be a network of receivers and go-betweens. The gangs also looked after those members unfortunate enough to get caught. In 1940, during a trial of three dockers accused of theft, a cargo superintendent of an export firm complained that men were making weekly collections at the Clearing House on Saturday and giving the money to those who had been fined. He cited the recent case of a man who had been fined and still ended up £3 in pocket.

Of the total number of people convicted of dock thefts only forty per cent were dock labourers, twenty per cent were seamen and the other forty per cent were spread over forty different occupations. Seventeen of those prosecuted were watchmen, responsible for preventing the pilfering. It is difficult to quantify how much was stolen, particularly with export thefts. It was only when the ship had reached its destination that the missing load would be discovered. At the docks, men would break open cases and rob the contents before filling up the boxes with rubbish and nailing them shut. In 1949, a consignment of 86,000 pairs of nylon stockings heading for South Africa was destined never to arrive. Customs officers investigating the cargo of a ship berthed in Liverpool found that thirty cases supposed to contain the hosiery were stuffed with rags and paper.

The authorities did their best to put a stop to the pilfering. They would, for example, separate a consignment of shoes into left and right feet, thereby thwarting the robbers who would end up with two useless left shoes. However, the practice only spurred the thieves to go looking for the other container to complete the pair.

Of course, dock thefts continued after the end of the war. The level of pilfering came under the spotlight in 1947 when Liverpool's stipendiary magistrate pointed out that the crime wave had become something of a pantomime joke. A local comedian used to quip that the docks were a training ground for thieves. Others didn't find the situation so amusing. Leaving aside petty thefts by individuals, the magistrate explained that well-organised and trained gangs were a major problem. Many men had just spent six years in the armed forces, where they had learned commando tactics and the cleverest tricks of violence. According to the magistrate, such skills were being put to nefarious use.

* * *

Even as the war was being fought in Europe, violence was spilling over on to the streets of Liverpool. Youths not yet called up for military service had enough time on their hands to cause a bit of mayhem. Most of the beatings were being dished out by the Peanut Gang in the south end of Liverpool but the rest of the city also suffered occasional outbursts of aggression from angry young men, particularly in the dancehalls, milk bars and cafes.

In 1940, Joseph Reilly was involved in a Saturday night fight with a man outside a milk bar in Breck Road. He shouted, 'I will kill him,' before both brawlers crashed through a window. Two policemen ran over and tried to intervene but Reilly's two brothers immediately set upon them. Both officers were knocked to the ground where the brothers jumped on them and seized them by the throats. One of them shouted, 'Smash them up,' as he invited the hostile crowd of spectators to join in the attack. The constables were left seriously injured and on sick leave for weeks after being given a good kicking.

In 1944, after a dance at the Orange Hall in Garston, a crowd of about 250 people gathered outside to take part in a fight. Girls from the south end would often travel to the dance. However, a crew from the Park Road area was under the impression that the Garston lads were stealing their women, so they made their way to the venue to confront their love rivals. The street was turned into a battlefield and the police had great difficulty restoring order. Eight young men and a sixteen-year-old ended up being fined for their part in the affray.

A year later, a sixteen-year-old was fined for using a broken bottle on a dancehall rival. The victim was dancing with a girl when another boy 'excused' him and took over the dance. Later that evening the victim went to the toilet where he was struck on the head. As he lay on the floor, his adversary kicked him in the body and punched him in the face. The lad's friends pulled him off but he returned with a broken bottle, which he smashed in the poor boy's face, putting him in hospital for three days.

The kicking outrages of late Victorian Liverpool were periodically re-enacted, as if to show that nothing had really changed. In 1945, Thomas Cullen, a seventeen-year-old absconder from an approved school, and Harold McCormick, a carter of the same age, attacked a detective in Lime Street. The officer observed Cullen, who was wanted for various burglaries enter a café with some lads. As he was being arrested, Cullen put up resistance and fell to the ground with the officer. A hostile rabble gathered and Cullen was dragged into Lime Street by his mates. The determined detective was pulled along the floor, refusing to let go of his prisoner. As somebody shouted, 'Boot him,' McCormick kicked the officer in the head. The dazed detective was held down and his stomach used as a trampoline. His shoes were then removed and thrown into the crowd. Cullen ran off but was later arrested along with McCormick. When accused of the assault, McCormick replied, 'He was my mate, wasn't he?' On being told that he was being arrested, he barked impatiently, 'Get on with it.' At Manchester Assizes, Justice Hallett sent the youths to borstal for three years. Addressing McCormick, whom he called 'a savage', he regretted not being able to have him flogged.

While the youth gangs of Liverpool were on the rampage, and the adult criminals stealing whatever they could lay their hands on, there was a new generation of young tearaways about to emerge. With their parents busy fighting a war against the Germans the children were ready to start their own war, against each other, against society, against anybody who stood in their path.

15

Dead End Kids:
Juvenile Gangs During the War

THE CHAOS OF war created new environments and opportunities for Liverpool's juveniles. While fathers were serving in Europe, and mothers working long hours in the local munitions factories, many children were left to their own devices. Some took full advantage of the freedom from parental discipline. The situation was exacerbated by the closure of many youth facilities as volunteers and Scout leaders joined the forces. Schools were often closed for lengthy periods. In 1940, the Rev. Heming Vaughan, Minister of the Ancient Chapel of Toxteth, wrote in his church publication about the thousands of school-less children who were running wild. Local residents were complaining about the 'gangs of youngsters bent on any mischief, property damaged, traffic a peril, and the lives of quiet people made unbearable'.[1]

Relentless bombing meant that many properties were damaged. Seventy thousand people were made homeless. Many families were forced to move in with friends and neighbours, with up to four families crammed into a single house. In such difficult environments children were often chased outside, where they caused mischief. After the war, when demobbed fathers again became part of their children's lives, it was often too late. They had become strangers and had difficulty exercising any parental control.

One of the worst cases of feral childhood was that of a five-year-old boy, described in court as a 'confirmed and persistent thief'. By 1940, the youngster had committed six offences. His size meant that he could easily slip behind shop counters to steal from the till. He had even stolen his teacher's handbag and shared the contents with his classmates. He was such a menace in the district that it had been necessary to furnish all the shopkeepers with his description. This did not stop him sneaking into a butchers shop and stealing some money. The boy's father was away in the navy and his mother worked as a barmaid. On several occasions, police had found him sheltering in shop doorways as late as 11pm. When an Education Officer visited the home one evening, no adults were present. There was a commotion in an upstairs bedroom where five children, aged from two months to nine years, were playing with lighted paper. The next night, the officer returned only to be told by a little girl that her mother had 'gone for a pint'. When the mother was questioned as to her absence she replied that it was her only night off and she 'needed some enjoyment'.

The war provided the ideal conditions for burglary. Parks and other public amenities were left vulnerable to vandalism after protective railings were pulled up to aid the war effort. Buildings, half destroyed by bombs, were looted while completely bombed out buildings were ideal places to hide stolen property. As families cowered in air raid shelters, kids would burgle deserted properties. In 1940, a fifteen-year-old called at a house claiming that his own home had been bombed. The householder took pity on the lad and after feeding him, allowed him to stay all day. Later, during an air raid, the man went on warden duty while his wife took refuge in a shelter. The ungrateful lad took the opportunity to plunder the gas meter.

In the same year, two children burgled a house. Not only did they have stockings on their hands to avoid fingerprints but the older boy was heard telling his accomplice to 'wait till the guns go' before breaking the window, thus taking perfect advantage of the distraction. The blackout also created ideal conditions for street robbery. There were many reports of bag snatches from lone women as they walked through the pitch-black streets. One case involved two youngsters wearing masks.

Wartime evacuation also disrupted the lives of many children. After being wrenched from their families, the youngsters became unsettled on their return. For those who stayed in Liverpool, the nightly destruction and violence must have had some adverse psychological effects. In 1939, two boys kidnapped and assaulted a seven-year-old. The young victim was found wandering in the road, dazed, wounded and naked. In court, his twelve-year-old attacker explained how they met the boy coming up Marsden Street, off West Derby Road:

> We got two bottles of lemonade and told the lad to come with us. When we got him into the yard in Winter Street we took him inside and jumped on him. We both kept hitting him in the face with our fists and I kept running to the gate to see if anyone was coming. The other boy hit the lad on the head with a brick. He was covered with blood so we pulled him into a shed and then took all his clothes off, and we both started to throw bricks at him. We both lifted him into a tin bath and then started to hit him to make him go to sleep. I did not hit him with a piece of iron, but only with a strap and some bricks. He was covered in blood. When he was in the tin bath and he said, 'I am warm. Let me go to sleep,' we got on the roof and dropped a lot more bricks on his head. When he was still, we went away and left him in the bath.

The accused boy was sent to a remand home for a week. His mother, seemingly unaware of the gravity of the offence, stunned the magistrate by asking, 'Can't he come home?'

The streets of Liverpool could be violent for even the youngest of boys. Also in 1939, a gang from Fazakerley battered and robbed a nine-year-old after shouting, 'Let's rag him.' The case involved 'gangster methods', said the prosecutor. A year later, the savagery of the young generation was again demonstrated by an attack on a four-year-old and his two-year-old brother. Three boys, aged seven, eight and eleven, dragged the two youngsters into an air raid shelter and beat them unmercifully with weapons until they screamed. One of the perpetrators was armed with a tree branch, one clutched a stick and the other boy brandished a wire spoke from an umbrella. The eight-year-old admitted thrashing the boys thirteen times. The seven-year-old revealed that he committed the attack because he was after the victim's jersey. The two younger attackers claimed that the eleven-year-old did most of the beating and had threatened them not to grass him up. The previous month, the older boy had suffered six strokes of the birch for another offence.

In 1941, a female magistrate expressed dismay that such vicious children existed in Liverpool. She was right to be concerned. A year later, a seven-year-old boy lost an eye after his ten-year-old tormentor deliberately threw lime in his face. Around the same time, teenagers would hunt in packs to ambush lone boys walking along Church Street and School Lane. Extra police had to be drafted to put a stop to the spate of unmerciful beatings.

The following year, a seventeen-year-old female was standing in a shop doorway in Walton as a group of lads passed. One of them hissed, 'Acid, you will burn away.' As the words were spoken, a thirteen-year-old boy threw the contents of a bottle at her before running away. The young woman immediately felt her face and neck burning and had to be rushed to Stanley Hospital where she was treated for burns. She was left with permanent scarring. The girl's mother later went to Walton Road where she spotted the attacker and apprehended him. The lad claimed that some older boys gave him the acid, telling him that it would burn through clothing. After the assault, the lads decided to stay away from the area for a few nights until it had all died down. Prior to attacking the girl, the boy had already thrown acid on the coats of two other females.

In 1943, a seven-year-old was walking down the street when he was punched in the back. As he turned around, he was slashed across the face with a razor. His attacker was eight years old.

Two years later, a reign of terror was brought to an end with the conviction of a ruthless gang who used their dog as a weapon. They would hang around school gates waiting for the pupils to leave. One eight-year-old victim gave his statement to the court: 'I saw four boys with a large brown dog. They came and got hold of me. One said, "Have you got any money?"' The boy replied, 'I have only got my mother's change.' They then searched his pockets and took some coppers. Before running away, they pushed him over and sat on him. A ten-year-old witness claimed that the pack of boys grabbed him and told the dog to 'seize him'. Other terrified children were chased down the street as the dog was let loose on them.

The war influenced children in more obvious ways. In 1942, while Britain and Germany battled for supremacy in Europe, a smaller scale re-enactment was being fought on an Anfield railway embankment. The opposing forces eventually appeared at

Liverpool Juvenile Court accused of trespassing on the railway. One battalion, consisting of five ten-year-olds, appeared first before the magistrate. The leader explained that they were waging war with a rival troop. He admitted throwing stones as 'hand grenades' at the enemy force holding another embankment.

The Clerk of the Court: 'Who was the general?'

The Leader: 'We had no general but I was the major.'

The Chairman of the Bench: 'Which side won?'

The Leader: 'We did.'

The boys were dismissed with a caution and the sound advice that in future it would be safer to carry out such manoeuvres on open ground. The 'vanquished forces' appeared next in the dock and were similarly discharged.

The influence of the war was also later demonstrated by the antics of a squadron of fourteen-year-olds from St Helens who modelled themselves on 'Bomber Command'. The boys would gather on Windle Bridge, over the East Lancs Road. Splitting into two groups, one party would spot approaching motors while the other group, facing the other side of the bridge, would shout 'bombs away' as they dropped missiles on the passing cars.

Perhaps the most disturbing aspect of the war was the availability of real weapons. In 1941, five lads smashed down the door of a munitions store to steal detonators, gunpowder and twelve hand grenades. In 1943, a fifteen-year-old, working as a tea boy at the Ministry of Supply, stole various weapons parts and a quantity of ammunition. Picking bits up here and there and taking them home, he was able to assemble a 'tommy gun' without any assistance. The boy, who was described in court as 'mechanically minded', claimed that he was keeping the firearm ready for when the Germans invaded. Unfortunately the stolen parts were rejects and if he had fired the weapon he would have seriously injured himself. A year later, eight boys broke the padlock of an army storehouse to steal a machine gun, three hand grenades and 384 rounds of ammunition. The gun was all ready to fire and it was only by luck that nobody was hurt. The youngest boy's father admitted that his son was 'soldier mad'.

Even after the end of the war, munitions stores were vulnerable to attack. In 1948, a gang broke into a store at a gun site in

Aigburth Road and armed themselves like a small regiment. A teenager was walking along the foreshore near Fulwood Park, Dingle when he saw an eleven-year-old carrying a revolver. The youngster proceeded along the cliff top and shouted to another boy, 'If you move I'll fire at you.' The boy did move and was lucky to avoid the bullet intended for him. Another youth then found five more boys on the foreshore, all armed to the hilt. He also confiscated the weaponry and handed it to the police. The boys were rounded up and admitted using an axe to break the lock off the stores. They had stolen seven revolvers, four rifles, three Sten machine carbines and enough ammunition to start a small war.

It was only a matter of time before a tragedy occurred. In 1946, in Norris Green, an eleven-year-old called George Gell was shot dead by a fourteen-year-old, using a rifle stolen from an army cadet barracks. The boy had been playing with friends in a field when he was shot through the heart. Mrs Gell raced to the scene and spoke to her son as he closed his eyes for the very last time. The culprit was later put on probation.

Many of these weapons and other wartime souvenirs were later used in hold ups and armed robberies throughout the city. The fact that the firearms often had no ammunition was irrelevant to the terrified shopkeepers staring down the barrel of the gun. The availability of such guns remained a problem for some years. In 1965, almost twenty years after a general nationwide amnesty, Bootle police held their own firearms amnesty in a bid to get the wartime armaments off the streets. The initiative was extended to cover all types of weapons. The final collection of revolvers, rifles, ammunition, bayonets and cavalry sabres was taken out to the River Mersey and dumped.

Another major effect of the war was that it galvanised children into forming gangs. The lack of adult supervision meant that children looked to each other for companionship, leadership and protection. In 1940, one Liverpool mob had their headquarters in a disused stable, where they had taken precautions against being surprised by visits from the police. The five boys were prolific thieves who targeted shops, mainly for tinned goods. In court, the prosecutor claimed that special police patrols had been sent to put an end to the boys' activities.

Another juvenile gang, from Middlewich, used a shed as an office and kept written records of all their robberies. The hideout was furnished with stolen stationery for clerical use. The office had a list of rules signed by one boy calling himself 'The Boss'. Fighting was forbidden and spitting in the office not allowed. The lads were not so stupid as to keep the stolen goods in the shed and a large amount of property remained missing when the scamps were finally brought to justice in the summer of 1940. Around the same time, three boys aged eight, nine and twelve, were responsible for a series of burglaries around Great Homer Street. In one raid, the crew pilfered some musical instruments with the intention of forming a 'miniature band'. They also broke into a house and stole from the gas meter. When caught, the youngest asked for fourteen other offences to be taken into consideration.

'This boy is a member of a little gang that cannot be called anything but "gangsters",' announced the prosecutor at Liverpool Juvenile Court in 1940 when a fifteen-year-old was accused of wounding a shop assistant. A team went into a fruit shop in the city centre where the lad asked for an orange. When told the price, he then requested an apple. The assistant suspected that the boys were waiting for an opportunity to steal and so ordered them out of the shop. The lad warned, 'I've got sixpence and I've got a razor too.' He then rushed at the young woman and slashed at her face. She raised her arm to protect herself but was sliced across the forearm. When arrested, the lad told a detective, 'I cut the woman to scare her.' The gang was rounded up and found guilty of another robbery in Ranelagh Street. The lads had posted themselves around the store and when the manageress approached they grabbed cigarettes and chocolate before making a hasty exit.

Liverpool University sociologist John Barron Mays researched the city's juvenile delinquents. He explains the modus operandi of a typical bunch of shop thieves:

One group used to carry a supply of paper bags with them for wrapping loot as a protection against accusations. They worked as a team, with one or two boys posted as attention-engagers and watch-dogs while the remainder helped themselves. In raiding small shops an effective method was to fill the shop with so many different boys that the assistants could not possibly keep an eye on what was actually taking place. One or two would make purchases while the others took what they could reach. The groups would then change places and carry out the same procedure so that all had a fair chance of getting something for nothing.[2]

One juvenile gang, specializing in Saturday morning shop raids, called themselves the 'Forty Thieves'.

The city was awash with gangs. In 1942, a nine-year-old led a group of prolific shop breakers. His companions were slightly older at ten and eleven but they deferred to the younger boy's greater experience. Another team targeted women in department stores. Upon being caught, an eleven-year-old admitted, 'I am out for what I can get.' A year later, some members of the twenty-strong Salisbury Street Gang appeared in court. In a written statement, one of them explained the scale of their operations around Islington: 'I have been breaking into shops with the gang for about eight months. We got into about four shops every week, generally on Wednesdays and Sundays.'

Also in 1943, some 'blitz kids' terrorised the Everton district. From their headquarters in a bombed-out house, they planned their burglary sprees. They were so experienced and well prepared that they each had a pair of rubber gloves hanging by a nail on the wall. Juvenile delinquents took forensics very seriously. The Chief Constable of Manchester recounted the time his officers raided a gang who had barricaded themselves in a cellar. In the hideout, the youngsters had pinned a list of rules, the chief one being that under no circumstances must any member do a job without gloves. Police in Norris Green tried to take fingerprints from a fifteen-year-old burglar only to discover that he had shaved layers of skin from his fingertips.

The ingenuity of Liverpool's young thieves knew no bounds. In 1940, some kids knocked the padlock off the back door of the cinema and replaced it with a different lock. Over a few weeks, the boys used their own key to take most of the local children to the pictures for free, leaving the cinema manager baffled as to how his accounts never seemed to match the full houses he was constantly attracting. In the same year, four scallywags snatched a clip of twenty £1 notes from the cash desk of a city store. They threw some notes into the Mersey because they were dirty but had enough money left over to go to the pictures, take a trip to New Brighton and generously donate some cash to the Lord Mayor's War Fund. A constable caught them the next day, dropping a trail of notes as they were being chased for breaking a street lamp.

Liverpool was also hit by a spate of brick theft as youths raided sites where air raid shelters were being built. Over 1,000 bricks, each one costing a penny, had already gone missing all over the city when two thirteen-year-olds were caught helping themselves from a site in Low Hill. In court, one of the boys explained that he wanted to build his own shelter in the back yard.

One daring young band from Bootle used a flotilla of rafts to row back and forth across a canal in the blackout in order to raid a warehouse. One eager lad even swam across to join his mates in the theft of tinned beef. Two equally enterprising fifteen-year-olds created a lucrative swindle. They would vandalise public pay telephones to make them useless and then plug the return coin slots. When people were unable to make calls, they found that they were not refunded. Afterwards, the boys would return, remove the plug and collect any money. Six telephones had been tampered with in the same day. Boys at Bootle's Strand invented their own scam. They would steal the early morning bundles of newspapers left outside newsagents in order to sell them to dockers on their way to work.

The presence of American servicemen on Liverpool's streets also created new rackets. Boys would ask soldiers and sailors for a penny for two halfpennies. The men would usually give the money and refuse the small change. Some boys were earning a pound a week through the ruse. In 1945, youngsters in Lime Street were doing a roaring trade collecting for some dubious church mission while brandishing homemade cardboard charity boxes.

The war years also saw an epidemic of bike theft. In 1942 a Bootle man had his special racing bike, worth fifteen guineas, stolen. Later, a boy knocked at his door and returned the wheel. The man was so grateful that he rewarded the lad with ten shillings. Little did he know that the same boy had stolen the bike. The thief, together with the rest of his team of fourteen-year-olds, later appeared in court. Over a three-month period the six-strong gang had stolen twenty-three bikes. As soon as they got their hands on a machine they would take it to a bombed-out house, dismantle it and grab parts either for their own use or to sell. A group of smaller boys would follow them and eagerly collect the unwanted remains of the stripped-down bikes, acting like hyenas feasting on a left over carcass. 'This is nothing less than racketeering,' was the verdict of the chairman of Bootle Juvenile Court.

Liverpool's tearaways were equally at home organising and planning elaborate and ingenious frauds or thinking on their feet in order to commit daring off-the-cuff crimes. In 1945, two policemen visited a Liverpool school to give a talk on juvenile crime. However, the officers forgot one of the golden rules of crime prevention: never leave your goods unattended. While they gave their lecture, two boys sneaked into the cloakroom and rifled the officers' coats, stealing warrant cards and travel passes.

The level of juvenile crime during the war caused the authorities great concern. In 1941, a magistrate stated, 'Something drastic will have to be done to check the crime wave among the young people of the city.'³ There were 1,000 youngsters on probation in Liverpool alone, a greater proportion of the juvenile population than anywhere else in Britain, including London. He added that 'hundreds of youngsters are just running wild in Liverpool – parents have a great deal to answer for in many instances'. A probation officer supported the magistrate. He pointed out that after the First World War there had been a similar situation with young people rampaging through the city. The problem was that the youngsters of those days had become the parents of today. As a solution, the magistrate urged teachers to use the cane more often while his legal colleagues also favoured greater use of the birch.

Others called for the naming and shaming of young offenders. The practice had ceased in 1933 but some thought that this was a step in the wrong direction. In 1941, the Chief Constable of Cheshire spoke in his annual report of a dramatic increase in juvenile crime. He felt that a major contributory factor was the anonymity granted to young villains. Keeping their identity secret led to indifference amongst youngsters who simply felt that they were getting away with their crimes. If anonymity had to be granted, one magistrate felt that the press should at least be able to name the school attended by the young offender. It was hoped that the shame brought upon the school might just prick the pupil's conscience and lead to improved behaviour. Hardened juveniles, however, were not likely to be bothered by such niceties. By 1949, it was being claimed that most Liverpool youths who appeared before the courts were exhibitionists who would love to see their own names in the papers.

The juvenile justice system was felt to be in meltdown. Throughout the war years, a steady stream of 'Dead End Kids' made their relentless journey through the various stages of criminal maturity: probation, broken probation, remand home, approved school, birch and borstal. The youngsters would appear in court showing little sign of repentance. 'They don't care,' was the verdict of one court official after watching boys leave the court smiling. Some lads would plead with the magistrate to send them to a particular approved school that had been recommended to them by their mates who had had such a good time there.

In 1941, a fifteen-year-old, with the cheeky demeanour of the young actor Mickey Rooney, prepared to take the stand by popping chewing gum into his mouth. In the next case, a mother appeared on behalf of her daughter who couldn't get out of bed. The magistrate asked, 'Couldn't you wake her?' She claimed that if she did so, her daughter would be in a foul mood. The following hearing involved a drunken sixteen-year-old charged with fighting. Another case involved a band of three boys, one of whom had used a rubber truncheon on a man during a burglary. In was not unusual for juveniles to ask for seventy other offences to be taken into consideration.

The leniency of the juvenile justice system came under constant attack. For example, a boy who set fire to a business premises, causing £1,000-worth of damage, was fined just ten shillings. Instead of trembling in the dock before an austere judge, expecting a flogging, bored youths would sit comfortably in the pleasant surroundings of a youth court, knowing that the most likely sentence would be a term of probation. Such namby-pamby treatment was seen as appeasement rather than punishment.

In 1942, an editorial in the *Evening Express* spoke with alarm at the increase in juvenile crime. Every night, shops were being raided and stripped of cigarettes and sweets by packs of feral youngsters aged between six and twelve. The loot was then divided amongst the members of the various gangs rather than sold to third parties, as was usually the case with older thieves. This made the job of tracing the goods all the more difficult for detectives. The newspaper urged magistrates to get tougher in the fight against crime. It was no use simply warning juvenile delinquents; they were too hardened and streetwise for mere words. What was needed was an example to be made of half a dozen of them by giving them a good thrashing in front of other offenders.[4]

In the same year, the Bishop of Liverpool, Dr David, felt obliged to add to the debate about juvenile crime. In a diocesan leaflet he acknowledged that children's home and school life had been severely disrupted by the war but nevertheless felt that what was needed was harsh discipline: 'The ideal punishment is one which begins by inflicting pain. It should be short and sharp. Many cases can best be met by a whipping as soon as possible after conviction.'[5] In addition to punishment, he also felt that Sunday schools and youth clubs were effective antidotes to crime. Dr David was convinced that not many children who attended such activities went on to appear before the magistrates. The usual explanation offered for juvenile crime is that children get up to mischief because there is nothing for them to do. Yet by the summer of 1942 it was becoming apparent that even when facilities and events were provided for young people, some children rejected them and continued to behave like hooligans.

The 'Holidays at Home' Committee was particularly concerned that boating facilities were being withdrawn from some Corporation parks due to the disorderly behaviour of the rowers. Circuses and fun fairs were also threatened by a wave of juvenile disorder, believed to be worse than ever before. One circus had to flee from Liverpool after a spate of vandalism. At both Newsham Park and Wavertree Playground, canvas tents and guy ropes were regularly being slashed and there were fears that some children would set the wild animals free from their cages.

One of the disturbing features of juvenile crime during the war years was the amount of wanton vandalism. The burglars were not interested in theft; they simply revelled in destroying anything they could lay their hands on. In 1942, a couple of years before the American 'action painter' Jackson Pollock made a name for himself by freely dripping paint over huge canvases, a group of Croxteth lads, calling themselves the Black Flash Gang, demonstrated their own take on Abstract Expressionism. The youths broke into an empty house on a building site in Hebden Road. The premises were being used as a paint store. Different coloured paints were poured over the floor and splashed around the walls. Electrical fittings and the tiled fireplace were also smeared with brightly coloured shades. Even the workers' tea cans were filled with paint.

In 1945, a vicar complained that teenage terrors had torn off the roof of his school. The culprits were apprehended but nobody in the community would go witness against them. He knew full well that the lads would simply intimidate and smash up the houses of anybody brave or foolish enough to give evidence. The vicar had even given up trying to protect his parish hall. After destroying and stealing anything of value, the vandals had lately turned their attention to ripping up the floorboards.

What to do with these young tearaways was a matter of urgent concern for the long-suffering residents of Liverpool. In a letter to the *Daily Post* a man calling himself 'Another Citizen' called for the introduction of a 'House Guard' as protection against the hordes of hooligans roaming the streets.[6] In tones that echoed the support for the Logwood Gang, who acted as vigilantes against the High Rip, the writer urged residents to unite to defeat the gangs. He boasted that he was more feared in his own neighbourhood than the local police. It seems that he was not averse to giving lads a slap if he saw them misbehaving. He claimed he was willing to pay any fines.

Others held different views. Shortly after, *The Evening Express* printed a letter from somebody called 'Chaddy'.[7] The writer asked why children were being blamed for running wild when it was obviously not their fault that their parents were too busy fighting a war. Chaddy instead blamed the system and called for better housing and social conditions together with the abolition of borstals, which were simply breeding cages of crime. The writer also wanted to eradicate corporal punishment, for it tended to make children harder.

Days later, Chaddy was firmly slapped down by somebody calling himself 'Justice for the Good People'.[8] In an angry reply, this correspondent called for the public flogging of young delinquents to put a stop to increasing levels of crime. He also demanded sterner judges, harsher regimes in prison and the return of bread and water to stop such institutions becoming places of enjoyment. His idea was to severely punish first-time offenders to stop them repeating their crimes. Being lenient to criminals had been tried and failed. 'Punish the young ones first, then there won't be any old ones,' was the writer's solution to crime.

On the day the letter was published an incident occurred that demonstrated what the police and public were up against. A thirteen-year-old, from Norris Green, was arrested after creating a miniature laboratory in his garden shed. The budding scientist had amassed a huge collection of dangerous chemicals, including cyanides. The bottles were obtained from older boys, who stole them from their employers and a school. Police discovered the haul when they were called to a house and found a lad unconscious from chloroform poisoning. After stealing the chemical for the young boffin, he had sniffed the contents with the rest of his boys but couldn't resist a swig of the bottle. Fortunately, he made a full recovery. When the lads appeared in court, it was revealed that the younger boy was known in the district by his ominous nickname 'Killer'. The magistrate explained that one of the chemical thieves was a 'terror of the boys in the neighbourhood'. In an unrelated incident, the fifteen-year-old had beaten a cat to death with a piece of lead piping while other boys looked on. Some of them vomited but were so afraid of the lad that they dared not intervene.

At the end of the war, as Britain looked forward to an era of peace and prosperity, a whole generation of lawless children and youths was about to destroy the party. 'Modern Youth – As Seen in Court' was one newspaper headline cataloguing a variety of disorderly incidents from the celebrations on VJ night in 1945.[9]

Three boys stole desks from an air raid shelter in Norris Green. The wood was needed for bonfires. Two lads chased some girls along Upper Hill Street in Toxteth, swinging large tin cans filled with burning rags round their heads on the ends of ropes. A teenage absconder from an approved school broke into a shop in Lime Street. When told that he would be remanded in Walton Gaol, he replied defiantly, 'I don't mind.' These examples were seen as representative of the kind of behaviour that faced the police and public in post-war Liverpool.

The view that the city's children were out of control was also illustrated by another shocking report. In October 1945, it was pointed out that the vandals were succeeding where the Germans had failed. Tens of thousands of pounds worth of damage was being caused to property by feral youths who roamed the streets wreaking havoc. Buildings that had been slightly damaged by enemy action were being completely destroyed by marauding armies of youths. One house facing a police station was wrecked so severely that it had to be demolished. The Liverpool and District Property Owners' Association called for action. It identified a lack of parental control together with the adventurous spirit of young people as causes of the disorder and suggested more playgrounds and sports activities as ways of channelling the misspent energy of youths. It was a call that had been made every decade since the 1880s when the High Rip Gang began decoying sailors near the docks. The call echoes to this day.

Meanwhile, a new generation of decoy gangs was busy at work.

16

Decoy Gangs

'Rolling has had a long tradition in Liverpool and been
traditionally associated with sailors and prostitution and the
taking of the pay packet which was flashed around too openly.'[1]

IN 1950, A SENIOR police officer claimed that females were
behind two-thirds of crime in Liverpool.[2] It seems that young
women were being enticed into gang life either through physical
attraction to the ringleader or as an act of rebellion against the
narrowness of post-war life. Transforming themselves with
bleached hair and bright red lipstick, they soon became gangster's
molls, losing all moral sense in the process. Some of these young
women, along with prostitutes, acted as decoys for the gangs. They
would entice sailors from cafes and bars and lead them down dark
alleys to secluded spots with the promise of sex, leaving the
victims at the mercy of waiting men who would rob and beat
them. In 1944, Justice Birkett called it 'one of the lowest forms of
crime to which human nature could stoop'.

Some victims would be persuaded to visit shabby shebeens
where they would be ripped off by paying for overpriced drinks.
The crime was well suited to ports like Liverpool where a steady
stream of seamen and soldiers would be eager for entertainment
after long voyages. With money in their pockets, they were ripe for
picking by Liverpool's decoy gangs. Sometimes respectable-
looking men were targeted and asked to escort a 'frightened'
woman through some dark street. Such gentlemanly conduct
would be rewarded with a severe beating along the journey. Due to
the embarrassment, many cases must have gone unreported.
Occasionally, decoys from other areas such as Manchester would
be used. When they had outlived their usefulness to the gang they
would return home and a fresh female face appointed. Another
version of the decoy trick was for the girls to accost a lone drinker

in a pub or café and act in such an outlandishly provocative manner so as to incite the man to utter an insult or tell her to get lost. This would be the excuse for the nearby crew to move in and sort him out, robbing as well as beating him.

Over a two-week period in November 1945, two women from Toxteth were part of a five-strong gang that lured Indian and Chinese seamen from cafés in the St James Street area. The men were then set upon and stripped of any valuables. In one incident, two Indian sailors met the decoys in a Chinese café known as the American Bar. Afterwards, the women offered to direct the men to the docks. While they were in Caryl Street, however, three men jumped them as the women ran away. The Indians were later found unconscious in the road with serious head injuries. One man suffered cuts about the head and face, a double fracture of the jaw and had five teeth knocked out. In another case, a Chinese man had to have twelve stitches inserted after a bloody encounter with the gang. A revolver or some other metal object was used in one attack and a heavy piece of wood in another. The attackers were rounded up and, despite their denials, received between eighteen months' and five years' imprisonment. The judge expressed regret that two of the men were unfit to receive a flogging.

In 1946, two young Liverpool women mated up with three penniless American soldiers to perform the decoy trick in Lime Street. The team noticed a South African soldier standing opposite the Adelphi Hotel. He was in fact wasting some time as he waited for his train to Glasgow. The gang decided to 'get him done'. The plan was for one of the women to entice him into a side street where the men would lay in wait. It worked. In a carefully executed crime, one soldier held the victim while another, called 'Tex', punched him and the third robbed his wallet. Despite his injuries, the South African was able to give descriptions to the police, leading to the capture of his attackers. The women were imprisoned for six months and the men dealt with by court martial.

The following year, a man and woman from Liverpool were arrested in Bristol after using the same scam. The couple were part of a gang that used a female decoy to lure a Canadian seaman to a hotel. Instead, the woman took him to a tree-lined square half a mile out of his way where the rest of the team pounced. First, an angry man appeared, claiming to be the woman's husband. He picked a fight with the seaman and knocked him to the floor. Three or four others jumped out of the bushes and held him down while his pockets were rifled. The woman told the court that, 'The Canadian was apparently loaded with money and my gang told me to let him get funny with me so that they could beat him up.'

Not all decoy gangs used women. In 1948, a ship's paymaster was walking through the town centre, just after midnight, when a youth asked him for a cigarette. When the man mentioned that he was looking for a hotel, the boy offered to fix him up. The man followed the lad into a passage at the back of Lime Street. He remembered nothing else until he woke up in hospital. It seems that the youth had punched him to the ground while two men, who had followed the pair into the back alley, rifled through the victim's pockets. Fortunately, police had followed the men and witnessed the assault. Although the youth got away he was later caught. He told the arresting officer that if he got bail he would be out of the country within twenty-four hours. He later made a statement that they went out that night to 'moll some bloke for a couple of quid'. The lad was sent to borstal while one of his accomplices got four years.

'Like the High Rip Gang' was how the prosecution described one ruthless decoy team. In 1949, a young married couple, John and Kathleen 'Kitty' Rooney, together with John's cousin Daniel Rooney, were charged with nine late-night decoy robberies. The Rooneys came from Ireland where they lived the life of nomads. They had arrived penniless in Liverpool expecting to find their fortune. Unfortunately, none of them could read or write and with employment opportunities limited they turned to crime. The desperadoes were active in the south end. In one incident, Kitty stopped a railway porter in Myrtle Street and asked him for a cigarette. The man continued walking with her. However, in St Bride Street he was grabbed by the collar and prodded in the back with a gun. John Rooney snarled, 'You are going to give me everything you've got,' before robbing him of twenty-five shillings.

A week later, a seaman was strolling along Strand Street, near the docks, when a woman stopped him for a cigarette. This time her accomplice carried a bottle, which he broke and held against his victim's neck. A watch and some money were taken. In the third incident, a woman stopped a man in James Street and asked him to walk with her, as she was afraid that she was being followed. The man's gallantry was repaid in Duke Street when a stranger jumped on his back and started punching him. The victim retaliated and was getting the better of his attacker when the female decoy repeatedly whacked him on the head with half a house brick. When he came round, the poor man discovered that he had been robbed.

Mrs Rooney was later spotted by her first victim and subsequently arrested. Ironically, her husband had been separately arrested for living off immoral earnings. When told of the allegations, Kitty came clean: 'You picked my husband up today for living on me and if he says "guilty" to them that goes for me.' The woman was shown an imitation revolver that had been found in the couple's lodgings. When told that it was believed by the police that this was the weapon used to rob their first victim, she replied, 'That's the thing we use. A mug would think it was real.'

John Rooney denied the charges. 'I don't know what you are talking about,' was his response. This was despite the fact that the gold watch he was wearing was identified as belonging to the second victim. He claimed that he had bought it in London months earlier. The victims all identified their attackers on an identity parade. Daniel Rooney was later arrested trying to board a Dublin-bound boat at Princes Landing Stage. The three appeared before the City Magistrates. As one victim described being struck with the brick, nineteen-year-old Kitty burst out laughing. She was warned by the magistrate to behave herself or she would be put out of court. However, moments later she giggled again. When a constable rebuked her, Kitty turned on him: 'Don't talk to me like that. My husband's here and he dare not talk to me that way.' The three accused had to be separated and placed in different parts of the court so that they could not whisper to one another. Kitty's statement, admitting to taking part in ten decoy robberies, was read out. John Rooney was sent down for three years while his cousin received thirty months imprisonment. Kitty got twenty-one months.

Liverpool detective Bert Balmer recalls that in the late 1940s, one of the most infamous decoy gangs operated out of Lime Street and the adjoining thoroughfares running through to Copperas Hill. The area was notorious for its prostitutes who would parade along its length looking for business. Girls flocked from Manchester, Wigan and Glasgow to work what Mr Hemmerde, the Recorder of Liverpool, once called, 'The street of illicit delights.' Lime Street was also known as Liverpool's Piccadilly, or simply 'Crime Street', after it became the focus of the city's seedy nightlife. During the war, youths would hang around the milk bars and pubs. 'Got any gum, chum?' was the familiar cry of children as they begged and touted from visiting American soldiers and foreign seamen. In 1945, a naval officer was outraged to be approached by a small boy and asked if he wanted to go out with his sister. Balmer discovered that the pretty decoy was an ex-artist's model and former call girl from London, working for the much-feared Throstle Gang. The leader had already served two sentences totalling eight years for robbery with violence and attempted murder.

A young constable once told this hard case to move on from the corner of Lime Street and Skelhorn Street. The gangster simply threatened the officer and warned him that if he weren't wearing a uniform he would be beaten up. However, he was trying to intimidate the wrong man. The tough officer pointed to an alley off Skelhorn Street and told the villain to meet him there. He promised to take off his tunic so there would be no excuses. The fight ended with the hoodlum unconscious and having to be carried away by his associates. The incident became the talk of Lime Street. From that moment on, the constable was treated with a lot more respect, although his superiors, on hearing about the incident, decided to move him to a different beat. No official complaint was made against him.

The moll who fronted the Throstles was a bit too high class to entice her men from the seedy streets. Instead, she worked the hotels and better class drinking establishments where a member of the gang shadowed her at all times. The lady would never make the first move on a gentleman but would skilfully lure him with her demeanour and actions. As she sat on her own, it wouldn't take long for someone to send over a drink and a request to join her. When the couple became more relaxed in each other's company the conversation would turn inevitably to sex. The moll would name her price, which was never cheap, and offer to take her friend to her flat. The dupe would never get to see the inside of the apartment. As he escorted the lady through some dark side street, the Throstles would set upon him. The poor man would not only be beaten up and robbed but also risked being blackmailed. If his identity and address could be ascertained from his wallet, the bandits would bleed him for all he was worth. Needless to say, such a 'respectable' man would never report the incident to the police for fear of the damning publicity.

Detective Balmer and his colleagues set out to trap the Throstles after speaking to two victims who, although unwilling to give formal statements, were glad to offer descriptions of the moll and one of her accomplices. Balmer himself posed as a dupe in the very hotel where the lady plied her trade. He sat at the bar flashing his cash about and it wasn't long before the moll made her approach. After some small talk she asked him to escort her to her flat in Rodney Street, explaining that she was afraid of walking alone through the dark streets. As the couple began to leave, Balmer noticed the moll's protector rise from his nearby chair. He was to be her shadow.

The pair walked along Lime Street into Mount Pleasant when the lady suddenly turned into a narrow thoroughfare called Benson Street. After fumbling in her handbag, she gave Balmer a cigarette and offered him a light. As he stooped towards the flame being held out to him, he waited with bated breath for the violent ambush that was the hallmark of the gang. The attack came from two directions. The protector was close behind while the leader, along with two accomplices, decamped from a car parked nearby. Fortunately for Balmer, his own colleagues were also following and in the ensuing fight the Throstles were arrested. Two of the ruffians had sandbags in their pockets, handy for whacking victims on the head, while a search of the moll's handbag revealed a knife with a five-inch blade. She was later jailed for twelve months while the rest of the gang received prison terms between three and seven years.

Detective Balmer's most famous case was the Cameo murder (see Chapter 19). In March 1949, the manager and assistant of the Cameo Cinema in Wavertree were gunned down during a botched robbery. George Kelly hanged for the crime while his alleged accomplice received ten years for robbery. In June 2003, three appeal judges decided that the verdict was unsafe. Kelly was a well-known figure in the Liverpool underworld. In the 1940s, the Kelly gang used women as decoys to lure men who showed signs of carrying a little too much cash. Sailors who had been paid off, or businessmen looking for pleasure, were the usual easy targets. It was also alleged that Kelly and his accomplices terrorised prostitutes. They would wait until a girl had finished with a client before demanding a slice of her earnings. Anyone foolish enough to refuse would receive a 'battering'.

George Kelly began his criminal career as a young thief in the 1930s. His offences were common juvenile capers, breaking into a school, stealing money from a house, robbing cash from a cigarette machine. In 1940, Kelly was sentenced to seven days imprisonment for assaulting an air raid warden who complained about an unscreened light. Kelly knocked the man down with a blow to the jaw before kicking him in the face, smashing his false teeth. Kelly's stint of national service then saw him posted to the navy. However, he deserted five times to resume his career as a local gangster. In one incident, Kelly became close to a lady friend whose husband was away. When she refused to let him into her home she was rewarded with a vicious beating. Kelly kicked her so hard that she suffered internal injuries. As she lay on the ground she was then kicked unconscious. He served nine months' hard labour.

Other spells of imprisonment did nothing to quell the Kelly legend. The bold announcement 'I am Kelly' was said to strike fear into the inhabitants of the Lime Street area, where he was known as 'Little Caesar'. The troublesome gangster and his underlings were barred from many pubs and clubs in Liverpool. According to the *Daily Mirror*, 'A jab in the face from a broken glass was their usual way of meeting opposition, and often the police tried in vain to persuade their victims to give evidence.'[3]

During the Cameo trial in January 1950, Kelly's alleged sidekick, Charles Connolly, was held in Walton Gaol. A fellow prisoner called Robert Graham, doing six months for receiving stolen property, later gave evidence against the pair. While in prison, Connolly was supposed to have revealed to him, 'My family is in a gang called the Peanut Gang – half of them are in here and the other half outside. They'll upset any evidence the police have.' The verity of these words is suspect, particularly in light of the unsafe verdict. However, whether the threat was uttered or not, the very mention of the Peanut Gang in this context demonstrates the fear in which they were held.

The Peanut Gang, also known as the Park Lane Gang, was based in the south end of Liverpool, near the docks. Members consisted not only of tough young bucks but also of hard-faced young women. In November 1945, a letter appeared in the newspaper headed 'Gangsters' Molls'. The writer described how the female members of the Peanut Gang would take part in the decoy trick:

> This area is frequented by a big number of sea-going men of all nationalities, including our own. These women make up to the sailors, and after several drinks caution and common sense are lost and when paying for rounds in most cases it is easy to see the amount of notes these sailors are carrying. From this moment they are marked men, the women passing the information to the male members of the gang.[4]

These women not only acted as decoys: they were notorious gangsters in their own right. As crime writer, Norman Lucas, points out:

> The Liverpool mobs also had their 'queens' – unkempt amoral girls, who provoked fights among the gangs, fought among themselves with fingernails and knives, and did as much wanton damage as their male counterparts. These female vandals, whose ages ranged from fourteen to twenty-two, were the despair of Liverpool probation officers. They were motivated by a love of notoriety, and they were completely beyond parental control.[5]

Two Liverpool drunks offer mutual support in this classic street study.

Troops of the Scots Greys guard an armoured car during the bitter Transport Strike of 1911. A similar convoy protecting prison vans was attacked by a huge mob, causing soldiers to open fire, killing two men.

Below, a crowd gathers at the spot where one of those fatally wounded, carter John Sutcliffe, fell. A police officer also died during the bitter dispute.

Boys and young men crowd outside the house of John Sutcliffe to pose for a photographer. The dispute began when unionised seamen went on strike and escalated to include carters, railwaymen and dockers. By mid-summer the city was at a standstill.

Rioting in the street during the 1911 strike. Eventually more than 2,300 soldiers patrolled the city and gunboats moored in the River Mersey

Bookmakers at race meeting shortly before the Great War. Gambling was a major source of entertainment and income for the working classes but a headache for the police.

A group of cornermen in Hill Street in 1934. Street corners were a popular hangout for ruffians and young tearaways.

A bomb-damaged house in 1942. The outbreak of war stretched the police and presented tempting opportunities for organised gangs of thieves.

A policeman silhouetted against street lights at St George's Hall, looking at Lime Street. Some of Liverpool's bobbies were as tough as any villain.

Church Street car park in 1947, a temptation for the growing number of joyriders and car thieves.

The flats at Caryl Gardens, home to members of the notorious Peanut Gang.

Park Lane was the headquarters of the Peanut Gang, the biggest in the city in the mid-Twentieth Century. The gang reputedly got its name when some young members tore open bags of peanuts in a raid on the docks.

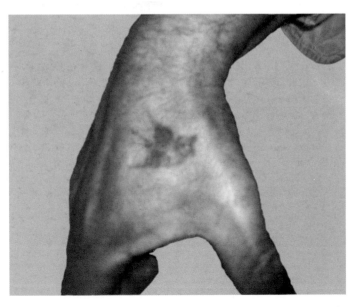

A swallow hand tattoo, sign of the Swallow Gang. Female members would have a shoulder or leg tattooed.

In 1948, one such streetwise fifteen-year-old girl was caught stealing money and clothing coupons. When questioned, she revealed that for years she had lived by her wits on the streets. Described as 'intelligent and sophisticated', she had run away from home so many times she could hardly remember the details. She had slept rough in parks, under the stalls at fun fairs and in air-raid shelters. She had even hitched rides to London and back in lorries. The girl was offered shelter at a local convent but ran away. After deserting three times she was sent to another convent in Manchester. From there she was sent home. Although the girl admitted that her parents were good to her, she hated life at home.

She claimed that members of the Peanut Gang gave her some money to go to the pictures, further explaining, 'These lads are all spivs. They call the women spivesses.' As she could offer no guarantees that she would go straight, the magistrate at the Juvenile Court had no option but to send her to an approved school for three years. He remarked, 'There is no doubt, in her own words, this girl will become a spivess unless she receives treatment.'

No doubt some other young 'spivess' was eager to take her place as a moll in the Peanut Gang. Not since the days of the High Rip had a mob instilled so much terror into the hearts of Liverpudlians, albeit this time in the south end rather than the north end of the city. And links between the two gangs were uncanny. Proximity to the docks was again a major point of advantage for these bandits who, harking back to the late Victorian period, combined robbery with outrageous violence. In 1884, the High Rip burst onto the scene with the murder of a Spanish seaman on his way back to his ship. Just over sixty years later, there was a similar attack on a seaman returning to base.

17

The Peanut Gang

I was a Gunmoll for the Peanut Gang
But I haven't always been
I never even clocked a cop till I was seventeen.
I started in a convent and now I often muses,
When doing a little lifting up at Owens's or Hughes's
That instead of hanging round for hours outside Walton Gaol
I might have been a better girl and even … Took the Veil
Since then I've took a lot of things, but one thing, this is straight,
I've never took no nonsense from a fellow, boss or mate.[1]

AT MIDNIGHT ON 14 July 1945, a Royal Navy Signaller called James Marsh was making his way back to his depot with two colleagues after a trip to New Brighton on the Wirral. In Hill Street, he met a group of five men, aged between nineteen and twenty-one. What happened next also has eerie echoes of the murder of Richard Morgan, who was set upon seventy-one years earlier returning from a day out in New Ferry.

Some of the young men stood on top of an air raid shelter and shouted abuse at the naval men. The gang included Moses Birch and Leonard Dixon. Henry Johnson, a native of Montreal, was not a member but just happened to be with the others. One of the sailors protested at the abuse but Dixon jumped down and punched him in the mouth. After a short fight, the men separated and one of the gang picked up a sailor's cap. The owner pleaded, 'You have had your fight. We have had our fun. Now give me back my cap.' Instead of handing back the cap, the man launched a kick. Another fight started and Marsh fell to the ground after he was bashed with a brick behind the ear.

In a nearby house, a soldier was awakened by the commotion outside. He got up and opened the window where he saw five men booting a body in the gutter. Suddenly, the window dropped and made a noise, alerting the attackers, who fled. If it hadn't been for the sound of the window, the pack would have continued their pitiless assault on Marsh's lifeless body. The victim's friends ran to the barracks 100 yards away. When they returned, their friend was lying dead. Marsh, who came from Ilford in Essex, had been stationed in Liverpool for a mere three days. The seaman's angry colleagues were out in force that night looking for the culprits.

The police, however, got there first. The suspects were soon rounded up and interviewed. Birch admitted, 'It was done in a fight.' His colleagues agreed. When charged, Dixon replied, 'I can only say that I did not think that I had done it so bad.' At the Assizes, Dixon and Birch were convicted of manslaughter and jailed for six years. Johnson went away for four years. The judge took into account the fact that when the three men were not at home terrorising the inhabitants of Liverpool, they nevertheless did their duty at sea.

The accused were in fact members of a notorious crew known to some as the Park Lane Gang and to others as the Peanut Gang. They lived in the south end streets, including Upper Mann Street, Brassey Street, Dombey Street and Caryl Gardens. In court, Detective-Inspector Culshaw claimed that the gang had about eleven members, a gross underestimate. In fact, because they were such a big group, they were also known as the 'Forty Strong'. D.I. Culshaw also revealed that two of them were already serving jail sentences for wounding.

At the time of the trial, the Peanut Gang was already infamous. The gang was a couple of years old and had developed out of the hordes of street corner tyrants that emerged in the hungry 1930s. According to crime writer James Morton, the Peanut Gang were 'so-called because they began their career by splitting open bags of peanuts on the docks, before they graduated to splitting open the heads of seamen decoyed into alleys off Lime Street for their wage packets'.[2] More specifically, they were named after their one-time leader, 'Peanut' McGlynn, who was one of the children with a taste for stolen peanuts. The mob, which included mixed-race members, grew out of this loose collective of south end juvenile dock thieves.

In his wartime annual report, covering the years 1939 to 1945, Liverpool's Head Constable makes reference to gangs who,

> although not organised under one leader, consist of members who are willing to assist each other in carrying out crimes, intimidating potential witnesses against them, or even providing perjured evidence to secure the acquittal of the prisoner. Members ... have been responsible for many most serious offences, such as robberies, woundings, breaking into all types of premises and even manslaughter.[3]

Although not specifically identified, the factions are undoubtedly tentacles of the Peanut Gang. The lack of an absolute leader made them all the more vicious, for they were out of control.

As their other name suggests, the gang was active around Park Lane where they targeted shopkeepers and pub licensees in what used to be known as the Sailor Town district but was more commonly referred to as 'Zone 10' by the Flying Squad. The thoroughfare was internationally famous, being the first port of call for the thousands of foreign seamen who visited Liverpool. The place included numerous sailors' outfitters, boarding houses and mariners' pubs. The area was once genteel. It was, literally, the lane leading to the respectable Toxteth Park. However, by the time of the Second World War the district contained some of the worst slums in the city. A century earlier, that accolade would certainly have gone to the cramped north end district of Scotland Road and adjacent courts. However, the authority's slum clearance programme had alleviated some of the housing problems in the north.

A north/south divide was becoming evident, even in the criminal profiles of each district. North-enders would probably have viewed their own misdemeanours as 'clean crime', usually consisting of petty thieving, breaking into business premises and snatching goods from shop counters. The south end, however, was home to the seedy dives, drugs and sex trade. Racial problems only complicated the criminal landscape.

By 1941, the Park Lane area was becoming notorious. In December, two detectives were on patrol in the district when they saw two boys acting suspiciously. When approached, a sixteen-year-old ran off and jumped onto a moving tram but his fifteen-year-old accomplice was caught with stolen property in his possession. When questioned, the boy admitted filching from motorcars during the previous nine months. 'I have stolen from about seventy motors and have also pinched about nine bikes. I was with my mates,' was the boy's frank admission. The boy's friends were members of the Peanut Gang.

Over a nine-month period the two lads, with or without the rest of their boys, had committed a total of 309 crimes. They spent the proceeds on trips to the pictures, days out to New Brighton and numerous visits to cafes. The culprits eventually appeared before Liverpool Juvenile Court accused of stealing jewellery, clothing, cosmetics and even surgical instruments. They were also charged with breaking into a shop and stealing 3,200 cigarettes, tobacco, cigars and chocolate. The stolen goods were stashed away in air raid shelters and bombed-out houses before being sold on to strangers. The number of vehicle thefts admitted to by the lad was grossly understated. He ended up admitting to breaking into 137 cars while his older friend put his hands up to stealing from 142 motors. After medical reports, the lads were sent to an approved school.

The neighbourhood would probably not even have noticed the absence of these prolific young criminals. There were plenty more where they came from. In May 1942, the press had become aware that Liverpool's south end hooligans were teaming up to terrorise the late night streets. The anonymous bandits were likened to the old-fashioned highway robbers known as 'footpads'. Particularly vulnerable were those returning home from nights out.

The warning came after two youths were attacked in Catharine Street, off Upper Parliament Street. A seventeen-year-old approached both lads and asked them for a match. One of them replied that they hadn't got a light but perhaps the man who was walking behind them could help. The speaker's companion turned around to see the identity of this other person but was immediately knocked unconscious by a vicious blow to the jaw. As his terrified mate made hasty plans to escape he was suddenly surrounded by about eight youths. He tried to break through the barrier but was tripped up and brutally beaten. When he woke up he found himself alone in an air raid shelter at the junction of Princes Road and Upper Parliament Street. This was about a quarter of a mile from the spot where he had been attacked. He had no idea how he got there but he managed to stagger home. Some passers-by discovered his friend and gave him first aid treatment. The motive for the attack was unclear since nothing was taken. The first victim still had his wallet, money and identity card.

The attack came shortly after an assault on a Dutch seaman who was leaving a public house. This time the motive was clear. He was struck on the head and robbed of his wallet containing twenty pounds. He remained in a serious condition in hospital for some time.

In August 1942, a lad was fatally injured shortly after being assaulted by two youths. The attack bore all the hallmarks of the Peanut Gang. Ralph Hall, aged eighteen, was a ship's pantry boy who had recently been paid off his vessel. He had £50 in his possession when he embarked on a Saturday night drinking session with shipmates around Lime Street. At 11.30pm a man was walking down Cornwallis Street, off St James Street, when he overheard voices from the other side of an air raid shelter. He also heard somebody groan in pain. The voices resumed: 'Shut up. Here's the police.' As he looked around the shelter, the man saw a body and two youths running away towards Park Lane.

The man asked the victim what had happened.

'Two or three fellows kicked me in the face and robbed me.' He added that it was his own fault, as he had been flashing his money about in the pubs.

The man dragged the lad to some steps and offered to inform the police. However the victim refused all help. He didn't even want his parents informed. He said that he had lost all his money and might as well commit suicide. As the man could do no more for the lad he left him and made his way to Seel Street Police Station to report the incident. Walking away, he noticed three men approach the victim. He shouted to them not to hurt the lad as he had just been robbed.

When the police went to investigate, all four men were missing but there was blood on the floor. Shortly after, the victim was killed in a hit-and-run incident in nearby Park Road. It was thought that a lorry was responsible. Mystery surrounds the lad's death but the mugging no doubt played its part. It was the type of assault that made the Peanut Gang feared throughout Liverpool, not only by the public but also by the police.

In 1942, two constables were ambushed while intervening in a disturbance that started outside the Pavilion Theatre in Lodge Lane after a pack of fifteen lads were refused admission. An officer went to investigate a scream from a woman in nearby Beaumont Street when a fifteen-year-old told him to mind his own business before punching him in the face. As the policeman tried to make an arrest, the shout went up, 'Get some bricks.' A volley of missiles found their target, fracturing an officer's skull. As he lay helpless on the floor, he was then whacked with a broom aimed at his colleague. The other officer had his finger twisted and broken as he tried to blow his whistle for assistance. Three brave servicemen were also assaulted as they tried to aid the constables. The five injured men sought refuge in a nearby house but the bricks continued, smashing the windows. Two lead-weighted coshes were later found discarded at the scene. In court, one of the policemen handed the magistrate all that remained of his helmet – the brim.

As two youths were gaoled and a third sent to an approved school, Inspector Culshaw told the judge that the lads were members of a gang that had been causing a lot of trouble in the south end. He added that the violence had been growing in recent months and was directed at not only the police but also shopkeepers and members of the public. The Peanut Gang or Park Lane Gang was not specifically mentioned in court but they certainly appear to be the main suspects.

Crime writer Norman Lucas attempted to explain the social psychology of such gangs. 'As in the early days of the Glasgow gangs,' he wrote, 'poverty and idleness in Liverpool, coupled with irrational human desire to wield power through brutality over others, led to the formation of groups of thugs. These social misfits, like their Glasgow counterparts, not only attracted rival gangs, but roamed the streets ready to beat up anyone just for the hell of it.'[4] Indeed, members of the Peanut Gang even turned upon themselves. In December 1942, it was reported that the gang had split in two and a fight arranged between the rival factions. During the disturbance, one Thomas Tigline was injured.

At the beginning of 1943, the name of the gang started to appear frequently in the newspapers. 'These youths are members of a gang forty strong, known as the "Park Lane Gang", which have been terrorising shopkeepers in the south-end of the city.' So said Mr Dalzell, the prosecutor at Liverpool Police Court. Before him were twelve lads, aged sixteen to twenty, accused of breaking into a lock-up and stealing 47,000 cigarettes, among other offences. Eight of the team were juveniles and couldn't be identified but Francis Burke, Patrick Rowan, Henry Dutton and George Bainbridge were named. Mr Dalzell asked that all twelve be remanded to prison. He argued that since being granted bail after they were caught, they had interfered with several witnesses. It seems that some witnesses had then refused to give evidence against the gang.

Shopkeepers were equally terrified. When the owner of a chip shop in Great-George Place complained to the police about the actions of the lads he was visited by four or five of them and threatened. The man closed his shop for two days. Burke, otherwise known as 'Piggy', admitted that they had used violence towards sailors. Extra police had to be drafted in to control the district. DI Culshaw described the lads as 'the worst gang of young toughs I have experienced for many years'.

When the gang reappeared in court the following week, a thirteenth member called John Fitzgerald joined them in the dock. Mr Silverman MP, the youths' defence lawyer, argued that it was wrong to keep such young lads in jail. He denied that the youths had interfered with witnesses and promised that this would not happen if his clients were given bail. But when the gang eventually appeared at the Assizes in February 1943, the judge had strong words for them:

It makes me wonder to what the country is coming. In the last war, boys of sixteen, and sometimes younger, from this city, were anxious to get into the Army. There are many of us who remember them out in France at the age of sixteen – some sometimes brought back when the authorities found out their ages, but others staying out and helping their country. Each of you, in the hour of your country's need, has been doing the very opposite.

The defendants all pleaded guilty. Fitzgerald, described by the police as one of the leaders, was given eighteen months with hard labour. Others were sent to borstal or were bound over and put on probation. Rose Heilbron, defending a number of them, explained that many of them came from large families and were of respectable parents. She claimed that the gang had now broken up and that the majority of the members had realised the error of their ways.

The lawyer was perhaps being a little optimistic. Not all of them had turned over a new leaf. In November 1944, a lad called Fogg innocently queued up in a fish and chip shop waiting for his supper. John Fitzgerald, not long released from prison, accused him of entering the wrong queue and stabbed him in the stomach. The victim staggered home, with Fitzgerald and his boys following. Fogg's mother claimed that up to nine lads tried to break down her front door. She explained, 'They all wanted to tear the boy to pieces. They meant to kill him. Four of them went round the back door and they would have killed him, but they pulled the wrong doors down.'

Fitzgerald was taken to court and found guilty of not only the stabbing but also the burglary of a pawnshop. He already had a previous conviction for housebreaking and had been discharged from the Merchant Navy for serious misconduct. In court it was alleged that Fitzgerald was the ringleader of a violent mob of young outlaws who terrorised pub licensees and shopkeepers in the south end. Members of the public who complained to the police were threatened with reprisals. The gang was, of course, the Peanut Gang.

In court, police read out a letter that Fitzgerald had written to a friend in Southampton: 'There are plenty of scouses up here. What a team? Cafes wrecked, battles with the Yanks night after night. It's sweet.' The message only confirmed the lad's hooligan credentials. The judge at Manchester Assizes imposed concurrent sentences of four years, warning the recidivist that he intended to put down the use of the knife in Liverpool. 'You had better mend your ways,' was the judge's final advice.

The loss of one of the leaders did nothing to stop the south end crime wave. In November 1945, four young men, believed to be members of the Peanut Gang, were accused of a number of break-ins around the Park Lane area. Jewellery, watches, cigarettes and whisky were favourite targets. When caught, the youths remained tight-lipped, refusing to say a word. However, during their trial at Manchester Assizes, they admitted the thefts but denied any involvement in the Peanut Gang.

A great many exploits of the Peanut Gang remain anonymous, since the names of juvenile offenders, and even the districts where they lived, were never made public. Although the gang included numerous underage lawbreakers, the newspapers were not allowed to reveal information that could lead to their identification. A great deal of the disorder described in Chapter 15 could well have been the handiwork of junior members of the Peanut Gang. Indeed, the gang was most likely responsible for many of the unspecified crimes committed around the south end district. In 1943, a man turned up for fire watch duty at a Park Lane store. A fifteen-year-old, who happened to be one of his own employees, lay in wait and beat him over the head with a hammer before ransacking the shop and ripping open the safe.

The Peanut Gang was not the only bunch of terrors active during the war in the south end of Liverpool. 'These young men can only be described as hooligans,' declared Mr Culshaw, prosecuting at Liverpool Police Court. In the dock were three black seamen, all aged nineteen, from the Toxteth area. The case recalls the High Rip rampage around Scotland Road where the members indulged in an orgy of violence against shopkeepers and pedestrians minding their own business.

In 1941, Raymond and Henry Williams, together with Patrick Johnson, roamed the streets randomly attacking complete strangers. One innocent man was looking in a shop window in Paradise Street when Johnson struck him between the eyes. The gang then walked off laughing. In Canning Place, Henry Williams smacked a man in the face and in Park Lane, Johnson struck a seventeen-year-old before turning on a seaman outside the offices of the Shipping Federation. Their excuse was that they were drunk. Raymond Williams was fined while his accomplices were sent to prison.

In 1944, a Chinese seaman was making his way home from the theatre when someone suddenly came up to him and struck him in the face before running away. As the poor man lay on the floor, Anthony Gobin kicked him in the stomach. The victim lost consciousness and awoke to find that he had been robbed of eight pounds. Seventeen-year-old Gobin had been released on licence from borstal a couple of months earlier. Described as a member of a notorious gang, Gobin had originally been sentenced to three years for breaking into shops. After the assault on the seaman, Gobin himself was severely beaten up by his colleagues who suspected that he had given the police information about the others involved in the assault. He ended up in hospital for several days. To cap it all he was then sentenced to eighteen months' imprisonment. The judge warned Gobin that if he had been physically fit he would also have faced twelve strokes of the birch.

Attacks on the Chinese and other foreign seamen bore the signature of the Peanut Gang. In August 1945, two sixteen-year-olds were arrested after two plain-clothed constables observed them trying to mug some Chinese men. The lads were seen waiting outside a Chinese boarding house not far from Park Lane. Every time somebody left the premises the two lads would follow him and try to strike up a conversation. The fourth Chinese man to leave was foolishly counting a roll of banknotes as he walked. The lads took their positions either side of him. However, before he was attacked, the police intervened and carried out a search. One of the youths was carrying a short iron bar, which he claimed to have picked up outside a billiards hall in Duke Street 'in case anybody got funny'. The alert constable knew that there was no billiards hall in Duke Street. The lads were therefore arrested.

In court, the pair claimed that they had merely gone out for a walk and picked up the iron bar in case anybody attacked them. They were both found guilty of loitering with intent to commit a felony and of being armed with an offensive weapon. They were remanded to prison with a view to being sent to borstal.

The Chinese man counting his cash was fortunate not to have been beaten to a pulp. Others were not so lucky. A Liverpool taxi driver recalls an incident from his youth when he witnessed an attack by the Peanut Gang on a defenceless Chinese man in High Park Street. The victim lost an eye in a motiveless and merciless kicking.

All nationalities were fair game to the Peanut Gang. In 1945, a sixteen-year-old was remanded to prison for stealing money from a domestic gas meter. His arrest came in curious circumstances after he called at Kingsley Road Police Station claiming to have been assaulted. After questioning, he admitted that his story was untrue. A policeman then noticed that his address matched the premises where the gas meter theft had recently taken place. The lad decided to come clean. He admitted to the robbery and also to being a member of the Peanut Gang who beat up a 'Yank' the previous weekend. He claimed to have been so drunk that he couldn't remember how much money they had robbed. The young gangster was an absconder from an approved school and was adamant that he didn't want to return. He asked to be sent to borstal instead.

A vicar pointed out the existence of a team of ruffians willing to beat up anyone for a few shillings. Although he did not name the gang, his horrific description of their handiwork points to the Peanut Gang. He claims to have seen victims so badly disfigured that it was easy to mistake them for wartime casualties.[5] The Peanut Gang was certainly in the news at the time. The *Evening Express* featured an editorial about the gang and spoke of a 'reign of terror' being waged in the south end of Liverpool. One shopkeeper was so fed up of being burgled that he left a poster in his window: 'Will the gentleman who had to smash our windows twice within six days call at the Head Office for the keys.'[6]

In November 1945, the newspaper started receiving letters from concerned citizens, just as sixty years earlier outraged Liverpudlians put pen to paper about the High Rip. One person pointed out that he was a businessman with contacts in the south end. For months he had listened to horror stories of the activities of the Peanut Gang and claimed that it was no longer safe for people to venture out after dark. He called for greater police action and the return of the 'cat'. Another businessman confirmed that people were no longer leaving their homes during the evening. Not only were the rogues breaking into shops but they were also beating people up, including policemen. This writer also felt that showing kindness to them was useless: 'Once they are whipped they will think twice before they do wrong again.'

The situation was so bad that by November 1945 the police decided to take new measures to stamp out the south end terrorism. This was at the time of the trial of the young men accused of killing the Royal Navy signaller James Marsh. Precise details of the police operation could not be given. However, it was revealed that whereas in the past a lone constable was helpless against a mob of twenty, the new commando-trained teams of officers were more than a match for the hooligans.

To check any improvements, a *Daily Post* reporter bravely decided to take a tour through the blighted areas just as years earlier his predecessors had undertaken similar late night trips to the north end to observe the High Rip in action. The journalist was pleased to report that during his two-hour expedition he saw no evidence of youths looking for trouble. A shopkeeper, whose premises had been raided four times, boasted that in the last fortnight there had been a marked change in the district. He had recently witnessed a police raid on the gang and was sure that it would take a long time for them to defy the officers again.

The responses from the public illustrate the level of fear in the city. Music writer and Beatles expert Bill Harry offers his own disturbing memories of Liverpool during the era of the street gangs:

> It was rough … There were gangs – the Chain Gang, the Peanut Gang. On your way to school, they'd stop you and search your pockets for money. I remember one guy throwing me to the ground while three others kicked the hell out of me. They'd smash bottles and stick them in people's faces. The violence was extreme because kids imagined themselves stuck there for the rest of their lives and felt hopeless.[7]

Yet even when opportunities to escape the violence on Liverpool's streets presented themselves, lads felt drawn back to gang life. In January 1946, an eighteen-year-old joined the army. He didn't last long. After four days he went absent without leave from his unit in

Freshfield. A week later he was caught back in the city, breaking into a house in Great George Street. He did not act alone: he was in fact another member of the Peanut Gang. When arrested, he offered to come clean: 'Since I ran away from the army I have been back with the gang in Park Lane and sleeping out.' He met two other lads in a café and they decided to commit the burglary. Despite stealing jewellery and money to the value of £290, he claimed to have received only £2 for his efforts.

The lure of gang life must have been irresistible to young people growing up in the catastrophic atmosphere of wartime Liverpool. Gangsters were looked up to and respected by their peers. For those not in the gang, there must have been the ever-present fear of becoming a target of violence. During the research for his book on Liverpool's juvenile delinquents, John Barron Mays interviewed a number of young hard cases. A former thief and bully, known only as 'J', offered the following account of gang life. Although the gang is not given a name, it is almost certainly the Peanut Gang:

> When he was about 14½ he made overtures to the leader of the most notorious juvenile gang operating along the dock-side. He spoke to the leader in the street familiarly and was rewarded with a 'thick ear.' That put him off joining the gang although he wanted to join and admired them. However, his own brother was 'beaten up' by the gang at about the same time because of some slight quarrel. The gang would 'beat up' sailors and rob them and left a trail of destruction wherever they went. They were feared in the city. His own cousin was a member and he was eventually caught and committed to Borstal. ... The gang has now dispersed and the one-time leader is a tap room loafer cadging drinks.[8]

The Peanut Gang, like the High Rip before them, eventually fizzled out. The members probably grew up, got jobs, found wives, had kids and spent the rest of their lives complaining about the behaviour of the young generation. It is fitting that the once feared leader became an 'ale house bum' just like Nick, the battle-scarred veteran of the High Rip who would tour the dockside pubs looking for free beer. Like their Victorian predecessors, the Peanut Gang also became bogeymen figures of Liverpool folklore. Parents would warn their children to watch out for the gang and stay clear of lads thought to be members. Terrified youngsters would run a mile if they thought a group of approaching youths was the Peanut Gang.

One theory has it that as the thousands of troops returned to Liverpool at the end of the war, the Peanut Gang was outclassed. Young tearaways, however vicious, were no match for tough, fit and fearless men trained in combat. Whereas the murder of the Spanish sailor in 1884 marked the beginning of the reign of the High Rip, the death of a Royal Navy seaman in 1945 signalled the beginning of the end of the Peanut Gang.

The district remained dangerous, particularly for sailors, but the worst was over. By 1951, crime reporter Richard Whittington Egan could conclude: 'The dreaded Park Lane where not so very many years ago the formidable Peanut Gang swaggered in undisputed mastery, is comparatively innocuous nowadays and no new mob of organised ruffianism has risen to take the place of the erstwhile terrorists.'[9]

But this was not the end of the gangs of Liverpool, 'organised' or not. In 1945, a journal published a catalogue of senseless juvenile crimes before warning its readers that, 'if something is not done, the whole city will soon be in the murderous grip of an organisation like the old Hi Rip Gang which Mr Justice Day years ago exterminated with the gallows and cat-o'-nine tails.'[10] The justifiable fear was that as the Second World War ended, yet another war was about to begin.

18

Little Gangsters

IN 1947, THE *Daily Mirror* carried an alarming headline: '1000 "little gangsters" are on the loose.'[1] After visiting Liverpool's police zone 10, the cosmopolitan area around Park Lane, a journalist called Joseph Garrity gave a grim assessment of the current state of juvenile crime. It came as the Chief Constable was about to launch an Easter crusade against juvenile delinquency, involving teachers, churchmen, sociologists and anybody else that could come up with some solutions to Liverpool's growing crime problem. The issue was not so much the actions of mischievous and high-spirited youngsters but of organised gangs who planned operations with ruthless precision. Indeed, so devious were some of the felonies committed by Liverpool youngsters that the police often focussed their inquiries on adult suspects.

Gang members were also interchangeable, with youths assisting each other for particular criminal operations. Not only did they band together to intimidate witnesses but they also provided each other with perjured statements to secure acquittals. One young hoodlum even made his own jemmies.

There was certainly cause for concern. Crime during the war had increased by fifty per cent. The Liverpool University School of Social Science did some research which showed that, before the war, the value of goods stolen amounted to £2½ million pounds. By 1947, the figure had risen to £12 million pounds. There were good reasons for this. War-damaged buildings were easy to break into. Abandoned premises were used as cover to smash a way into adjacent buildings. A landscape of mangled architecture and craters provided ideal hiding places for stolen goods. A black market thrived on providing items that were impossible to purchase legally. Food and clothing shortages meant that buyers eagerly snapped up any contraband.

The reporter trotted out a crook's roll call of vicious mobs, including the Commando Gang, the Black Hand Gang and the Peanut Gang. The Chief Constable had reported that during 1946 the police had broken up over 163 juvenile gangs, totalling 700 young hoodlums. The statistical breakdown revealed eighty-six gangs consisting of three members, forty-nine with four members, twenty-three with five members, eight with six members, six with seven members and five with eight members. There was one gang with nine members and one with twelve. These were only the official figures. A senior policeman admitted, 'It's difficult to arrive at an estimate but I should say that there are at least a thousand boy gangsters on the loose in the town tonight.'

The bandits were usually teenagers but tinier terrors also prowled the streets. The Chief Constable's figures included 187 children under the age of ten, many of them nevertheless veterans of the courts. A 1947 police report showed that of 840 burglars and shop breakers arrested, fifty-six were boys and girls aged only eight.

'More trouble than any other boy in the school, a habitual criminal, a menace to the community, and a persistent truant' was the grave judgement of an education report on a twelve-year-old boy, one of the ringleaders of a notorious juvenile crew active throughout 1946. The nine boys, ranging in age from nine to fourteen, were convicted of an epidemic of burglaries of shops and houses in Everton, Anfield and Kensington. Bicycles, cash, clothing coupons, ration books, jewellery and cigarettes were plundered. Only the bicycles were ever recovered. In every case, the boys had gained entry to homes by breaking the back windows and inserting a piece of wire to release the catches. Once inside, they ransacked each room. The lads would split into smaller factions to do different jobs.

A policeman arrested the two ringleaders, who were also the youngest members, at 11pm. They were riding bicycles they had just stolen. Fingerprint evidence helped convict the boys, some of whom were already on bail when the offences were committed. In December 1946, their reign of terror was ended. Four lads, including the youngest, were sent to an approved school for three years while others were given a spell in a remand home or put on probation.

The youngsters aped their lawless elders. Stealing cars was not restricted to adults. Three boys aged ten, twelve and sixteen described their love of 'joyriding' when they appeared before the Juvenile Court in 1946. They were caught when a policeman saw them acting suspiciously, examining a car with a torch late at night. When questioned, they explained that they were merely checking the mileage. On further examination the door handle was damaged. When searched, the older lad was found to be carrying twenty-eight car ignition keys, a tyre lever and a pair of gloves. His father explained to the court that his son had been a good boy until he started work. He then went off the rails.

The wicked ingenuity of some boys led to outrageous assaults. In 1946, three Seaforth boys, aged twelve and thirteen, decided to fire staples from pieces of bicycle inner tube. One female shopper was hit in the eye and had to have her eyeball removed at St Paul's Eye Hospital. Another missile narrowly missed a delivery boy. When caught by a passing policeman each boy was found to have a well-stocked armoury of staples and pieces of rubber. In court, the culprits refused to speak but the father of one of them explained it was purely an accident for which they were sorry. Firing at people was a popular juvenile sport. A year earlier, Liverpool police seized 300 catapults from children.

In 1948, there were more warnings of a growing post-war crime wave.[2] The lawlessness was said to be getting as bad as Chicago and New York. Although Britain did not have the same problem with organised gangs, the level of individual crime was believed to be comparable with America. British gaols were overflowing, with up to three men sharing a cell. Murder and violent robbery were so common that mere burglary was felt to be no longer newsworthy. The fault was said to lie with a lack of police on the beat. The call went out for urgent government action.

It seems that Liverpool youths were being influenced on two fronts. In addition to the violence of the war in Europe there was also the powerful attraction of American crime films. The lads were beginning to model themselves on the gangsters they had seen or heard about from Hollywood films. There has been a link between Liverpool and America ever since ships first sailed between the two countries. However, after the Second World War a culturally fruitful relationship was forged on the North Atlantic passenger ships. Local seamen, stewards on the transatlantic run, were known as 'Cunard Yanks'. They had regular contact with American lifestyle and customs. Liverpool tailors were instructed to copy the cut of American fashions. Long overcoats were worn in the manner of the big screen hoodlums. American slang words crept into the local vernacular. Recordings of American rhythm and blues and country music were heard in Liverpool long before the rest of the country discovered them.

Yet even before the war, American culture reached Liverpudlians through the cinema. In 1939, Liverpool boasted ninety-six picture houses, offering a daily diet of comedies, love stories and, most importantly, gangster films. During the 1930s and 1940s local cinemas showed the latest films about machine-gun toting hoodlums and their enemies, the G-men from the Federal Bureau of Investigation. In 1949, a Birmingham University research team discovered that, while in the past cowboy films had proved hugely influential, a new generation of young men was being seduced by the cool violence of the big screen gangsters.

Ironically, there were hardly any gritty British-made crime films on show since the British Board of Film Censors banned anything that involved drugs, prostitution or brutality. Realistic depictions of criminal techniques or attempts to show crime from the gangster's point of view were also rejected as immoral. Local youngsters were forced to look across the Atlantic for inspiration. Throughout the 1930s over seventy-five per cent of movies shown in British cinemas were American. The authorities deplored the importation of such un-British examples of culture. While some police chiefs welcomed the cinema as a means of keeping kids off the streets and reducing drunkenness amongst adults, for others the big screen glamorised crime and eroded respect for the law.

In 1938, at a meeting of magistrates and social workers, Alexander Paterson, the Prison Commissioner, offered some reasons for juvenile crime. He claimed that thirteen was the most dangerous age for young people. A Liverpool probation officer further explained that this was a boy's last year of freedom before leaving school. He would therefore have one last criminal fling before entering adulthood. It was also the age when boys formed gangs and started playing at being gangsters, copying their celluloid heroes. This often led to more serious trouble.

An early example of a youngster aping the blackmail and extortion rackets of American gangsters is the case of the fifteen-year-old who, in 1934, sent a letter to a married woman living off Breck Road. The lady opened the unstamped letter and read:

> Dear Madam,
> I have in my possession a number of photos of you in a very alarming state – to be precise in the nude. . . . My price for same is £10. If the money is not forthcoming, or if you mention the matter to anyone, no matter who it is, I will send one photo to each of your relatives, and also to your husband.

The letter went on to give directions and a sketched map of the drop-off point in nearby Wolverton Street, where the money was to be collected and the photos returned. The letter concluded, 'Come by yourself and remember what I said about keeping it dark. Burn after reading.'

Detectives set a trap and observed a boy covering his face with a scarf before going into an entry. He was arrested and, although he denied the offence, a handwriting test showed him to be the author of the threatening letter. The lad then admitted it had been a practical joke that had gone too far. There were no photos. He had simply discovered details about the woman while doing his milk round. His father put the blame on his son's reading habits: 'He reads any kind of rubbish he can get hold of.'

In 1949, a sixteen-year-old youth from North Wales tried a similar blackmail attempt on a married woman. After threatening to make public some scurrilous allegations about the lady's moral character, he demanded £10. Like the previous lad, he was caught as he tried to collect the money. This boy was also an avid reader of gangster fiction. He claimed that he discovered the details of the scam in the plot of a book.

Pulp gangster fiction replaced the old 'penny dreadful' tales of daring highwaymen. In 1940, some lads stole a motorcar from the United Co-operation Laundries in West Derby and used it to break into a shop, where they stole air rifles and pistols. Later, police spotted the car. While searching Joseph Davies, a constable was struck on the head with the butt of a pistol. In court, a police inspector explained that Davies was the ringleader and had been reading gangster novels. He was sent to borstal for three years for the 'dastardly and cowardly' attack.

It wasn't only novels and the cinema that gave criminals ideas. In 1931, Liverpool's Head Constable pointed the finger at press reports that described in too much detail how crimes were committed. Some newspapers included graphic photographs. Indeed, one young hoodlum sent a letter to the editor of a Liverpool daily correcting the inaccurate reporting of a crime he had committed. He also complained that the headline was not in bold enough typeface.

Young people from all over the country latched onto the gangster craze. In 1938, three members of the Red Skull Gang from the unlikely setting of Herne Bay in Kent, pleaded guilty to several burglaries. Each boy had his own gang name. One was called 'The Boss', another 'The Brains' and the third 'Slick'. An eight-year-old, too young to be charged, was known as 'Al Capone'.

It was from the celluloid version of the American criminal underworld that Liverpool's own homebred hoodlums drew their inspiration. Actors such as James Cagney and Humphrey Bogart became icons for their portrayal of hard, ruthless mobsters. In 1948, a lad wearing a scarf tied around his face entered a store in St. Domingo Vale, Everton, pulled out a knife and ordered the lady at the counter to 'stick 'em up'. However, she put up such a fuss that he fled empty handed. When captured, he admitted to the police, 'I got the idea from Humphrey Bogart.' The influence of the cinema was also apparent in the actions of two youths who, in 1946, burgled a house and then set it on fire to destroy their fingerprints. It was something they had learned from a film.

The cult of the gangster took hold. Boys aped not only the methods but also the language of their heroes. It has been claimed that in order to communicate with each other, some delinquents learnt by heart about 500 words of underworld slang and criminal jargon. In 1944, two twelve-year-olds appeared in court accused of stealing from a shop in Marsh Lane, Bootle. During intense questioning, one of the accused turned to his accomplice and shouted, 'It's all a frame-up. Take that.' He then smacked his mate in the mouth. His tearful friend explained, 'The jacks [police] have got it against me.'

In 1940, a fifteen-year-old Liverpool lad was charged with sending his former employer, a timber merchant, a threatening letter demanding money. On being sacked for bad timekeeping, the lad decided to wreak revenge. He wrote:

> As far as we know you are very rich, two cars and a very big timber yard: but suppose that the yard went on fire. If you like to stop it, you will put six pounds in packages and put it in the air raid shelter round the corner, and by the way, it is no use going to the police about it, because we have many big shots in with us.

'Big shots' indeed. In fact the boy was working alone.

As well as sending threatening letters, the leaving of signed notes at the crime scene was another classic American gangster trick and was to prove very influential with Liverpool's juvenile gangs. Such notes were not an entirely new phenomenon, although, again, there seems to be some American connection. In 1918, a shop in Derby Lane suffered several burglaries. On the final occasion, a note was left at the scene for the owner: 'Mrs Milburn – I took the shutters down. You can find me if you want to. I go to sea at two o'clock.' It was signed, 'Dick, the American ball tosser.'

'Dick' was in fact an eighteen-year-old girl who lived above the shop and once worked for the owner. The note did little to throw police off the scent and she was soon arrested and fined.

The craze was popularised partly through the Black Hand Gang series of popular films and partly through American gangsterism. Indeed, the Black Hand Gang can also be traced back to the wave of Italians who settled in America in the early twentieth century. Underworld figures such as 'Lupo the Wolf' were responsible for extortion rackets amongst shops and businesses in the Italian sectors. Letters would be sent demanding money, each note bearing a black palm print.

In 1941, there was an epidemic of burglary around Wavertree and Everton. Bricks would be removed from the walls at the rear of shops to afford entry. Suspicion fell on a gang of four men. Two were arrested but the shop breaking continued, with a sinister difference. After each robbery a note was left on the premises claiming that it was the work of the 'Black Hand Gang'. The other suspects were eventually arrested and some of the stolen property found in their homes. The gang was a familiar name in Liverpool. In 1944, a sixteen-year-old was caught behind a shop in Bootle wearing a silk stocking mask with menacing eye slits. He was carrying a file in one hand and a chisel in the other. The magistrate declared that the lad had 'behaved like one of the Black Hand Gang'.

In 1940, two men from the Park Road area broke into several premises, including a tobacconists shop in Lodge Lane and a pawnshop in Smithdown Road. Each time, they left behind a note signed, 'The Ringer.' *The Ringer* was the title of a movie made in 1931. Based on an Edgar Wallace thriller, it depicted a master of disguise who commits a series of daring crimes. The name remained popular for some years. In 1965, police questioned a suspect at the scene of a burglary in Litherland. The youth held up his hands and enquired cheekily, 'Was it the Ringer?'

The level of crime committed by disenchanted youths in post-war Liverpool led to the chairman of the juvenile court issuing a dire warning: 'Every boys' gang in this city that appears before me is going to be broken. We have fought two wars to make this a decent country to live in. We are not going to have gangs of boys breaking it up.'

The words were prompted by a court appearance in 1947 of a group of five lads known as 'Snake Eye's Gang'. The boys, aged between ten and sixteen, pleaded guilty to a spate of burglaries and vandalism in the Walton area. As well as stealing sports equipment from schools, breaking into a church offertory box and attempting to smash a safe, the boys had broken into the gas meters of their own homes. After wrecking machinery in a factory, they left a note with the name of their gang. The youngest child, who couldn't read or write, was placed on probation. The others, including one lad described as 'anti-social and of a warped mentality', were sent to an approved school. The chairman regretted not being able to order a good flogging.

Another juvenile mob from 1947, known as the 'Skull Gang', was active in the Smithdown Road area, where they committed burglaries and vandalism. The children, aged ten to twelve, broke into a stonemason's office and smeared memorials with black paint, ruining them. They then smashed up the place, causing £300 worth of damage. A calling card was placed on a table, 'With compliments of the Skull.' They burgled another stonemasons but on this occasion they refrained from vandalism and merely stole a few tools. They left another note: 'You are lucky this time. The Skull.' After being caught, three of them were fined and sent to an approved school for a month.

In the same year, three boys aged twelve and thirteen decided to leave behind the pressures of life in post-war Liverpool in search of something better down south. First, they selected a 'secretary' to dictate farewell messages to their parents. The crumpled note read, 'Dear Mam and Dad – I am running away forever, but don't worry about me because I will be all right. If you come after us you will never see us again. We are going to London so as to be there for the Cup Final.' It then mentioned the names of the other boys before continuing, 'Pass this to their mothers. I am fed up with that house because I am always getting hit. I will send some money (£5) as soon as I get it.' The message from the second boy was equally bitter about home life: 'Dear Mrs ___ , You've always been asking me to go messages and going for the milk, I am fed up with that.' The third boy's domestic circumstances were also oppressive: 'Dear Mam, I'm always getting battered and having to do the grate and the rooms so I am running away for ever. Your son.'

To prepare for their journey the boys broke into some shops in Islington, stealing food. They spent their first night in a blitzed building next to the water tank in St Anne Street. However, the boys were caught and later achieved their dream of living away from home. They were each sent to a remand home for a month.

In 1948, three outlaws, aged thirteen and fourteen, called themselves the 'Just William' gang, after the hero featured in the series of books by Richmal Crompton. Calling themselves 'William', 'Ginger' and 'Douglas', the lads broke into the pavilion of Quarry Bank High School and stole watches and cash. In court, 'Douglas' explained his gang had read all the *William* books and listened avidly to the radio shows. The magistrate pointed out to the boy that William may have been mischievous but he certainly did not steal. The lad was put on probation while his colleague 'William' was discharged.

The glut of young rascals on Liverpool's streets sparked yet another debate about juvenile lawlessness. In 1948, letters were sent to the newspapers criticising the laxity of the criminal justice system. One correspondent blamed rising levels of crime on lenient magistrates and dreaming sentimentalists: 'We have to face the fact that there is a "jungle generation" in our midst, which calls for drastic and forceful action.'[3]

The 'jungle generation' was in evidence during the summer of 1948. Over a period of a few months, schools in Bootle suffered an epidemic of wanton vandalism as youths went on the rampage. In one incident, 154 panes of glass were broken. Ten boys, aged eight to fourteen, were rounded up and dealt with at the juvenile court. One admitted that he smashed twenty windows and another stated that he had broken light bulbs and thrown empty milk bottles against the classroom walls. A picture of the headmaster was also chalked on the blackboard. Asked to explain their behaviour, two of the boys admitted that they wanted to get their revenge on the teachers, who caned them 'for nothing'. After meting out punishments ranging from fines to probation, the magistrate warned future offenders that they would be named and shamed in the press despite their youth.

Yet vandalism, robbery and violence continued. One team of boys, aged eight to fourteen, pulled off a despicable robbery in a restaurant in London Road. In 1948, they stole a charity collection box belonging to the Liverpool Child's Welfare Centre. Despite being a close-knit gang, when caught they all turned on the youngest member and blamed him. The magistrate, disgusted by the lack of group loyalty and solidarity as much as by the theft itself, concluded, 'You are not even fit to be a gang.'

Another juvenile gang, who listened to the radio but completely misunderstood what they were listening to, were the 'Dick Barton' gang. Dick Barton was a 'special agent' on a popular radio show broadcast between 1945-1951. At its height, the programme attracted 15 million listeners and was widely seen as responsible for inspiring a generation of juvenile delinquents.

In March 1950, five youths, aged fifteen and sixteen, from the Great Howard Street area were accused of burglary and vandalism. In one raid on the Hornby Docks, the premises had been entered from a low roof and the entire window frame removed. Furniture was smashed and a heavy safe pushed from one room to another before the bottom was hacked off. Keys were taken which were then used to open the main safe containing £66. A building in Regent Road, near the docks, was also hit. The place was left in a shocking state. A door had been torn from its hinges and the telephone wire cut. Pictures were plucked from the wall, an electric fire smashed beyond repair and an attaché case ripped to shreds. The gang, who acted like a plague of locusts, left a note for the police: 'Dick Barton strikes again.' They seemed unaware that Dick Barton was on the side of law and order.

The boys also broke into a public house and helped themselves to some beer. They were tracked down and prosecuted. One lad revealed that he got £10 as his share of the raids, which he spent 'knocking about town'. The magistrate was not amused by their antics and sentenced four of them to an approved school and one to a detention home. He even allowed their names to be published in the press, despite the usual suppression of juvenile identities.

In 1950, eleven boys were caught after Liverpool College suffered four burglaries in a single week. The gang would run amok, emptying drawers, throwing salt and pepper around and tearing up documents. Either as a sign of his repentance, or for a bit of cheek, one of the boys left behind a note saying, 'Sorry about the damage.' It was signed, 'The Black Robe'. This was in fact the title of a short story by Victorian novelist Wilkie Collins. These lads might have been vandals but they were well read.

Others had office skills. Also in 1950, junior bandits broke into a business premises in Bootle and left a note on the typewriter saying, 'The Dillinger Brothers Strike Again.' The boys also burgled a school and left the same slogan on the blackboard, next to a rude message. Around the same time, the Tennyson Street Gang, consisting of eight youngsters, were ripping off the wire grills protecting numerous shop windows in the Toxteth Park area. They would then use glasscutters, or sometimes bricks, to get at the goods on display.

Juvenile gang life was not simply about thieving, vandalism, exciting adventures and leaving menacing notes behind. Turf warfare was also part of gang culture. In 1947, territorial hooliganism was rife in Fazakerley. Two juvenile mobs ruled the area, one led by a thirteen-year-old and the other by a fourteen-year-old. One night, the older lad stepped from a bus with his mate, only to meet his younger rival who was standing with the rest of his boys. The younger leader shouted, 'I'm mad,' before attempting to plunge a blade into the older boy's shoulder. The weapon, an old table knife, was too blunt to penetrate the lad's clothing. The 'mad' assailant ran off but was caught by the older boy. Their fight resumed and the younger boy was stabbed in a swift act of revenge. 'I fought till blood spurted out of my back,' the victim later said. In a statement, the knifeman claimed self-defence. Three years earlier, the older boy had been placed under supervision because he was out of control. He had also suffered a spell in an approved school for theft. For the stabbing, he was bound over for twelve months.

Whether the cinema was a major influence on juvenile crime is a matter for sociologists and criminologists. What is certain is that there was as much crime happening on the streets of Liverpool as there was in the latest American gangster film. For some victims, real life outside the cinema was a great deal more violent than anything being shown on the big screen.

The Cameo Cinema in Wavertree was the subject of another raid, this time by a juvenile crew. In February 1949, William Carr, the relief manager, turned away some lads for misbehaving. A few minutes later, an aggrieved fifteen-year-old approached Carr and asked him why his gang had been barred. Not satisfied with the answer he was given, the youth butted Carr before kneeing him in the groin. Carr suffered two black eyes and three broken teeth. The lad was arrested and sent to a remand home for twenty-eight days. The streetwise chairman of the bench warned him, 'Next time you will go to the Assizes and get imprisonment. I know all about the old "butt, knee and boot" trick.'

It could be argued that the city's young tearaways didn't need to ape the antics of the big screen American gangsters. Their older brothers provided a set of role models much closer to home, for the post-war period also saw the adult gangs bringing their own little bit of Chicago to Liverpool.

19

After the War:
Hostilities Continue

WHILE THE PEANUT Gang took over parts of south Liverpool, across the river on the Wirral, the Falcon Gang held its own reign of terror. In 1946, four youths were accused of various break-ins around Bromborough. Shops, a library and a social club were targeted. When Henry, or Harry, Adamson, alias 'The Falcon', was arrested he admitted to being a member of the gang, along with Stanley Kimberley. It was suggested that Adamson went around terrorising the neighbourhood with a bodyguard of six or seven men. Before binding them over for twelve months, the magistrate claimed that the gang sounded like something from an Edgar Wallace thriller.

The following month, Adamson, who boasted a fearsome reputation, was the victim of an assault by the former leader of a defunct gang. In a café in New Ferry, Adamson approached John Roberts, who was with his girlfriend. A few words were passed and Adamson invited Roberts outside. His rival refused but as he left the café Adamson shouted, 'I'll kill you, you bastard.'

An incensed Roberts then followed him and a mass brawl erupted. As Adamson went to the assistance of a colleague who had been floored, Roberts and a lad called Whitty gave him a severe beating. The factions scattered as the police arrived. However, they soon met up again at the bus depot down the road. Whitty and Roberts again singled out Adamson who was smacked in the face, knocked down and dragged unconscious into the gutter. He spent the next eight days in hospital.

In the court case following the attack, Roberts' defence asked Adamson where he acquired the nickname of The Falcon. He claimed that he'd made it up. The defence probed further: 'Does that mean that one of your peculiarities is that you swoop down without warning?' A puzzled Adamson muttered that he didn't understand. Roberts and Whitty claimed that it was a fair fight but were found guilty of assault and sentenced to one month's imprisonment with hard labour.

In November 1947, a Sunday newspaper ran an article criticising the level of crime in Liverpool, particularly in the Park Road area. In response, Liverpool's Chief Constable, Herbert Winstanley, wrote to the Lord Mayor offering his own observations. He denied the existence of armed gangs around the Park Road area, pointing out that the district had never been difficult to police. He felt that the article probably meant to refer to Park Lane, the nearby headquarters of the infamous Peanut Gang.

However, the original newspaper report was probably not far off the mark since Park Road was also a rough area. The following month it was the scene of an orgy of violence after a mob went on the rampage. About eighteen youths, including girls, left a dancehall in Steble Street shortly after eleven o'clock. The group, aged between sixteen and twenty, went along Park Road into Northumberland Street where they smashed the window of a shop. They continued down Park Road and put in another plate glass shop window. The owner came out and confronted the gang as they tried to smash a third window. He grabbed hold of one lad who promptly butted him in the face. The pack then split into two, one group running down Hill Street where another window was broken. No goods were stolen; the aim was simply wanton vandalism.

An innocent man on his way home from the same dance bumped into the gang and was whacked twice over the back of the head with a blunt instrument. He was taken to hospital with concussion. Police patrols combed the area but the troublemakers had dispersed.

* * *

While the south end crime spots were making regular headlines, the old High Rip stamping grounds in the north end continued to host scenes of violent disorder. With war now over, 1946 brought more dancehall hooliganism. Three youths, including the two

Murphy brothers, went to the Acacia House club in Everton Brow. They knocked on the rear door but were refused admission. They then broke the glass panel. As the licensee opened up, he was struck on the head. One of the lads brandished a bottle while the others clutched pieces of timber. Bursting inside, the brothers went on the rampage, attacking the dancers, smashing furniture and ripping the radiator from the wall. The licensee had to be taken to hospital where he received stitches to two head wounds and treatment to five damaged teeth. One of the brothers received a month's hard labour while his accomplices were fined.

In 1946, yet another Kelly gang was on the warpath. William Kelly, from Bootle, was standing with four other men outside a public house in Derby Road. Two passing policemen suspected that they were drunk. They were shouting and singing a song containing the line, 'Watch out cops, when the Kellys are about.' Kelly boasted to one of the officers, 'I am the twelve stone champion of the Somersets and I would like a few minutes with you.'

The policemen told the group to move on, which they did. However, ten minutes later they bumped into them again. Kelly led the men, shouting, 'Out of the ___ way', as he walked right into one of the constables, almost pushing him off the pavement. He then turned to the gang and shouted, 'Let's get these ___ coppers.' Kelly threw a punch but the policeman dodged it and closed in on him. Both fell to the floor, with the constable on top. A large crowd gathered and the officer felt his coat being torn from his back. A ferocious kick to his groin forced him to release his grip on Kelly, who jumped up and booted him in the face. The crowd closed in with their own kicks. The officer rose and drew his truncheon but somebody jumped on his back and snatched it from his hand. The victim was left with one eye badly swollen and the other bleeding. Kelly later received twelve months' imprisonment.

Three years later, Phillip and James Kelly, from the same Bootle address, were convicted of a similar assault on a policeman. In October 1949, the brothers were cautioned for being drunk and disorderly. However, Phillip then turned on the policeman and kicked him in the ribs, shouting, 'Take that, you ___.'

As the officer got up, James thumped him. Fortunately, a patrol car arrived before further harm could be inflicted. The Kelly brothers were arrested and put in the car. As they drove off, Phillip screamed, 'Let's get the _____ driver,' and both brothers lunged forward from the back seat. The constable had to beat them off with his truncheon. Although the brothers denied any assaults, and despite claims that they were the real victims, they were both found guilty.

The idea of criminals going quietly and admitting to a 'fair cop, guv' remained something of a myth, seen only in cinema films. Rescue attacks on policemen trying to make arrests decreased as the century progressed but never completely died out in certain rough areas. It seems that almost every time a young constable made an arrest in the Scotland Road district, he was assaulted. The situation became so bad that the superintendent in charge of the division made the decision to put officers patrolling the area in pairs for their own protection.

In 1948, two men appeared in the Magistrates Court accused of being drunk and assaulting police officers. The constables stated that they were surrounded by a 300-strong, hostile mob as they tried to escort the prisoners to the bridewell. After sending the men to prison, the Stipendiary Magistrate made the point that the inhabitants of Scotland Road rightly expected the police to help them whenever they were in trouble yet not one of the crowd had enough British spirit to offer assistance to the constables.

Angry crowds were one danger facing the police; desperate criminals with guns were another. One of the biggest crime problems in post-war Britain was the amount of weapons circulating. Lugers and Berettas brought home and kept as war souvenirs were sometimes stolen from the owners' homes and ended up in the underworld, to be used in armed robberies. During the First World War, only officers had carried revolvers and so the problem of surplus firearms had not been as severe.

At the end of 1945, the *Evening Express* ran a prophetic editorial:

The volume of violent crime that is sweeping the country is alarming. Hold-ups, burglaries, thefts and wilful damage have

increased immeasurably since the end of the war and the
'Gunman' complex seems to be animating more and more of the
lawbreakers as the days go by. Even boys – they can hardly be
dignified by the term 'Youths' – are numbered amongst the
revolver brandishers.[1]

The crime situation was made worse by the fact that police
numbers were still severely depleted due to the war. There simply
weren't enough officers on the beat to cope with the crime wave.
The newspaper offered three solutions: demobbed soldiers were to
be encouraged to help reinforce police numbers by volunteering as
'specials', the public was urged to report cases of illegal firearm
possession, and judges were asked to enforce stiffer penalties. In
particular, the newspaper longed for the introduction of life
sentences and flogging for trigger-happy thugs and pointed out
that the 'naughty-boy-don't-do-it-again' approach to criminal
justice had failed and only encouraged further violence.

The incident that perhaps prompted the newspaper's tough
stance had occurred a few days earlier when a sixteen-year-old
youth appeared at Liverpool Juvenile Court. The lad was a
member of an armed gang that travelled the country burgling
houses and shops. They had already visited Birkenhead, St Helens,
Manchester, Southampton, Swansea, London and Blackpool. The
youth, an escapee from an approved school, wasn't from Liverpool
but was caught after detectives learned that the gang was visiting
the city.

As a result of information received, a couple of detectives
tailed two lads behaving suspiciously in a doorway in the city
centre. The officers followed on foot while their colleagues
approached in a car from the other end of the street. The lads
started to walk away. Upon becoming aware that they were being
followed, one turned and pointed a revolver at the detectives, while
his mate covered the car. The officers bravely ran towards the
gunmen while their fellow detectives also attempted to cut them
off. The lads turned into Renshaw Street when the sixteen-year-old
realised that he was being overtaken. He again pointed his gun at
the officer but was overwhelmed by the man's colleagues, who
wrestled him to the ground and confiscated his loaded weapon.

On being charged, the dejected youth sighed, 'I don't care if you shoot me now.' Back at the station he added, 'I am glad you got me before I shot anybody.' He claimed to have bought the gun for £10 from an American soldier in a Liverpool milk bar.

Also in December 1945, three armed youths, aged about sixteen, attempted to hold up the Post Office in Shaw Street, Everton. One of the lads produced a revolver and demanded, 'Hand over your dough.' Only the sound of the alarm prompted the gang to run for it.

The gun menace continued on Liverpool's streets. Friday, 23 January 1948, was the date of 'one of the most dastardly acts of crime committed in Liverpool for some time'. At 2.40pm, Sidney Brown, a London Road tailor, was standing behind his counter when a man entered the shop, stooped down and fastened the door from the inside. As the short-sighted shopkeeper approached the customer, he noticed that there was a second man behind a partition inside the shop porch. Suddenly, the first man stuck a revolver into the tailor's stomach and declared, 'This is a stick up.'

As the terrified man screamed for help, his colleague shouted, 'Hit him. Hit him.' The shopkeeper was then whacked several times on the head with a truncheon known as a blackjack. His screams for help continued and were met by more shouts of, 'Hit him again. Hit him again.' He fell to the ground semi-conscious. As he lay bleeding on the floor, one of the raiders asked him for money and again threatened to assault him. The tailor promised the men that he would give them cash if they would leave him alone. The robbers searched him and took his money. After looking for clothing coupons, they then returned to their victim and tied his hands and feet before wrapping an overcoat belt around his mouth to stifle his cries.

Lying in a puddle of blood, the tailor heard one of the men ask, 'How much did you get?' His accomplice replied, 'Only a lousy few bob, and they told me I'd get plenty here.' The wounded man, blind from the blood in his eyes, eventually crawled to the door, and staggered onto the crowded pavement. He muttered behind his gag, 'I've been hit over the head with a gun.' His false teeth, spectacles and wristwatch lay behind him in the doorway.

After inquiries, led by Chief Inspector Balmer, Frederick Seiga, aged nineteen, and his twenty-three-year-old brother Edward were arrested and charged with attempted murder and robbery. Balmer later found the revolver, loaded with three rounds of ammunition, in a house on the outskirts of the city. Police also found two bloodstained blackjacks and the clothing used in the robbery hidden in a locked chest at a Corporation yard. Forensics also provided a crucial piece of evidence. Samples scraped from Frederick's fingernails bore traces of blood of the same group as the victim.

A sixteen-year-old was also arrested. The lad, an unemployed seaman, claimed that before the robbery, the other men took him to a public house in London Road and got him drunk on six pints of beer. He revealed that they then went to the tailor's shop where one of the men pulled him inside, told him to shut the door and put a blackjack in his hand. The boy admitted attacking the shopkeeper while one of his accomplices pistol-whipped him. He also told the police that he saw a man pull the trigger of a loaded revolver during the hold-up 'but the safety catch or something prevented it from firing'. The lad received a fiver for his part in the robbery.

In court, it was alleged that the tailor had been targeted days before the crime was committed. The robbers had also prepared a hideout, to which they could escape, change their clothes and wait until the hue and cry had died down. The place was in fact a gas locker containing meters serving a block of tenements. The prosecution's case was that it was Frederick who carried the revolver. The youth's own confession stated that it was Frederick who bought him the beer, handed him the blackjack and told him to hit the shopkeeper. Frederick Seiga received ten years' imprisonment while his brother got five years. The youth was sent to borstal for three years.[2]

Once again, concerned Liverpudlians put pen to paper to protest at the latest crime wave. In February 1948, the *Liverpool Echo* published letters from readers angry that the legal system was being too soft on offenders. One letter-writer expressed outrage that campaigners were calling for the abolition of the death sentence and the cat at the very time when they were most needed to tackle violent crime. Another pro-flogging correspondent, shocked at the leniency shown by some judges, called for another Justice Day 'who put an end to crime and robbery in Liverpool some years ago'.[3] Unfortunately, as earlier chapters have shown, he didn't.

At the time, the London Road robbery was unique both for its choice of weapons and the level of its violence. Unfortunately, it was a mere prelude to an even more outrageous and cold-blooded gun crime in Liverpool. It was against this post-war background of a ready use of firearms amongst hardened criminals that the so-called Cameo Murder took place. On 14 March 1949, the manager of the Cameo Cinema in Wavertree was busy in his office counting the night's takings with his assistant when a gunman burst in and shot both men dead. Fifty pounds was stolen in the raid.

Much has already been written about the crime.[4] During a massive police inquiry, 70,000 people were interviewed and every gangster and known ruffian on Liverpool's streets was pulled in for questioning. A prostitute, her pimp and a conman pointed the finger at local hard-case George Kelly and ex-seaman Charles Connolly. Despite a lack of forensic evidence, and claims that the men didn't even know each other, Kelly and Connolly were eventually convicted. Kelly was hanged for murder while Connolly was imprisoned for ten years for robbery. After a long campaign by the men's friends and family, both convictions were posthumously quashed in 2003.

The death of Kelly may well have served as a warning to would-be gunmen. Most robbers preferred a less violent means of earning a living. Safes in town centre stores and offices were ripe for picking by clever and organised crooks. In 1948, film director David Lean's version of the Charles Dickens novel *Oliver Twist* was shown on the big screen. It wasn't long before the newspapers reckoned that thieves were copying Fagin's method of using small children to break into premises.

On a Saturday night in January 1949, a carefully planned raid on the premises of the Merseyside Hide and Skin Association left a steel safe weighing more than two hundredweight wrenched from the wall with its back torn off. The various entrances to the premises were securely locked up, the only vulnerable point being a narrow gap in a trellis gate. It was thought that a small boy was lifted through the aperture in order to open the gate from the inside. The child's bulkier minders then entered the building and scrambled over the half-treated hides on their way to the office where they smashed the door. Taking the workers' smocks and overalls, they carefully shielded every electric light in the room. It would have taken three men to move the safe from the wall. To deaden the noise, towels and other materials were spread over the floor before the safe was pushed over on its front. With the aid of a jemmy and screwdriver, the back was then ripped away and the steel drawers inside battered to reveal their contents. Unfortunately for the thieves, most of the cash had already been removed before the weekend. They left their tools but took a number of tablets of soap.

In 1949, eight men were remanded on a charge of burglary. It was feared that they were part of a well-organised gang, using motors, responsible for an epidemic of break-ins around Liverpool. For four months, shops, offices and factories had been hit. Safes were either forced open or actually taken from the premises. A number of cracked safes had been found dumped on waste ground in various parts of the city. During the night of February 27, on the eve of their appearance at Manchester Assizes, three of the prisoners decided to break free from Walton Gaol. Joseph Bennett, John Lewis and John Hanley cut through their cell bars with a hacksaw before employing the classic trick of a rope of knotted bed-sheets to complete their escape. The prisoners then scaled a twenty-five-foot wall at the rear of the prison, backing on to Broomfield Gardens, near to the main Liverpool to Preston railway line. Although prison warders lived in the dwellings that bordered the wall, nobody heard or saw anything.

Upon the discovery of the audacious escape, a massive police operation swung into action. Patrols combed the districts of Walton and Aintree while all sidings at Walton Junction and Preston Road Stations were searched. Every truck and coal wagon was inspected without success. Meanwhile the men had fled to a house in Walker Street, off West Derby Road, just a stone's throw from where they lived. On Wednesday, March 2, just before ten o'clock in the morning, five patrol cars converged upon the house. About twenty officers, led by Chief Inspector Balmer, surrounded the property prior to two detectives going in. Minutes later the three unshaven men emerged and were quickly escorted to nearby Harper Street police station. After sixty hours of freedom the escapees were back in custody awaiting an appearance at Manchester Assizes. Bennett later received five years while Hanley got four years. Lewis was sentenced to twelve months. The other five men also received prison sentences. In court, D.I. Bonner claimed that Bennett and Hanley were the ringleaders of a large gang that had stolen property worth £1,600.

Yet cracking safes continued. In the same month as the gaol break, Henderson and Glass Ltd, a firm of constructional engineers in Regent Road, suffered a burglary. Nothing was taken for the thieves were merely sussing the place out for a much more lucrative job. Three weeks later, they were back with a cunning plan. Using the firm's own oxy-acetylene equipment, they ran the tubes from the ground floor workshop through a window on the first floor into the cashier's office. They then burned out the side of the safe before ripping open the inner lining with metal shears. Up to £200 in cash was stolen.

Safe-blowing was for professional teams with technical expertise. Some villains preferred to continue with the more primitive and merciless tradition of randomly mugging strangers. In 1948, an armed robbery took place in Mill Lane, off William Brown Street. After a trip to the cinema, a man was returning home through the narrow unlit street when a figure approached and demanded his wallet. Before he knew what was happening, two others had joined in to attack him. Although one shouted to his mate, 'Don't use the knife,' the ringleader repeatedly tried to stab the victim. He succeeded in slicing his cheek and hand. A knife and safety razor were later found discarded on the pavement. A policeman witnessed the assault and was able to arrest the men. Amazingly, the attacker tried to convince the constable that the victim was trying to rob him. In court, the accusation was dismissed and the knifeman received four years and his accomplices two years.

The following year, a gang of eight men led by John White attacked a man as he left a dancehall in West Derby Road. At 12.45am the victim was walking towards the town centre when he heard a voice behind him. Although he quickened his pace, White overtook him, grabbed his lapels and butted him in the jaw. The man broke away and ran down a side street pursued by the men who caught up with him and gave him a beating. White and a colleague called Thomas Flynn marched their victim to another side street where they repeatedly punched him as they ordered him to surrender his overcoat, sports jacket and tie. He was also robbed of £9 and had to spend three weeks off work due to his injuries.

The attackers were caught and each sentenced to five years' imprisonment. Flynn got an extra year for a separate assault on a policeman. The judge lamented, 'In this great city it would seem it was not uncommon for a gang of roughs to attack peaceful citizens. That might seem to be a rather appalling situation.' The judge's damning words could have been uttered seventy-five years earlier, at the trial of the three Cornermen convicted of the murder of Richard Morgan. As the century neared its half-way mark, the question posed itself. Had the situation on Liverpool's streets improved much since the infamous Tithebarn Street murder?

20

Our Wickedest City

POST-WAR BRITAIN seemed to hark back to the violence and street anarchy of the beginning of the century. Some revenge attacks on witnesses were as shocking as anything committed by the High Rip or the Victorian Amazons. In the early 1950s, Liverpool's Brodie Gang appeared in court. The formidable wife of one member was known as the 'Strong Arm Man'. She attacked one female witness with a razor as she left the court. For this she received four years' imprisonment and the gang faded.

Yet gangs are like the mythical many-headed Hydra: as one head is cut off, another grows in its place. The Fifties began with horror stories about the activities of organised bands of teenagers terrorising various parts of the country. Although Glasgow police had largely rid their city of the notorious razor gangs, new criminal fraternities had sprung up in their wake, including the Chain Gang and the Hammer Gang, the names offering an alarming hint as to their favoured weapons. More disturbingly, it was reported that junior versions of the gangs also existed, including the 'Wee Chains' and the 'Wee Hammers', ready to step in their brothers' shoes. Like Glasgow, Norwood in South London boasted a gang called the Billy Boys. Indeed the capital was awash with gangs, echoing the Hooligan era of fifty years earlier. There was the Diamond Gang of Islington, the Kilburn Gang of Hampstead and the Eagle Gang of Stepney. Old Kent Road was home to the Brick Gang.

According to *Daily Herald* journalist Alan Clarke, the conviction of George Kelly split up the big, organised criminal gangs in Liverpool.[1] It was noted at the time of Kelly's execution in March 1950 that his colleagues had promised to avenge his death. However, nothing seemed to have happened. A journalist tracked four associates to a Merseyside holiday resort where they waited for the pub to open. They then drank pints of mild in mourning for their boss. 'Old George might have got us into trouble by saying we would avenge him,' explained one of the men. 'We want to say here and now that we don't want any trouble.'[2] The police never even bothered to take special precautions against potential revenge attacks on witnesses.

Whether the hanging of Kelly had any deterrent effect on Liverpool's gangsters is debatable but by 1950 there were at least some indications that the post-war crime wave was receding. This was certainly the view of Arthur McFarland, the Liverpool Stipendiary Magistrate. Yet for every statistic offered to show that the situation was improving there was other evidence to suggest that crime was at best remaining the same or even getting worse. In February 1950, Justice Oliver told the Liverpool Assizes, 'Violence in Liverpool is rife.' In the same year, the *Daily Herald* felt compelled to ask of Liverpool, 'What makes it our wickedest city?'[3]

With the death of Kelly, there were other hoodlums waiting in the wings ready to stake their own claims, including shadowy underworld figures. In 1952, customs officers and plain-clothed police combed Liverpool looking for leads to the criminal mastermind behind a cigarette racket at Liverpool docks. Seamen who were entitled to duty-free smokes were selling their entitlement to the gang who then scoured the pubs offering them to customers for sixpence less than the normal price. Supplies were also obtained from American soldiers based at Burtonwood. A mysterious villain known as the 'Cigarette Man' was believed to be behind a huge team of pedlars and touts.

However, it was out on the street corners rather than in the shadowy depths of the underworld that the next big threat came. The 1950s saw the birth of rock 'n' roll music, brought to British teenagers largely through the efforts of white American musicians such as Bill Haley and Elvis Presley. This imported craze coincided with the creation of a decidedly English teenage style that slavishly copied, or rather parodied, the sharp cut of earlier upper-class fashions from the beginning of the century. The very name 'Teddy Boys' derived from the Edwardian suits revived by Savile Row tailors in 1950. Working-class teenagers soon filched the style and made it their own.

The term 'Teddy Boy' first appeared in print in March 1954. However, the lads were already strutting the streets a year earlier when they were referred to as 'Edwardian hooligans'. They wore long drape jackets with velvet collars, drainpipe trousers and crepe-soled shoes, a look that was at once both dandy and menacing. Liverpool MP Bessie Braddock once saw some Teddy Boys wearing the tightest trousers imaginable.

She asked, 'How do you get into them pants?'

'Dead easy,' came the reply. 'We grease our boots.'

Grease was also applied to the hair to form an impressive quiff or elephant's trunk. The style originated in London but, aided by a series of sensational headlines in the press following the first 'Teddy Boy murder' on Clapham Common in 1953, soon made its way up north into the waiting arms of a new generation of bored young delinquents.

Liverpool's 'Dead End Kids' and 'Little Gangsters' from the previous decade had come of age and were ready for the next assault on public morals. Whereas their parents had faced an austere life of slum housing, dead-end jobs or the dole and the prospect of being packed off to war, these youths had money in their pockets and time on their hands. Between 1945 and 1950, the average real wage of teenagers increased at twice the adult rate. Living in the post-war economic boom, with the safety net of the welfare state, young people had it relatively easy. However, instead of giving thanks, they rebelled by rioting in the cinemas and beating up strangers in the street.

The very strangeness of the Teddy Boy's attire brought terror to neighbourhoods. They were such a visible presence on the streets. Not since the days of the High Rip, with their 'bucco caps' and mufflers, had a gang stood out so menacingly from the crowd. People were assaulted for simply staring at the Teddy Boys. Indeed, the first Teddy Boy murder saw a teenager killed for calling one of the lads a 'flash cunt'. It was felt that without the uniform, the Teds were cowards. 'Take away the suit and you take away the trouble,' was one maxim uttered at the time.

The drape jacket became a focal point. In Edge Hill, the Teddy Boys were known as 'Mississippi Gamblers'. Tailors were blamed for selling the suits on the 'never never', thereby allowing teenagers to become gangsters overnight. Youth clubs complained that membership was falling because lads were using their subs money to pay for suits. When two Teddy Boys were arrested, one admitted, 'I can't pay any fines. I've got the suit to pay for.' His mate was more annoyed: 'OK Jack, don't crease the suit,' was his message to the arresting officer. Another lad was disgusted to hear his drape jacket being described in court as 'black'. 'Midnight blue' was his more accurate description.

In 1954, four members of Walton's Midnight Blue Gang used a broken bottle to assault a lad walking a girl home from a dance. The sadistic attack left the victim needing fifteen stitches to a face wound. The lads, aged between seventeen and eighteen, were each jailed for two years. As they were led away from the dock, parents and girlfriends wept openly in court. 'Oh no, my poor boy,' was the cry from one distraught mother. The judge asked a detective whether such violence was common amongst teenagers. D.I. Bonner informed him that the police had recently dealt with three similar cases in dancehalls and skating rinks. In one case, ice skates were used as a weapon.

In 1954, the chairman of Liverpool Juvenile Court told three Teddy Boys accused of burglary in Fazakerley, 'You seem only to ape Edwardians in their dress. It would be far better if you adopted their code of honour.' Yet earlier chapters have shown that no such golden age of high moral standards ever existed. In fact, the new Edwardians of the Fifties had a great deal in common with their original predecessors who were active between 1901 and 1910.

The bloody street-warfare, vandalism and wearing of a uniform adapted for fighting all had their origins in an earlier age. Early twentieth-century gangs, such as London's Hooligans and Birmingham's Peaky Blinders, made improvised weapons out of belts, hob-nailed boots and razors fixed to their peaked caps. Their modern heirs hid razor blades and bicycle chains inside coat collars and used large rings as knuckledusters. Like earlier gangs, the Teddy Boys' best weapon was their sheer numbers, which they used to intimidate the public.

Indeed, the Teddy Boy craze for randomly beating up strangers went right back to the murder of Richard Morgan and beyond. There were numerous reports of savage attacks by Teds on defenceless victims minding their own business. In August 1954, ten Teddy Boys set upon two youths in Aintree, kicking one unconscious. The following month a gang ambushed three boys off Smithdown Road. One was butted in the face and booted while on the ground. In the same month another youth was attacked at the Pier Head. A mob repeatedly kicked him, leaving him writhing and groaning on the floor. Also at the Pier Head, two lads walking with their girlfriends were left battered.

In 1955, a funfair at Bootle's North Park attracted the usual crowd of Teddy Boys. A bunch of younger lads started some trouble with a soldier and a sailor before calling on their older protectors. The Teddy Boys then pounced, using their belts to crack heads. One of the men was left with several smashed teeth after he was kicked in the face three times. His mate sustained a fractured skull and was left with a gaping wound in his forehead that exposed the bone. He was then thrown head first into the paddling pool. After members of the gang were found guilty, the victims received anonymous letters threatening to 'do them in'.

Whereas the menace of the Peanut Gang was largely confined to the south end, the Teddy Boy phenomenon spread like wildfire throughout Merseyside. Women in Norris Green voiced concern that they were afraid of walking past the groups who congregated on the corner of Utting Avenue East and Broadway. The Capitol Cinema in Edge Hill was forced to display notices banning lads in Edwardian dress. Various café owners and dancehall proprietors on the Wirral kept a close watch on the Teddy Boy situation.

Cinema managers in Huyton and Prescot, just outside Liverpool, were often faced with Teddy Boy disorder. The lads would shout to each other from opposite sides during the film. Girls were often the source of the problem. They would incite and encourage their boyfriends to cause trouble. In 1954, a crowd of drunken Teddy Boys from Huyton caused a disturbance in Prescot. As policemen tried to arrest two of them, one threatened to 'bring their mobs down on them'. The constables had to draw truncheons to stave off the rest of the hostile rabble.

The following year, at a Bill Haley concert at the Odeon cinema, police were called to control the scores of Teddy Boys jiving in the aisles and the management had to repair 140 wrecked seats. A Birkenhead lad on his way to the youth club to play basketball was ambushed by four Teddy Boys armed with razors, who slashed him about the head. In the same year, some Teds piled on the top deck of a bus as it stopped in Wavertree. Two men sitting quietly with their partners objected to the lads' bad language. One was punched and beaten. As his girlfriend tried to stop the assault, a Ted stood on the seat and booted her in the face. The police later brought the women to a local dancehall where they were able to identify their attackers.

In 1956, in Stanley Road, Bootle, a twenty-strong mob stood outside a dancehall and defied the police. One lad shouted, '____ cops. We'll throw them over the ___ canal bridge.' Around this time, the Chief Constable of Bootle reported that incidents in which bottles and belt buckles were used as weapons had increased from six to twenty-two during the previous year. The old beat system of policing was felt to be inadequate in dealing with the ferocity and size of the gangs. Individual constables stood no chance. Trouble was also flaring up over such a wide area that police back-up was often too slow to respond. The authorities therefore introduced Land Rover patrols throughout the city to target trouble spots such as the Locarno and Grafton dancehalls in West Derby Road. The aim was to disperse the gangs before they caused any mischief. The problem was that the lads simply caused trouble elsewhere. It was felt that the squeeze being put on the Teddy Boys was driving them to fresh pastures such as New Brighton.

Fairs became the focal point for youth disorder. In May 1955, police issued whistles to female stallholders at New Brighton fairground after a wave of terrorism caused by Teddy Boys. Strong-arm patrols also mingled with the crowds listening for the blast of a whistle that would signal the first sign of trouble. The precautions were taken after one lady cashier was assaulted as a gang robbed her till. The 'Wall of Death' nearly lost the day's takings after an attempted snatch. At a firing range, some Teddy Boys ignored the targets and shot all the prizes before pointing their rifles at the terrified stallholder. A ride attendant was beaten up on his way home after clashing with a gang the previous week. Teddy boys also damaged the slot machines in an amusement arcade before fighting with staff who tried to evict them.

Teddy Boys started to be accused of almost every violent crime and bout of hooliganism. In 1954, there were reports that Teds were costing Liverpool ratepayers an extra £1,500 a year. This was the amount the Corporation had to set aside to build fences around the playgrounds to keep out vandals. During the hours of darkness, when the beat constables had left the district, the Teddy Boys began their orgies of destruction. They even threatened elderly watchmen on night duty, resulting in some of the terrified men resigning from the job. In Bootle's North Park, a bowling green was torn up by 'screamagers', as the press labelled them.

When a brawl broke out amongst the crew on the British liner *Georgic*, in 1955, Liverpool Teddy Boys were blamed. They were said to be fighting over girls smuggled on board. The previous week, when the ship was docked in Melbourne, thirty-one seamen were arrested for being drunk and disorderly. A ship's officer explained that Teddy Boys had been allowed to sign on in Liverpool after it had proved impossible to muster an experienced crew in time.

In 1956, a South American left a city centre pub at closing time and turned from St James Street into a dark side street. Two lads appeared and demanded money. When the man refused he was stabbed in the back and remained critical in hospital for some time. The lads then ran towards the docks without even robbing their victim. The fact that one of them was wearing narrow trousers, a slim-jim tie and a leather jacket was enough for them to be labelled Teddy Boys in the press. In fact, so appalled were they by the crime that dozens of Teddy Boys came forward voluntarily to help the police with their inquiries.

The Teds did not have it all their own way. Some became victims of outrageous assaults. In 1956, a lone Teddy Boy was walking through the fruit and vegetable market in Queens Square in the city centre. A cheeky eight-year-old made some disparaging remarks about his ridiculous clothes, whereupon the Ted turned around and slapped him. However, the tearaway then blew on a whistle and summoned about twenty ten-year-olds who appeared from every direction and began to pelt the bully with the rotten fruit that was lying discarded in the street. The Teddy Boy ran for it but was cornered and bombarded with mushy pears, bananas and tomatoes. He went home looking like a fruit salad, with his £20 suit ruined.

In addition to the Teddy Boys, there were flocks of 'bird gangs'. In 1955, a Huyton youth appeared in court dressed in a drape jacket, blue jeans and a check shirt. His mother had called the police because she was at the end of her tether and could no longer control him. She had asked her son to tidy his room but he replied, 'You're the _____ housekeeper,' before assaulting her. In court, the lad was asked to exhibit the bird tattoos on his wrist. A policeman explained that a gang called the Bluebirds was active in the city. The lad denied any involvement but was sent to a remand home until the authorities could decide what to do with him.

The 1950s also saw the Swallow Gang waiting to spread its wings. Girls aged about fifteen underwent initiation ceremonies in which they allowed boys to tattoo a leg or shoulder with a blue swallow. Members would use a pin and dye to create the image on the inside of their moll's thigh, just above the knee. The lads sported their own tattoos on the back of their hands, above the thumb.

In 1955, police cautioned a mob of twenty youths causing trouble in Earle Road. Most heeded the warning and moved on but a sixteen-year-old shouted, 'Don't go … we are the Swallow Gang.' He then lashed out at a constable with his fist, around which was wrapped an army belt. In court, he denied being a member of the gang until asked to show his hands to the magistrate. The swallow tattoos put an end to his argument and he was found guilty.

Female members were also said to act as decoys, luring their victims into back alleys where the lads would be waiting. The story, of course, was nothing new. The practice had being going on since the days of the High Rip right through to the Peanut Gang. Only the names of the gangs changed.

On the other hand, some of Liverpool's post-war young louts certainly surpassed any previous generation's attempts at depravity and sadism. In 1956, the city suffered a spate of cat cruelty. First, there was the disappearance of hundreds of cats, some of which, it was suspected, were being turned into Davy Crockett caps. In the Bull Ring area of St Andrews Gardens, more than fifty cats were reported missing by their owners. Apparently, Teddy Boys and their girlfriends were playing a disturbing new game called 'Throw the Cat', whereby a rope was tied around the animal's neck in order to swing it around before letting it go. The winner was the one who obtained the furthest distance. Five cats had been found with shattered skulls and ropes attached. When the RSPCA went to investigate, a group of Teddy Boys pelted them with bottles and bricks. Officials from the Society also received a threatening phone call: 'Call off your investigations or the boys will tear you and your place apart.'

As with the threat from the High Rip and Peanut Gangs, the local newspapers and journals were bombarded with letters and comments from angry Liverpudlians. There were renewed calls for vigilante action. One correspondent called for fifty volunteers to be drawn from university students, teachers, solicitors and off-duty policemen. Aided by five cars, three gallons of tar, a bale of feathers and some hairdressing shears, the vigilantes were to seek out the Teddy Boys and publicly humiliate them. More sensible suggestions included putting the ruffians in the army and packing them off to the world's danger zones. Forcing the yobs to do military service has always been a popular antidote to hooliganism. This was despite the fact that young men in the 1950s were already forced to undertake two years' National Service.

Yet for some, conscription was part of the problem. Between the ages of fifteen, when they left school, and eighteen, when they entered the forces, lads were often at a loose end. It was argued that the interruption of the transition from school to work resulted in many youths causing mayhem during their years of freedom. An MP proposed deporting the thugs to a deserted Commonwealth island and letting them fend for themselves. A barrister suggested withholding the parents' family allowance until they made their children behave. Flogging the Teddy Boys was the inevitable solution. In 1955, at Liverpool City Quarter Sessions, two seventeen-year-olds from Walton were found guilty of assaulting an off-duty policeman. The Assistant Recorder advised their fathers to give them the biggest thrashing of their lives if they continued to hang around with the gang.

From the more liberal-minded, there were reminders that not all Teddy Boys were thugs. There had been reports that some Teds had recently helped an old lady across Byrom Street. One commentator claimed that the ruthless bullying of children by school headmasters was partly responsible for producing the sort of delinquents who went on to seek revenge against society.

Yet others rubbished such sociological explanations. Writing in the *Police Chronicle and Constabulary World* in December 1955, an anonymous writer, believed to be a high-ranking officer, criticised the current attempts at tackling crime and proclaimed that violent behaviour was worse than at any time in living memory.[4] In particular, he blamed the 1948 Criminal Justice Act for making life easier for criminals and more difficult for law-abiding citizens. The Act had abolished corporal punishment, except for breaches of prison discipline, and laid the emphasis on corrective training and treatment rather than punishment. The writer objected to the view that Teddy Boys were misunderstood and discriminated against by society. He accused those who held such notions of studying the brutes from the safety of an office or the back of a law court, and proposed that they meet the drunken hooligans up close on a Saturday night when they were on the rampage.

The debate about the Teddy Boys followed the same pattern as previous discussions. During earlier panics about juvenile delinquency there were repeated calls for more education and leisure facilities. There was nowhere for the lads to go and nothing for them to do. Yet in the 1950s, when facilities were provided, they were not only rejected but also smashed to bits. Victims were even beaten up outside youth clubs. Schools and playgrounds were vandalised. Cinemas and dancehalls became focal points for riots. Ice skates were used not for skating but for smashing over opponents' skulls. Fun fairs were turned into places of terror and some local parks reduced to no-go areas for respectable people. In 1956, the Liverpool park police were given self-defence lessons after the Corporation Parks and Gardens Committee registered with the British Judo Association.

Even public libraries, those bastions of self-improvement, were under siege. By 1957, Liverpool City Libraries were considering a policy of employing only 'physically fit' attendants in order to combat the Teddy Boy menace. One attendant refused to go back to work after being threatened. The chairman of Liverpool Libraries, Arts and Museums Committee suggested that Alsatian dogs might also be of help.

Yet the authorities never gave up on disaffected young people. Throughout the 1950s, new initiatives were created in order to stem the rising tide of violence. In 1953, students from Liverpool University were recruited to help break up the swarms of teenage toughs congregating in Liverpool's dockland. The undergraduates, working for the Mill Street Domestic Mission, would patrol the evening streets to hunt out and persuade troublesome youths to join the mission's youth club.

In 1954, a team of eight dedicated policemen, known as the 'Mercy Patrol', would spend their time seeking out and weaning youngsters from a life of crime. The Chief Constable had set up the initiative in 1949. Head teachers, parents and shopkeepers would forward to police the names of children at risk, particularly those kids who were beginning to steal or mix with gangs. The policeman or policewoman, officially titled a Special Liaison Officer for Juveniles, would then visit the children and their families to try to discover the root cause of the offending. Youths would then be encouraged to join sports clubs or the Scouts in order to channel their energies into more productive pursuits. The officer became the youth's friend and would keep in touch to offer direction and advice. The scheme was a great success, with the number of juvenile prosecutions in the city dropping from 2,248 in 1949 to 1,465 in 1953.

Whether the situation on Liverpool's streets improved or deteriorated during the 1950s is partly a matter of opinion and partly a matter of available crime statistics. If rock 'n' roll music and the accompanying Teddy Boy craze were a catalyst for violence, music could also turn young people away from crime. According to Colin Fletcher, a former member of the Holly Road Gang turned sociologist and writer, the arrival of rock 'n' roll on Merseyside in the mid-1950s helped distract youths from joining gangs. Beat music rather than beating people up became the way to attract the girls: 'What mattered now was not how many boys a gang could muster for a Friday night fight but how well their group played on Saturday night.'[5]

Yet music never put a stop to violence and disorder, as the numerous fights in dancehalls testify. Indeed, early performances by The Beatles were sometimes accompanied by flying chairs and mini riots. The provision of entertainment for young people was clearly no guarantee of good behaviour and some teenagers became more accomplished in the use of the bicycle chain than the guitar. Nor did the growth and popularity of sport put an end to thuggery. Some youths simply became football hooligans.

21

Mersey Maniacs

THE 1960S SAW the rise of modern football hooliganism. The label originally given to gangs of late-Victorian troublemakers was resurrected to describe the hordes of young tearaways spreading terror on the trains and terraces. It is ironic that a game promoted as a safe outlet for young people's aggression became marred by the violence of those watching it. On the other hand, football-related disorder has a long history. Indeed Edward II banned the game for that very reason in 1314. The modern sport began with the establishment of the Football Association in 1863. By 1868, thirty clubs had joined the FA. St Domingo Sunday FC was founded in 1878 and renamed Everton a year later. It was one of the founder members of the Football League in 1888. A dispute over the ground rent saw the club move to Goodison Park in 1892, leaving the existing premises to a newly formed club called Liverpool FC.

During the nineteenth century there were occasional outbreaks of unrest at matches. In 1886, an Everton/Bootle cup-tie was interrupted by crowd trouble. Two year later, when the Aston Villa team visited Liverpool, they were greeted by 'an army of young ragamuffins who met them at the station at Everton, hooting and threatening them'.[1] As the whistle blew to signal the end of a Wolves/Everton game in 1895, the crowd rushed at the referee and he had to be escorted to the press box by the police and some Wolves players. After half an hour, it was thought safe for him to leave. However, a large crowd continued to hassle him outside the ground until a quick-thinking policeman commandeered a passing taxicab. The referee was bundled into the vehicle, much to the alarm of the lady occupant. Two policemen sat in front and one either side of the official in order to shield him from the baying crowd. Unable to attack the man, the angry mob turned their attention to the cabman and tried to pull him from his box. His coat was ripped from his back and but for the actions of the police he would have been seriously injured. The vehicle sped away under a shower of missiles and a chorus of groans.[2] As Everton won the match 3-2, the disgruntled supporters were unlikely to be Evertonians.

Victorian fans were not afraid to show their displeasure. In the same year, an Everton/Small Heath game was halted prematurely at half-time owing to heavy rain. An incensed section of the crowd demanded their money back. After giving the Everton directors some verbal abuse they had to content themselves with smashing a clock and the windows of the committee room. Small Heath, of course, were the predecessors to Manchester United.

Despite such rowdiness, Liverpool's Head Constable believed that watching football led to a decrease in drunkenness. Speaking to a Royal Commission on Liquor Licensing in 1895, Captain Nott Bower explained that men would normally have a few pints after being paid on their Saturday half day off. However, if a match was being played they would rush home for a wash and brush up and leave their wages with their wives. In this way, the men didn't drink as much.[3]

However, this didn't stop some fans having a pint after the game. One of the earliest incidents of a football-related tragedy in Liverpool occurred in 1896. At a public house in Mill Street, two men started arguing over the match. A fierce fistfight broke out and was stopped before a second round ensued. One of the men went home to bed but became so ill that he had to be taken to the workhouse hospital. He later died of pneumonia accelerated by his injuries from the brawl. His opponent's plea of self-defence was accepted and he was discharged at the Police Court.

Disorder continued into the new century. The 1914 cup final between Liverpool and Burnley was watched by 15,000 Burnley fans and 20,000 Liverpudlians, plus supporters from various Lancashire districts. The threat of violence was never far away. *The Times* published the following report:

> The Northerners were more peaceable than on previous occasions. If they indulged in fraternal fights, they waited until they reached their native platforms. Then perhaps one would say to another,

'Has t' fowten?' and when the answer was in the negative would reply, 'Then let's get fowten an' go whoam!' There is more than a touch of the Celtic fighting-spirit in these solid, enduring, low-statured folk.[4]

Judging by the dialects of the fans, they appear to be Burnley rather than Liverpool troublemakers. This is not to say that Merseyside was without hooligans. In 1915, during an Everton/Barnsley cup-tie, a well-aimed orange hit one of the visiting players. The crowd calmed down only after a lecture on sportsmanship from the Everton captain.

Nevertheless, the inter-war years were relatively quiet, as was the decade following the Second World War. Yet Merseyside fans were still able to make an impression, particularly on away trips. When Everton fans visited Leicester in 1933:

A long special train brought over 600 boisterous supporters, who crowded out of the station and made a terrific din with rattles, whistles and sirens. 'Here are the Leicester,' they yelled. 'One step nearer Wembley,' and they held up trams and buses and scores of cars as they pushed their way across London Road. One party stopped in the middle of the road and held up a stream of traffic while they were photographed ... With shouts of 'Good old Everton' and 'Everton for the cup', 600 visitors surged down Granby Street behind one of their number, who carried a large jar of beer on his shoulder.[5]

Such behaviour was lively rather than threatening. Indeed, the Everton crowd could police themselves. A 1937 Everton match programme congratulated the supporters for taking exception to a recent bottle-throwing incident. It seems that the fans gave the hooligan a 'hot' time for his indiscretion. He was said to be 'sorry for himself long before the end of the game'.

However, by the mid-Fifties violence was creeping back into the game, with occasional pitch invasions, crowd disturbances and attacks on referees. In 1954, during a match between Everton and Bolton Wanderers Reserves, hundreds of fans stormed the pitch. Fireworks were thrown and an angry supporter booted a linesman. Two years later, Doncaster played host to Liverpool. After the home team scored a dubious goal, the crowd was incensed that the referee hadn't ruled it offside. Fights broke out and a policeman lost his helmet. A volley of missiles, including a pepper pot, was thrown onto the pitch, hitting two Doncaster players. A couple of table knives were later found behind the goal and a window in the Doncaster director's office was smashed. Liverpool supporters of the 'Teddy Boy type' were blamed.

In 1957, more Teddy Boys from Liverpool invaded the pitch at Preston North End to play a 'practice' game in the goalmouth before the kick-off. In the same year, at Goodison Park, West Bromwich players were assaulted as they boarded the team bus. Merseyside was beginning to gain a reputation for its inhospitable reception of visiting clubs. It was noted that in 1957, six teams suffered prolonged booing and jeering at Anfield or Goodison Park.[6]

Yet despite such isolated and spontaneous incidents, it was in the Sixties that football hooliganism developed into its current organised form. Patriotic support of the local team turned into fierce animosity between rival fans. It was as if the traditional Catholic/Orange hostilities were being re-channelled and redirected along tribal sporting lines. Youths were finding new reasons and opportunities for causing mayhem and rival teams replaced rival religions as a focus of hostility. A Catholic (Everton) and Protestant (Liverpool) division was already in existence from the 1950s, although less intense than the infamous Celtic-Rangers rivalry.

The growth of modern football hooliganism as a routine and organised weekly event can be traced through the behaviour of Everton and Liverpool supporters during the Sixties. Rather than merely respond to trouble, youths began actively looking for it. Televised matches may have played a part in publicising the disorder. Also, during this time, the away followings of both Merseyside clubs were bigger than most other teams'. The national press credited both Everton and Liverpool supporters with playing a major role in the growing hooliganism, awarding them a reputation as Britain's 'roughest, rowdiest rabble'.[7]

The trouble was not confined to the terraces. Train journeys home from away matches were often marred by bouts of mindless vandalism. The tradition of wrecking trains began in the Fifties. In 1956, Everton fans ransacked a number of trains on their way home from a match with Manchester City. The damage was extensive: eight door windows smashed, five side windows shattered, fourteen pictures broken, two mirrors cracked, one whole door missing, another door damaged, a door handle missing, dozens of light bulbs removed, several compartments spattered with blood, luggage racks torn from the walls and a number of seats slashed.[8]

In 1962, Everton fans on their way back from Bolton wrecked three compartments and the toilet of a 'football special'. Again, they smashed windows, pulled down luggage racks, slashed seats and broke lampshades. A water can, which was kept in the toilet for emergencies, was also hurled through the window. Finally, the train was delayed at Kirkby for twenty minutes after somebody pulled the communication cord, a regular prank on such trips. The Christmas holiday fixtures of 1963 were particularly destructive. A train packed with Everton supporters returning from Leicester was wrecked. Thirty-six light bulbs, four windows and a door were vandalised. As the result, the authorities threatened to put a stop to the football specials.

The clampdown spread to the terraces. Close the grounds or fence them in was the message from some newspapers in 1963. 'Let's save the game from Merseyside's hooligan hordes,' was one typical headline.[9] In November, for the first time at an English ground, temporary barriers were erected at Goodison Park after the Football League issued a warning: 'behave or the grounds will close.' The action followed a potentially dangerous incident when a dart, thrown by an Everton supporter, speared the Spurs goalkeeper. The secretary of the League claimed that the trouble had grown in the last two years. Referees were also being attacked by youths running onto the pitch at the end of the game. To prevent disruption from the younger supporters, Everton FC placed a ban on unaccompanied children using their parents' stand tickets for central league games. A staunch Evertonian explained the volatile atmosphere of the matches: 'We are a tremendously possessive people. If anyone lifts a boot to our Alex Young, that sets us off.'

Liverpool supporters could be just as 'possessive', if not equally violent. When Liverpool played host to Leicester in 1963, an apple core and a half-chewed pork chop were thrown from the Kop. The crowd taunted visiting goalkeeper Gordon Banks, 'Don't worry about the arrows Gordon – We've got the dartboard.' A piece of plywood later found its way onto the pitch. In another incident, a Spurs goalkeeper was pelted with marbles and stung by rice fired from peashooters. Young, but deadly accurate, Liverpool fans were blamed.

In January 1964, play between West Ham and Liverpool was paused to allow the referee to pick up shards of broken glass thrown at the Londoners' goalkeeper. At the other end of the pitch, keeper Tommy Lawrence had to retrieve a beer bottle from his own goal. In the same month, 150 drunken Everton supporters, dubbed 'Mersey Maniacs' by a railways boss, caused mayhem on the train home from a Leeds cup-tie. The fans decided to spend the journey fighting, shouting, slashing mailbags and throwing toilet rolls out the windows. A British Rail spokesman revealed that every soccer special train from Liverpool had suffered damage from supporters. The specials were duly suspended, the first time such trains had been banned in Britain.

On the same weekend, as Liverpool visited Port Vale for a fourth-round cup-tie, thousands of fans got in free after a gate was forced open. Some agile Liverpudlians managed to climb onto the grandstand roof for a better view. After a late goal made Liverpool the winner, two excited supporters crashed through the roof, one of them landing on and injuring two alarmed fans below.

By 1964, the Goodison Park crowd had gained a notorious reputation for vandalism particularly away from home. 'Shopkeepers lock up when Everton are in town,' was the verdict of one newspaper.[10] Meanwhile, Leeds had been labelled the 'dirtiest team' in the league. When both sides met in a November fixture, particularly following two contentious cup-ties the previous season, the scene was set for an explosive encounter, a modern War of the Roses. In a game described as more of a reckless scrimmage than a football match, both teams engaged in some vicious tackling. Everton's Sandy Brown was sent off after four minutes for thumping Johnny Giles. Just before half-time, Derek Temple collided with Willie Bell from Leeds. As the injured players were being carried off, sections of the 43,000-strong crowd went wild, littering the pitch with missiles and forcing the referee to temporarily abandon the game. For the first time in the history of the Football League, both sides were ordered off the field for five minutes until order was restored. The crowd's tempers were cooled only after the referee threatened to abandon the game.

In 1966, Liverpool Boys Association held their Senior Cup Final at Anfield. At one point, a group of teenagers invaded the pitch. Afterwards, young police cadets tried to remove the boys from the Kop. The situation escalated into a mini riot as fifty youths began scrapping with the cadets. An official from the club said, 'It was the Celtic game all over again – but thank heavens there were no bottles this time.' The League secretary claimed that the culprits had no interest in football and came only to invade the pitch.

Yet it wasn't only youngsters that caused trouble at matches. In 1965, the average age of thirteen Liverpool fans charged with offences at a Sheffield game was twenty-seven. Merseyside supporters can also lay claim to initiating a trend in more disrespectful and indecent songs and chants. Although tame by modern standards, there was said to be something unsporting and gloating in such antagonistic ditties as, 'Ee, aye, addio, Chelsea's out the cup', sung by Liverpool wags at an FA cup semi-final at Villa Park in 1965.

In August 1967, both Merseyside clubs faced their two Manchester rivals. Trouble was almost guaranteed. At Goodison Park, during a 3-1 win against United, thirty-three rowdy fans were arrested, a British record at a time when the average number of arrests was ten per game. After a nil-nil draw with City, Liverpool fans smashed the lights and fittings of the special train carrying them home.

The national success of Merseyside football teams during the sixties, together with the worldwide triumph of the Merseybeat sound, certainly put Liverpool on the map. Yet the ascendancy of

Scouse popular culture only served to mask some severe social problems back on the streets of the town. A massive redevelopment programme was to disperse some of the city's landmark communities and see the dreams of town planners become the nightmares of uprooted residents of the new overspill estates. The tearaways responded by smashing up the place and turning on each other.

22

The Sixties:
Vandalism and Violence

POST-WAR LIVERPOOL also suffered a housing crisis. There were 20,000 unfit houses together with thousands of bomb-damaged properties. People desperately needed somewhere to escape their damp, overcrowded rooms. Throughout the 1950s, families were moved from central Liverpool to newly built homes in Kirkby, Halewood and Speke. The Sixties saw another stage of slum clearance, with 38,000 families transferred to places such as Netherley and Cantril Farm. Expanding industries also jumped at the opportunity of relocating to the wide-open spaces. In response, thousands of homes were thrown up to meet the demand for local labour. The shifts in population were dramatic. In 1921, just over 3,500 people lived in Speke. Forty years later, the figure had grown to 27,000.

Yet for some, the high hopes of a new life in a modern home fell flat. Despite the central heating and spacious gardens, people complained that houses were being built before essential social and cultural amenities such as shops and libraries. The new residents came largely from the town centre slums. For generations they had lived in close proximity to family and neighbours. They knew each other's business and helped each other during crises. People were uprooted from the security and warmth of such tight-knit neighbourhoods to live in vast soulless estates. The extended families were scattered, the social networks fragmented.

In the upheaval, rising crime levels began to cause some concern, both locally and nationally. Nineteen sixty-four became the landmark year when the number of indictable offences reported to the police in England and Wales reached the one million mark.[1] In the following year, it was announced that in the past decade, crime in Liverpool had doubled to its highest level.

The figures got worse. In 1966, robberies in the city had increased 90% on the previous year. James Haughton, Liverpool's Chief Constable, warned, 'Many of these robberies are being committed by gangs of youths roaming the city late at night. They are attacking unsuspecting people who walk alone.'[2]

The crime epidemics of the past, particularly during wartime and the economic depression of the 1930s, could be partly explained. Poverty, family disruption and a generation of young people trained in commando tactics were all seen as contributing to the crime waves. However, over fifteen years after the war had ended, the city was enjoying relative prosperity and high living standards. Yet crime continued to rise.

Before the Second World War, the city's social reformers faced three major tasks: the abolition of poverty, the clearance of slums and the elimination of crime. It was believed that when the first two problems had been solved, the third would be easy to tackle. It seems that they got it wrong. In 1961, J.P. Eddy, QC, visited Liverpool and gave his own verdict on the city's crime problems.[3] He concluded that with prosperity, delinquency had also increased. As people became wealthier, robbery became more popular because there was more to steal. Also, higher wages simply meant that youths had more money for alcohol, which often led to violence. In 1964, sociologists cited affluence, leisure, better food and earlier puberty as contributory factors in wild behaviour.[4] A year later, Dick Crawshaw, MP for Toxteth, spoke of teenagers brought up in a society whose only aim is to get rich quick.[5] He pointed out that many youths appearing before the magistrates came from relatively well-off families. Their only crime was getting caught.

If poverty was not responsible for bad behaviour, some other reason had to be found. Some people pointed the finger at the breakdown of the traditional family structure. During the war, women had found independence by going out to work. After hostilities ended, some married women found it difficult to relinquish that freedom. It was felt that too many children were coming home from school to empty houses, as both parents were at work. These 'latchkey kids' were not being taught how to behave themselves and were left to cause mischief on the streets.

Feckless parents who renounced their responsibilities were also blamed for children's anti-social behaviour. In 1963, a former Speke resident was damning in his criticism of local families:

> In Speke Road Gardens today, children are brought up no better than natives in the jungle – illiterate and completely ignorant. Playing truant is a regular occurrence, so too is the Tuesday night booze-up by couldn't-care-less parents who decide the family allowance is better spent in pubs rather than on clothing for their own children.[6]

Speke Road Gardens consisted of modern two-bedroom flats with all mod cons. Yet the area was labelled corrupt, filthy and 'one hell of a rat hole'. Parents from Dingle were also slated after a youth leader hit out at those who put bingo and pubs before an interest in their own children. He complained that some parents had no knowledge of what their children got up to and were just glad to get them out of the house.[7]

The view that children were running wild was supported by endless reports of vandalism throughout the city. In 1963, another youth leader lamented, 'There is a tradition of destruction and non-appreciation of public property in this city.'[8] Communities in the south end certainly felt under siege. In the early Sixties, large areas of the district were in the process of being rebuilt. The dirt, dust and daily demolition had become a way of life, polluting the very heart of the community.

The civic vandalism of the architects was more than matched by mindless wrecking sprees of children and teenagers. In 1962, a bench provided for Dingle pensioners to enjoy the view of the River Mersey lasted six hours before being torn from its concrete footings and thrown into the river. Forty residents protested to the Lord Mayor about the epidemic of vandalism around Asbridge Street. As the slums were being flattened around Princes Road, youths were using the debris as ammunition to target neighbouring houses. Almost every day a window was smashed, leaving families cowering in fear of the next attack.

As Toxteth's Grenville Street Playground was being built, youths gathered nightly to cause trouble. The elderly watchman had to pack in his job after being stoned repeatedly. Equipment and fittings were regularly wrecked, walls torn down the day after they had been built and toys stolen from the pavilion. Volunteers who worked on the project had their personal belonging taken. One brave man was bricked as he tried to stop the vandals. When the local vicar tried to intervene, during another bout of stoning, two men gave him a volley of abuse. They defended the vandals, claiming 'they had the right to throw stones at anybody'. The playground leader deplored the vandalism and said that they were waiting for the 'erection of railings, to keep the children out'.

Also in 1962, a wave of robberies swept the Princes Park area. A shop suffered six break-ins in four months while another business endured six smash and grab raids. A gang removed part of the outside wall of an off-licence and plundered the spirits. One shopkeeper boarded up his window after it had been smashed only to find that the thieves had returned to remove the boards a few hours later to continue the burglary. Shopkeepers in Granby Street and Kingsley Road were also victims of daring smash and grab raids. Bricks were put through windows after metal grills had been ripped off. Insurance companies said that they had never known it so bad. A desperate shopkeeper electrified the interior of his premises to give intruders a powerful shock.

In November 1962, 300 residents, shopkeepers and businessmen from the Falkner Street area of Princes Park signed a petition calling for an end to the violence and vandalism plaguing the district. One local hotel manager claimed, 'Not a night goes by without someone having their window put in or another unfortunate being attacked. Only recently my friend's son was stopped on his way home and robbed at open razor-point.'[9]

Vandalism in the south end continued for a number of years. One resident warned, 'The area is rapidly degenerating into uncivilisation.' In 1965, Park Road shopkeepers offered their own rewards ranging from £25-100 for information leading to the arrest of the vandals, some of them armed with air guns. The windows would be cracked with a pellet then kicked in. The situation was so bad that some traders had moved from the district while those who remained were refused insurance cover for their plate glass windows. On one occasion, twelve people witnessed some lads break a shop window but only one brave lady was prepared to give her name and act as a witness. The problem, as one policeman put it, was that people didn't want to be viewed as a 'copper's nark'.

Residents of the new estates such as Speke were also plagued by vandalism. In 1965, adults were complaining of being terrorised. Twenty youths, aged between fourteen and eighteen, were said to be responsible for numerous burglaries, window smashing and graffiti. One resident grumbled, 'It's terrible round here at night. They've turned our life into hell. I had a bottle thrown at me as I came up the stairs the other night.'[10] Other residents claimed to have witnessed younger lads staggering around drunk. Once again, a petition was organised to highlight the problems.

In 1967, after a spate of late-night attacks on Speke's South Parade and Central Parade precincts, a group of shopkeepers banded together to ask the Chief Constable for police protection from the hordes of children, many below the age of criminal responsibility. Over the previous three years there had been nearly 100 incidents. Youngsters had used a crowbar to smash their way into a bakers shop. Nothing was stolen but the toilet was blocked with cakes. Two small girls cost a shopkeeper £100 to replace a window shattered in the effort to steal a bunch of grapes.

The north end also suffered from mindless vandalism. In 1962, Springwell Road Presbyterian Church in Bootle was threatened with closure after it was revealed that it was costing £100 a year to repair damage. The waste ground adjoining the church had become a battleground as youngsters lobbed bricks and bottles at the building. In 1964, the green at Bootle golf course was torn up and a wall pushed over. Rocks littered the verges while shrubs and hedges were uprooted. 'Everton' was scrawled in paint across the bowling green. Park benches were smashed and a post box set on fire.

British Rail transport police were forced to introduce dog patrols to prevent vandalism at Marsh Lane Station after numerous windows had been broken and a porter's hat knocked off by hooligans. Shopkeepers sent a petition to the Mayor after the spate of window smashing spread to nearby shops. Nothing was ever stolen. At Christmas 1965, vandals took the statue of Jesus from the manger at Litherland Town Hall and threw it through a window. The smashed figure was rescued and returned to its crib. The next year only the broken head of the damaged Christ was displayed, carefully wrapped in swaddling clothes. Thieves then stole the head. The senselessness of the vandalism begged explanation. For some sociologists, the wrecking sprees were a means for youngsters to vent their frustrations against an uncaring society. For others, the vandalism was explained by youths simply having nothing better to do.

In Liverpool, the problem was twofold. One the one hand, the old communities were in the process of being demolished. Young people in the south end were living in areas where the infrastructure was already half wrecked. On the other hand, thousand of people were being moved to new estates that were only half built. In Speke, for example, planning was said to have run wild, with houses being erected without consideration being given to accommodating social needs. Described as a desert of concrete, Speke was too far from Liverpool city centre for residents to partake in leisure activities. Yet there were not enough local facilities to keep people occupied. In the mid-Sixties there were 16,000 young people but the community centre could only hold 100.

Kirkby, a town of 60,000 newly built on the edge of Liverpool, presented a similar picture. In the mid-Sixties, half the population was below twenty-one years of age yet there was no cinema or dancehall. Some kids were running wild. The town's thirteen- and fourteen-year-olds were the most prolific offenders. Shop windows were regularly smashed and telephone kiosks were vandalised at the rate of one a day. When a warehouse was set ablaze in 1964, between 2,000 and 3,000 kids descended on the ruins to salvage what they could, pausing only to throw bricks at the salvage corps on duty.

Faced with a lack of facilities, youths were forced to make their own entertainment and create their own spaces. In 1964, at the Clough Road subway in Speke, groups of youths would regularly smash the fuses in the fuse box in order to plunge their subterranean hangout into menacing darkness. When a lock was put on the box to deter the vandals, they retaliated by smashing every light bulb in the subway.

Yet having few legitimate youth facilities was only half the problem. There was also a feeling that young people needed something a little less formal and organised than the traditional establishments. A vicar from Speke claimed that lads preferred dark street corners to youth clubs. Teenagers were attracted to risk and danger, not the safe provision of the welfare state. They needed freedom from adults to do their own thing. What the providers of authorized leisure pursuits could not appreciate was that youths liked to hang around apparently doing nothing.

In 1961, four lads appeared in court for obstructing the highway in Marsh Lane, Bootle. The youths were seen jostling each other, laughing and shouting. When a policeman tried to move them on they asked some pertinent questions, 'Why? Where can we go?' The lads were fined after the magistrate refused to accept that they had nothing to occupy them. The point is that the boys didn't want to go anywhere. Their first question was as important as the second. They were quite happy where they were, messing about and amusing themselves.

Teenagers made their own entertainment and created their own excitement, regardless of the law. In 1961, three fifteen-year-olds entered the private car park of a Bootle building contractor, started up various coaches and drove them around. Unfortunately, they crashed one into a wall. Two nights later, they repeated the stunt. Six years later, packs of up to twenty bikers and scooter boys from various districts would descend on the library car park in the sedate neighbourhood of Allerton. Rather than borrow books, the riders would stage road races, much to the annoyance of local residents.

The public facilities and pursuits that enlightened Victorians thought would help put a stop to crime and disorder were not only rejected, they were treated with contempt and even violence. Some teenagers spurned the officially sanctioned outlets for their energy. They didn't want to submit to the authority of leaders and they despised the uniformed organisations with their rules and discipline. In 1962, some sea cadets were sailing their unit's rowing boat down the Leeds/Liverpool canal when they got into difficulties after hitting a sunken barge. A cadet attempted to free his vessel but fell into the water. Five youths from a nearby factory then pelted the sailors with stones, further damaging the boat. The cadets had to seek shelter to escape the bombardment.

The gang situation in Toxteth became so bad in the summer of 1963 that the local Boy Scout Association held a recruiting campaign in schools and local parks. Leaders felt that if lads attended evening meetings they would not get into trouble. A financial aid scheme was launched so that boys from poorer families could be given free uniforms. Yet despite Baden Powell's belief that his organisation attracted the hooligan type, the tearaways preferred to wreak havoc. Liverpool Boys Outdoor Club, an independent youth facility run voluntarily by two brothers, was forced to close after nine months. The headquarters, in Linnet Lane, suffered three break-ins, a member was beaten up outside and snooker balls were thrown through the windows. The club was later re-opened after police promised to keep a close eye on it. One of the brothers lamented, 'I know for a fact that all the child psychiatrists in the world could not alter some of these boys . . . they want a good hiding.'[11]

The authorities cited the toughness of Liverpool teenagers as a reason for the shortage of social workers. In 1964, the lack of youth leaders in Liverpool was blamed on the place being 'the toughest in the country'.[12] Staff preferred to work in other, less intimidating areas. In 1968, the premises of the 12th Bootle Scout group were twice set on fire. The following year, the Bootle Sea Cadet Corps had to close its headquarters after repeated vandalism. In 1969, Speke marksmen used air rifles to shoot out the windows of the local swimming baths. Yet the facility did have its uses. A couple of years earlier, youngsters were involved in a protection racket, demanding money for looking after cars parked outside. In response, the Corporation agreed to hire a parking attendant

Many teenagers preferred music and dancing to camping and sailing. Nevertheless, some of them still couldn't be trusted to behave themselves. In 1963, in the south end, the only Saturday night dance in the area, at St Finbar's R.C. School, had to close after a thirteen-year-old was stabbed outside the hall. The club, which was home to 400 'beat fans', considered implementing a passport-style membership scheme with photographs in order to keep out the troublemakers. At the previous two dances, police had to guard the doors.

While some people bemoaned the lack of youth facilities, the youths themselves often displayed a complete lack of regard for local amenities. A catalogue of incidents from 1964 shows what the authorities were up against. At the Halewood Village Hall Hop, a sixteen-year-old was head-butted and clobbered with a chair after he accidentally knocked into another lad. A special dance reception to welcome a new priest at St Peters Church, Halewood, was brought to a dramatic halt by a battalion of teenagers who stood outside peppering the windows with air rifles. The Empire Kofe-Club, Garston's only Saturday night dance for teenagers, was forced to close its doors after youths repeatedly tried to smash up the place. The teenage dance night at Speke Boys Club was also marred by trouble. In 1966, Allerton Cinema was forced to ban teenage gangs after a spate of vandalism. In one month, fifty seats needed replacing after being slashed with flick knives. Lighted cigarette butts were also flicked into the audience. The manager blamed youths from Speke Road Gardens and Garston. The lads had even rung up the young female cashier and threatened to rape her when her shift finished.

Youths often attended events not to keep out of trouble but to look for trouble. In 1967, at a concert at Liverpool Empire, five mischief-makers from Speke and Dingle were refused admission. As they were being ejected from the foyer, three of them stabbed the theatre manager and two attendants. The gang, aged fifteen to seventeen, had previously robbed watches from younger boys in Lodge Lane and Ranelagh Street. Another victim had his coat taken at knifepoint in the town centre.

In 1968, Saturday night dances at Litherland Town Hall were turning into chaos. Blood on the floor, broken windows and beer bottles discarded in the street were a regular occurrence according to residents fed up with the noise, drunken brawls and bad language. The area also suffered disorder from drunks armed with hammers who would smash windows as they walked home down Linacre Road.

* * *

When teenagers were not smashing up their neighbourhoods, they were turning on each other. The beginning of the Sixties saw an escalation of territorial feuds, as lads from different districts, or even different parts of the same council estates, battled for street supremacy. With National Service recently abolished, and with no foreign wars to fight, teenagers formed their own armies and staged their own conflicts.

The year 1962 saw spiralling gang rivalries in Toxteth. A group of predominantly black lads given the derogatory nickname the Shiners went to war with a white mob called the John Bulls, or Jays. Their hostility was in fact racially complicated since some white lads fought for the black side and vice versa. The feud was as much territorial as racial, the Shiners deriving from the mainly black Rialto area and the John Bulls from the Park Road end of Upper Warwick Street. Nevertheless, racial slogans such as 'Keep Britain White' began to appear scrawled on pavements and walls around Princes Park, countered by 'Up the Shiners' messages on flats in Toxteth. In 1963, a black family campaigned to be re-housed from the Grafton House area of Toxteth after running a gauntlet of race hate from members of the John Bulls. After their children were subjected to verbal abuse and stone throwing, the family requested a move back to Kent Gardens where black and white families lived more in harmony.

Nobody was quite sure how the trouble started but rumour had it that it originated around 1960 when black teenagers assaulted a white lad. Gradually the black and white youths, who had grown up together and attended the same schools, became enemies and began to segregate themselves by frequenting different youth clubs. The black lads, who had previously attended mixed race clubs, withdrew to a youth centre in Princes Park. Unintentionally, the youth clubs became bases for the rival mobs.

One evening in May 1962, the warring factions hurled bricks and bottles at each other across a demolition site in Hampton Street. A sixteen-year-old was stabbed in the face and throat. Days later, a fourteen-year-old black boy had his clothing torn by a rival carrying a 'docker's hook'. The Central Ambulance Station in Upper Stanhope Street was forced to minister to a steady stream of victims injured by missiles and knives. A journalist spoke to a group of youths armed with blades. One explained that to go out without protection was asking for trouble.

Youth leaders believed that the glorification of gang violence in films such as the *West Side Story*, together with sensationalist news reports about New York gangs and the Notting Hill race riots of 1958, had helped inspire the troubles. Unemployment was also said to have played a part. One community leader felt that youths had become hard and embittered and carried chips on their shoulders against society for the injustices imposed upon them.[13] Schoolteachers, councillors and youth leaders made efforts to stop the feud by touring the trouble spots, speaking to parents and youths and campaigning for more sports facilities. Liverpool Corporation came in for criticism for not clearing the demolition sites that provided plentiful ammunition for the stone-throwers.

In August 1962, at 11.30pm, thirty to forty youths were said to be blocking the pavement at the corner of Park Road and Warwick Street. Two constables were attacked as they tried to make arrests after the group refused to disperse. When the case came to court, the Stipendiary Magistrate had some harsh words to say about Toxteth, 'The name of this district is becoming notorious and I intend to do something about it.' He certainly had his work cut out. The following month, another outbreak of gang warfare erupted. On three consecutive evenings, groups of teenagers clashed in High Park Street. The blame was laid on a crew from Sussex Gardens who regularly entered the area to cause trouble. The disturbances led to 2,000 residents signing a petition, urging their local MP to support the reintroduction of the birch. In one incident, over thirty lads roamed the streets looking for their enemies. Bottles and bricks were used to smash shop windows, including a chip shop after a rival sought sanctuary inside. The local bingo hall had to keep back its members to prevent them being caught up in the crossfire of missiles on their way home.

Other parts of the south end experienced periodic outbreaks of warfare. In October 1962, special police patrols were stepped up in the Lodge Lane area of Wavertree after rumours spread that cars packed with lads armed with axes and bottles were touring the district. The area had a history of trouble. A youth had recently been rushed to hospital with concussion after being attacked by a gang in Earle Road. The victim had been involved in another disturbance the previous night. Indeed, the disorder came weeks after a policeman was beaten up by a crowd of youths in the same area. In another incident, members of the local youth club had to shelter inside while two rival gangs fought it out on the street outside. The Girl Guides had to leave by the back door to avoid the trouble.

Also in 1962, territorial warfare broke out on the eastern side of Speke, as the lads from Alderwood Avenue clashed with their counterparts from Central Avenue. When the gangs were not fighting each other they were randomly beating up innocent boys. A councillor appealed for extra police protection after a schoolboy was battered on his way home. He sustained a fractured skull after being punched to the floor and kicked in the head by three youths.

After reading about the incident in the press, a contingent of five Alderwood lads visited the office of the *Liverpool Weekly News* to give their side of the story. They admitted the assault but pointed out that their victim had in fact left school and was therefore not a schoolboy. The newspaper noted that the culprits were all out of work, a fact that led to a discussion about the link between unemployment and gang behaviour. The beginnings of the Sixties saw a rise in young people leaving school, the result of the post-war population boom. This led to problems with finding work. Current opinion was that bored teenagers became frustrated and felt the need to let off steam. It was also suggested that these 'school-to-dole youngsters' suffered psychologically from not feeling wanted by society.[14] However, one of the Alderwood lads admitted that he once had a job but packed it in because he couldn't be bothered working on Saturdays. Two fifteen-year-olds and a fourteen-year-old were later fined for the attack.

The feud also resulted in several knifings, fortunately none of them serious. There were stories that fathers had to escort their sons to and from bus stops to save them from beatings along the way. In 1963, police approached fifteen rowdy youths in Central Way. The lads fled, some of them throwing bottles as they ran. The officers later caught up with three of them as they fumbled with their clothing in a passageway off Alderwood Avenue. It appears that they were putting on the army webbing belts that they had earlier wielded as weapons. One of the lads was also armed with a sickle. He explained, 'Two of my mates got jumped last week and I had it for protection. You need something around here.' Police played down the scale of the disturbances but residents continued to speak out against the climate of fear. One man wrote to the Chief Constable asking for permission to form a team of vigilantes to tackle the thugs. Consent was refused.

Teenage gangs were also on the move, looking for trouble in other areas. In November 1962, police stopped a ten-strong mob from Garston. A fourteen-year-old, armed with a studded belt and length of chain, explained, 'A lad got bottled last night. It's for the Dingle lads if they try anything.' The following year, elderly residents of Netherton Grange, which backed onto the canal, drew up a petition requesting more police patrols across the footpath. Roaming gangs, thought to come from Bootle or Kirkby, were smashing their way into their premises. One child was hit by a pellet from an air rifle. When a resident's son went into the back garden to investigate a noise, thugs armed with flick knives confronted him and ordered him back into the house. One lady was awakened late at night by a disturbance, only to find a number of lads in uniform, either scouts or cadets, hiding in her garden after being chased by a gang.

A year later, a disturbance in St Mary's Road, Garston, led to seventeen youths appearing before the magistrate. The lads, from Dingle, had travelled to the district searching for their rivals. A policeman spotted them disembarking from a bus and strutting down the street in a menacing fashion, shouting and jostling each other. They walked five abreast and obstructed the entire pavement for approaching pedestrians, who had to nervously step into the road. The practice was the old Victorian trick called 'holding the pavement'. One of the lads swung a chain and dog lead. Another clutched a chisel. An inventive thug had a piece of string tied to his thumb. At the other end of the string was a hammer hidden up his sleeve. In his pocket was a knuckleduster. 'We didn't mean any harm,' he protested, on being told that they were under arrest. Asked to account for the weapons, he explained, 'The Garston lads got me last week.'

The mid-Sixties also saw an outbreak of disorder in the north end. Gangs thirty-strong were seen running along Netherton streets, shouting and screaming as if in full battle. At the trial of three teenagers, the Chairman of Bootle Juvenile Panel criticised 'street warfare with sticks and knuckledusters'. In February, a policeman spotted some lads carrying wooden staves. They claimed they needed the weapons to defend themselves against the 'The Dodge', a crew from a rougher part of Netherton nicknamed 'Dodge City'.

Ten years after the Teddy Boys first plagued Liverpool, another youth craze was about to be unleashed. The Mods and Rockers hit the national headlines after a series of bank holiday disturbances in 1964. On a cold, wet Easter Monday, youths on scooters and motorbikes arrived at Clacton, only to be disappointed at the lack of leisure facilities. In their frustration, the Mods wrecked the beach huts and smashed some windows as they roared up and down the promenade. The press reports presented the disturbances as a confrontation between rival gangs and this led to further clashes. Other southern seaside towns such as Margate, Brighton and Hastings hosted reruns of the riots on subsequent holidays. In fact, bank holiday disorder was nothing new. Liverpool's Cornermen murdered Richard Morgan on a bank holiday in 1874. London's Hooligans came to public attention with a bank holiday disturbance in 1898. Liverpool's race riots of 1919 and 1948 also took place over bank holiday weekends.

The nearest Liverpool got to the Mods and Rockers seaside riots was a front-page headline in the local press about a disturbance in Blackpool. In May, 200 teenagers gathered on the Golden Mile. Nothing much happened except that three girls shouted such incendiary comments as, 'Down with the Mods ... Let's get rid of them ... What a poor lot.' The girls, aged fifteen to eighteen, were arrested and fined for using insulting words with intent to cause a breach of the peace.

Yet despite the lack of a local angle on the seaside warfare that was shocking the nation, Liverpool newspapers also decided to have a slice of the action. Reports surfaced of a Mods and Rockers style feud being settled in Derby Park, Bootle. Although the combatants included some lads on motorbikes and scooters, the trouble was probably more of a territorial dispute since one of the factions had travelled from the Walton area. On one occasion, eighty youths, some with hair down to their shoulders and armed with wooden staves and metal bars, fought until broken up by the police. The following day, twice that number staged another battle. 'Make the punishment fit the crime,' pleaded one outraged female witness.

The press also began to treat the internal squabbles in Speke as a war between Mods and Rockers. In March 1964, the Alderwood/Central feud had flared up again with numerous skirmishes involving knives and bottles. 'Animals on the loose,' was the verdict of one newspaper, which concluded that nobody was safe after dark.[15] Rampaging youths from Speke were also blamed for causing trouble in nearby Hunts Cross. Lads marched down Woodend Avenue picking up empty milk bottles from the doorsteps to hurl about the street.

A couple of months later, the 'animals' had been transformed into Mods. In June, it was reported that a truce had been hammered out on the troubled estate.[16] A man, who didn't want to be identified, had brokered the ceasefire between rival gangs of Cuban-heeled, cravat-wearing Mods and leather-clad Rockers. On a Thursday evening, the gangs met the mysterious 'Mr X' at a Boy Scout training ground, which had previously been vandalised. The peacemaker outlined his hopes for an end to the feud before arranging for the lads to help clear up the area as an act of community goodwill. The factions agreed to meet on the Sunday morning to plant some trees. However, only two youths turned up. They went off to look for the others and were never seen again.

Mr X's hopes of arranging another meeting were shattered a week later when the fragile truce was broken and violence flared up again. At 10.30pm some of the Alderwood lads invaded Central territory to buy fish and chips. A rival spotted them and an argument soon developed. A policeman approached and grabbed one of the Alderwood who snarled, 'If you want it you can have it.' Another policeman appeared but the Alderwood surrounded them. The officers were beaten to the ground and given a kicking. A compassionate bystander commented, 'It's the first time I've ever felt sorry for a copper.'

It seems that there had also been a running battle between the gangs the previous evening. Girls had caused the feud by going to each group and accusing the others of having assaulted them. A spokesman for the Central lads said, 'We don't want trouble ... especially when this involves beating up the police.' He also revealed that one of his own gang was assaulted for refusing to join in the attack on the constables. He claimed he wanted the truce to continue but only if the Alderwood agreed to keep out of their area.

Girls not only incited warfare, they could also dish it out as well as the lads. In March 1967, a new peril descended on Liverpool. Gangs of mini-skirted teenagers began terrorising the city centre. Three girls were beaten up in Lime Street. The victims were butted in the face, kneed in the stomach and pushed to the ground. One had her head repeatedly smashed against the pavement. The attack ended with the theft of a watch and handbag. Shortly after, three shops in nearby Bold Street had their windows smashed. Again, a group of girls was blamed. On another occasion, three young women, brandishing a toy pistol, held up a shopkeeper in the same street.

It seems that the Amazons of Liverpool never went away. Nor did the violence around the dockside areas previously haunted by the Peanut Gang and the High Rip before them.

23

Déjà Vu

THE SWINGING SIXTIES ended with yet another moral panic. 'Liverpool's new wave of terror,' declared the headline in the *Daily Post* at the end of 1969.[1] The sweeping arc of south end waterfront, from the Pier Head right down to Dingle and Park Road, was said to be a no-go area for innocent pedestrians at the mercy of roaming gangs. The problem was considered to be worse than the Teddy Boy epidemic ten years earlier. It was pointed out – wrongly – that the Teddy Boys, however vicious they were, only fought amongst themselves. The new breed of ruffian was targeting innocent members of the public. There was nothing 'new' about this, however, since it was almost a hundred years since Richard Morgan was battered to death by a very similar breed of thug.

The city had seen an alarming increase in stabbings, razor slashing and kicking outrages. The newspaper compiled a catalogue of brutality committed during the previous twelve months: seven people wounded by firearms, twenty-nine marked for life and two dead from knife and razor wounds, thirty victims injured after having broken bottles and glasses thrust in their faces, nineteen people seriously injured by kicking, a further twenty-four booted while being robbed, 245 sent to hospital after being punched while mugged, with another sixty being punched for no apparent reason. Finally, six individuals had pepper thrown in their eyes during robberies. A large number of these attacks were aimed at seamen, both foreign and 'homeward bounders' foolishly brandishing wads of notes in the local pubs. The old decoy trick was also still going strong.

Faced with the crime waves of the Sixties, the public were desperate for the return of the old-style bobby on the beat. Shopkeepers and residents slated the patrol cars that sped past too quickly to spot the hooligans in action. The police were torn between a traditional 'Dixon of Dock Green' approach to friendly community policing and a speedy and high-tech response to violent flare-ups. The authorities responded with a three-pronged attack that acknowledged the need for eyes and ears on the ground whilst also exploiting the advantages of the latest technology. In 1964, they formed a squad of plain-clothed 'commandos' to patrol crime hot spots. One hundred hand-picked officers, variously disguised as businessmen, Mods and scruffy 'beatniks', complete with wigs, would hang about the jukeboxes and street corners gathering intelligence and arresting unsuspecting criminals. The problem was that some suspects mistook the officers for layabouts and had a go at them, only to be charged with assaulting the police. Lawyers complained about such underhand tactics.

Police in Speke became the first in the country to start using portable walkie-talkie radios. The technology, introduced in 1964, was ideal for summoning assistance as disorder broke out on the various parts of the estate. In the same year, 'Big Brother' arrived in the form of CCTV cameras fixed at high vantage points in the city centre. Beady-eyed officers back at headquarters pored over images of car parks and notorious streets for signs of lawless behaviour. The press reported enthusiastically that the days of Liverpool's lawbreakers were numbered. Unfortunately, after some promising early signs of a reduction in crime, the city's hooligans, shoplifters, vandals, burglars and muggers carried on as normal.

Assaults on policemen in Speke continued. In 1965, teenagers beat up a constable outside a snack bar. The officer suffered a broken nose and collarbone after a gang tried to rescue a colleague who had been arrested. The following year, about twenty-five youths besieged the police station in the South Parade as two of their mates were being put into police cars. The mob punched, kicked and head-butted police officers in the effort to liberate the prisoners.

Animosity towards the police in Liverpool sunk to new depths. A policeman and a bus driver jumped into the River Mersey to save a drowning woman. As they tried to resuscitate the lady, hooligans poured hot tea over them and pelted them with bricks and sticks. The constable returned to the riverbank to find his watch had been stolen from inside his boots.

Lacking a sense of protection, even from the police, the public felt increasingly at the mercy of young villains. It was as if the rule of law was being demolished along with Liverpool's crumbling slums. Youths were seen as no longer having any respect for traditional authority figures such as teachers, policemen, watchmen and park attendants. Six lads, one of them armed with a knife, confronted the elderly caretaker at Springwood Bowling Green, Allerton, and threatened to 'do him over'. The terrified pensioner failed to report for duty the next day.

Faced with the impotence of such aging guardians, businesses began to employ more effective means of security. Yet the criminals simply upped their game. Attempts to stop them were met with even greater ingenuity and barbarity. In 1968, thieves enticed two Alsatian guard dogs to put their heads through the barbed wire fence protecting a building site. They then strangled them with a noose.

Throughout the Sixties, the public responded to the violence and disorder with endless public meetings, petitions and letters to the local press. The overwhelming feeling from such correspondence was that things were getting worse; the hooligans were winning the war; the country was degenerating into lawless anarchy. One such letter from 1969 couldn't have been more pessimistic: 'Wrecked telephone kiosks, wrecked schools, shop and factory break-ins, elderly folk coshed and robbed in their homes, school children defiant and destructive. What a tragic decline of behaviour in a one-time top nation of the world.'[2] The writer seemed unaware that when Britain was a 'top nation', the High Rip were terrorising the north end of Liverpool.

Yet the public had all the answers: bring back flogging, put more bobbies on the beat, fine the parents, make prisons a deterrent rather than a guesthouse, force prisoners to wear a ball and chain to prevent escapes, publicly ridicule the thugs by putting them in the stocks. Some thought that while great thought and effort were being put into the rehabilitation of the villains, no consideration was being given to the victims. Others felt that offenders should be punished first and reformed later.

Newspaper editors, local MPs and councillors had their own solutions: better education, improved parenting, a tightening of moral standards, re-housing and the promotion of youth clubs. Members of the public were asked to intervene rather than walk away from crimes and anti-social behaviour. Able-bodied men were invited to assist the police by joining the 'specials'. Magistrates and judges were urged to impose heavy sentences on convicted gangsters. Yet most of these solutions had been offered before, even as early as the High Rip reign of terror in the mid 1880s. Despite the best efforts of the criminal justice system, each decade continues to see yet another moral panic unleashed on the long-suffering public, from 'bovver boys' to 'lager louts' to the 'hoodies' of today.

One would be forgiven for concluding that gangs of tearaways will always exist. They simply transform themselves from time to time in order to adapt to changes in social conditions and technology. Violent computer games and gangsta rap might replace the old cowboy and gangster films as possible causes of juvenile crime, but the beating and kicking of innocent victims will remain pretty much the same. Emails and texting might replace handwritten notes furtively shoved under victims' doors but bullying and menacing intimidation remain the desired aim. Some other ethnic group might replace black people as a focus of bigotry and xenophobia but racism is still racism. Guns might replace knives as the gangster's weapons of choice but a murder is a murder for all that.

Today, as parts of Liverpool degenerate into gun wars, fuelled by the battle for drug trade supremacy and partly motivated by a twisted desire for 'respect', the same old solutions to crime are still being proposed. While the tearaways fight it out on the streets, politicians and social commentators continue to debate ways of stopping them.

Nothing changes.

Glossary of Underworld Slang

Artful Dodgers – Young thieves. After the Dickens character in *Oliver Twist*

At the wash – Robbery from somebody washing themselves in the public toilets or wash room

Bang – Hashish

Belt man – Man who keeps order at gambling schools by clearing the area with his belt

Blab – Inform to the police, to 'grass'

Blackjack – Truncheon with flexible handle

Bondy – A bonded warehouse

Bottling team – Gang of pickpockets

Brasses – Prostitutes

Buck – A working-man or street corner rough

Burst – Burglary

Cane – Jemmy

Card marker – Tipster who passes on information about potentially lucrative jobs

Carpet – Short for carpet bag, rhyming slang for 'drag', a three month prison sentence

Carrier-outer – Thief whose job it is to remove goods from a shop once they have been prepared. See Wrapper

Casing a joint – Checking a place before burgling it

Cat's paw – Person used as a dupe, e.g. when unwittingly used as a decoy in a crime

Coggers – Catholics

Coiner – Maker of counterfeit coins

Copper's nark – Police informer

Covers – Burglar's gloves

Creeper – Cat-burglar

Creepers – Rubber-soled shoes, ideal for wearing when burgling

Danny – Motorcar

Dip – Pickpocket

Dixy – Look out

Double banked – Having to fight two people

Douse – Look out

Drag – Car thief or person who robs from cars

Dropsy – Backhander, tip or pay off

Fence – Buyer of stolen goods

Flash – Of the underworld, hence illicit or dishonest

Flat catchers – Cheap watches or other items used to dupe customers, e.g. at auctions

Glim – Torch

Going to the butchers – Looking over the joint with a view to burgling it

Grafter – Crook

Granny – Legitimate business used as a cover by a fence

Grass – Police informer

Guttersnipe – Street urchin or slum child

H.B.I. – House-breaking implements

Hoister – Shoplifter, usually female

Hook – Pickpocket

Hot ice – Stolen diamonds

Jacks – Police

Jelly – Gelignite

Jemmy – Tool used for break-ins

Jigger – Back alley

Joe M'Gurk's – Gaol

Jowler – Back alley

Lag – Criminal who has served sentence

Lagged – Sent to prison

Life preserver – Short stick with heavy loaded end

Lingo – Language

Lloyd – A celluloid strip used to force Yale-type locks

Lorry-skipping – Jumping on and off moving lorries to steal goods

Love weed – Hashish

Mary Warner reefer – Sweepings from butts found in the gutter, re-rolled in fresh paper and passed off as new

Men catchers – Criminals who preyed on immigrants

Moll – Gangster's girlfriend. Girl, or person, used as decoy in robberies

Moll buzzer – Thief specialising in robbing from women, usually in department stores

Mooch – To go out on the 'mooch' is to embark upon a thieving expedition

Mopsed – Half-drunk

Mug – To mug somebody originally meant to buy them a drink. It eventually came to mean stealing the money from them

Mushers – Seamen

Napoo – First World War slang term meaning 'finished' or 'gone away'. It is from the French, 'il n'y en a plus', meaning 'there is no more'. A Manchester gang started using the word

Nicks or **Nix** – Keep watch

Ounce men – Drug pushers

Passer – Accomplice of pickpocket. Is passed the money before making a quick exit

Patter man – A mock auctioneer

Peter – Safe

Peterman – Safe-breaker

Pinched – Arrested

Pipe – To observe. 'Piping' is to look for an opportunity to rob

Plug Ugly – A ruffian used as a bouncer at mock auctions

PO'eys – Post Offices.

Poke – Money

Prigs – Juvenile thieves

Rolling – Mugging a drunken man, usually a sailor

Screw – Small fragments of hashish, sold in a screw of paper.

Screwsman – House-breaker

Shebeen – Illegal drinking den

Shiv – Knife

Smashers – People who pass off fake coins

Snide (or **Schneid**) – Fake, especially counterfeit money

Sniffing brigade – Cocaine users

Snout – Police informer

Sprawl – Fight

Squeak – Police informer

Stick – Jemmy

Stick carrier – Prostitute's protector. Alternatively pimp or ponce

Stool pigeon – Police informer

Stooley – To inform or split on someone

Swordsman – Fence

Tapper – Accomplice to pickpocket. Finds out where victim's money is held

Tolas – Small blocks of hashish

Twirls – Set of keys used to enter premises

Villainy – Theft or burglary

Whizzed – Robbed

Whizzer – Pickpocket

Windy – Scared

Wrap – Hashish cigarette

Wrapper – Thief specialising in wrapping stolen goods into a tight ball ready for removal from shop

Background Chronology

1893   Birth of Socialism
1901   Death of Queen Victoria. Beginning of Edwardian age
1905   Aliens Act attempts to regulate immigration
1907   700th anniversary of Liverpool Town Charter
        Birth of the Boy Scouts
        The Probation of Offenders Act introduces probation as
        an alternative to prison
1908   Childrens Act establishes a separate juvenile court system
        Crime Prevention Act establishes borstals for children too
        young for prison
1909   Liverpool's sectarian civil war
1911   Liverpool Transport Strike
1914-18 First World War
1915   Sinking of the Lusitania
1916   The Defence of the Realm Act prohibits the possession of
        cocaine and opium without a prescription
1917   Report of the National Council of Public Morals looks at
        the effect of cinema films on children's behaviour
1919   Racial disturbances in the south end
        Police strike
1920   The Dangerous Drugs Act
1924   First Labour Government
1926   General Strike
1929   Beginning of the Great Depression
1933   Children and Young Persons Act enables the State to
        intervene in family affairs, e.g. take children into care
1939-45 Second World War
1947   Anti-Jewish riots
1948   Racial disturbances in the south end
        Beginning of the Welfare State
        Criminal Justice Act abolishes corporal punishment
1953   Beginning of the Edwardian hooligans, better known as
        Teddy Boys
1954   Birth of rock 'n' roll music

1963   Last intake of National Servicemen demobbed
        Merseybeat music takes the world by storm
1964   Mods and Rockers begin to riot at seaside towns
        Final two prisoners hanged in England
1965   Murder (Abolition of Death Penalty) Act passed

References

Preface

1. Norman Lucas, *Britain's Gangland* (London, 1969), p.45.
2. Richard Whittington-Egan, *Liverpool Roundabout* (Manchester, 1976), p.277. Originally published by Philip Son & Nephew, 1957.
3. Quoted in James Morton, *Gangland, vol. 2: The Underworld in Britain and Ireland* (London, 1995), p.130.
4. Watch Committee, *Report on the Police Establishment and the State of Crime, For the Year Ending 1939-45.*
5. Sir William Nott-Bower, *Fifty-Two Years a Policeman* (London, 1926), p.142.
6. Quoted in *Bootle Times Herald*, June 23, 1967.
7. David Murray Lowson, *City Lads in Borstal: a Study Based on 100 Lads Discharged to Addresses in Liverpool*, Social Research Series (Liverpool, 1970), p.105.

Chapter 1

1. Letter in *Liverpool Echo*, October 15, 1960.
2. Letter in *Daily Post*, February 18, 1955.
3. Letter in *Liverpool Echo*, November 2, 1960.
4. *Evening Express*, March 23, 1950.
5. *Liverpool Review*, February 20, 1904.

Chapter 2

1. *Liverpool Review*, April 23, 1892.

Chapter 6

1. *Liverpool Review*, July 5, 1890.
2. *Liverpool Review*, February 28, 1891.
3. *Liverpool Review*, April 28, 1892.
4. J. & E. Braddock, *The Braddocks* (London, 1963), p.9.
5. 'Report of the Departmental Committee on the "Probation of Offenders Act, 1907", quoted in James Samuelson, *The Children Of Our Slums: Their Sufferings, Protection, Rescue, Training, &*

Afterlife (Liverpool, 1911), pp.54-55.
6. *Report on the Police Establishment and the State of Crime, For the Year Ending 31 December 1910*.
7. *Daily Post*, October 17, 1916.
8. *Daily Post*, October 24, 1916.

Chapter 7

1. *Liverpool Review*, September 17, 1892.
2. John Bohstedt quoted in John Belchem, ed. *Popular Politics, Riot and Labour: Essays in Liverpool History, 1790-1940*, Liverpool Historical Studies, 8 (Liverpool, 1992), p.188.
3. P.J. Waller, *Democracy and Sectarianism: A Political and Social History of Liverpool, 1868-1939* (Liverpool, 1981), p.209.
4. A.J. Ashton, *Proceedings and Report of the Liverpool Inquiry, conducted by A.J. Ashton, under the Police Act of 1909*, p.474. Liverpool Records Office.
5. *Report on the Police Establishment and the State of Crime, For the Year Ending 31 December 1912*.

Chapter 9

1. *Liverpool Review*, November 28, 1891.
2. *Daily Courier*, December 6, 1906.
3. *Report on the Police Establishment and the State of Crime, For the Year Ending 31 December 1910*.
4. For a fuller discussion see Andrea Murphy, *From the Empire to the Rialto: Racism and Reaction in Liverpool 1918-1948* (Birkenhead, 1995).
5. John Barron Mays, *Growing Up In The City: a Study of Juvenile Delinquency in an Urban Neighbourhood*, rev. ed., Social Research Series (Liverpool, 1964), p.45.

Chapter 10

1. *Daily Sketch*, quoted in *Liverpool Weekly Post*, January 25, 1919.
2. Licensing statistics, quoted in *Liverpool Weekly Post*, July 23, 1921.
3. Richard Whittington-Egan, *Liverpool Roundabout* (Manchester, 1976), p.282.
4. *Liverpool Review*, February 7, 1891.

5. *Liverpool Weekly Post*, November 6, 1937.
6. *Evening Express*, November 26, 1947.
7. *Daily Mirror*, August 8, 1948.

Chapter 11
1. *Review of Reviews*, quoted in *Daily Post*, September 12, 1911.
2. *Daily Post*, September 6, 1911.
3. *Evening Express*, November 20, 1935.

Chapter 13
1. Mike Brogden, *On the Mersey Beat: Policing Liverpool between the Wars* (Oxford, 1991), p.92.
2. *On the Mersey Beat*, pp.108-9.
3. *Liverpool Echo*, November 10, 1967 – February 3, 1968.
4. *Liverpool Weekly Post*, October 29, 1938.

Chapter 14
1. James Morton, *Gangland: vol.2*, p.134.

Chapter 15
1. Quoted in *Evening Express*, January 12, 1940.
2. John Barron Mays, *Growing Up In The City*, p.108.
3. *Evening Express*, April 14, 1941.
4. *Evening Express*, June 10, 1942.
5. Quoted in *Evening Express*, August 19, 1942.
6. *Daily Post*, September 4, 1945.
7. *Evening Express*, September 10, 1945.
8. *Evening Express*, September 12, 1945.
9. *Evening Express*, October 3, 1945.

Chapter 16
1. *Crime in the City: Report of the Steering Group,* November 1974, p.30.
2. *Daily Herald*, July 27, 1950.
3. *Daily Mirror*, March 11, 1950.
4. *Evening Express*, Nov 7, 1945.
5. Norman Lucas, *Britain's Gangland*, p.29.

Chapter 17

1. Lines from a poem by Frank Shaw, *My Liverpool* (London, 1971), p.68.
2. James Morton, *Gangland: vol.2*, pp.136-37.
3. *Report on the Police Establishment and the State of Crime, For the Year Ending 1939-45*.
4. Norman Lucas, *Britain's Gangland*, pp.28-29.
5. Letter in *Daily Post*, September 6, 1945.
6. *Evening Express*, October 27, 1945.
7. Joshua Greene, *Here Comes the Sun: the Spiritual and Musical Journey of George Harrison* (London, 2006), p.18.
8. John Barron Mays, *Growing Up In The City*, pp.200-201.
9. *Liverpolitan, vol.XVI, no.6* (June, 1951), p.20.
10. *Liverpolitan, vol.X, no.8* (August, 1945), p.3.

Chapter 18

1. *Daily Mirror*, March 16, 1947.
2. *Evening Express*, August 11, 1948.
3. *Evening Express*, August 30, 1948.

Chapter 19

1. *Evening Express*, December 13, 1945.
2. For further information on this crime, see Charlie Seiga, *A Liverpool Streetwise Kid: the Early Years* (2005).
3. *Liverpool Echo*, February 20, 1948.
4. See Barry Shortall, *The Cameo Murders* (Liverpool, 1999) and George Skelly, *The Cameo Conspiracy: the Real Story of the Cameo Cinema Murders* (2001).

Chapter 20

1. *Daily Herald*, July 27, 1950.
2. *Daily Mirror*, March 29, 1950.
3. *Daily Herald*, July 27, 1950.
4. Quoted in *Evening Express*, 23 December 1955.
5.Colin Fletcher, 'Beat and Gangs on Merseyside', in Timothy Raison (ed.) *Youth in New Society* (London, 1966), pp. 148-59, p.155.

Chapter 21

This chapter is indebted to the research done by Eric Dunning, Patrick Murphy and John Williams in their book, *The Roots of Football Hooliganism: an Historical and Sociological Study* (London, 1988).
1. *Birmingham Daily Mail*, October 10, 1888.
2. *Leicester Daily Mercury*, September 30, 1895.
3. Royal Commission on the Liquor Licensing Laws, P.P. 1898, XXXVI, 26310, 26311.
4. *The Times*, April 27 1914.
5. *Leicester Mercury*, January 14, 1933.
6. *Leicester Mercury*, November 14, 1957.
7. *Liverpool Weekly News*, November 9, 1963.
8. *The Times*, March 5, 1956.
9. *Liverpool Weekly News*, November 14, 1963.
10. *Daily Express*, November 13, 1964.

Chapter 22

1. *The Times*, February 2,1965.
2. *Report on the Police Establishment and the State of Crime, For the Year Ending 1966*
3. *Daily Post*, December 12, 1961.
4. *Liverpool Weekly News*, November 19, 1964.
5. *Liverpool Weekly News*, April 29, 1965.
6. *Liverpool Weekly News*, August 15, 1963.
7. Quoted in *Liverpool Weekly News*, February 14, 1963.
8. *Liverpool Weekly News*, May 16, 1963.
9. *Liverpool Weekly News*, November 1, 1962.
10. *Liverpool Weekly News*, June 3, 1965.
11. *Liverpool Weekly News*, April 9, 1964.
12. *Liverpool Weekly News*, February 6, 1964.
13. *Liverpool Weekly News*, November 15, 1962.
14. *Liverpool Weekly News*, May 3, 1962.
15. *Liverpool Weekly News*, March 25, 1964.
16. *Liverpool Weekly News*, June 18, 1964.

Chapter 23

1. *Daily Post*, December 1, 1969.
2. Letter to the *Liverpool Weekly News*, April 17, 1969.

Bibliography

Newspapers and journals
Birmingham Daily Mail
Bootle Times (Bootle Times Herald)
Daily Courier
Daily Express
Daily Herald
Daily Mirror
Daily Sketch
Illustrated London News
Illustrated Police News
Leicester Daily Mercury (Leicester Mercury)
Liverpolitan
Liverpool Daily Post
Liverpool Echo
Liverpool Evening Express
Liverpool Mercury
Liverpool Review
Liverpool Weekly News
Liverpool Weekly Post
Police Chronicle and Constabulary World
Police Review
Review of Reviews
Shetland Times
The Times

Ashton, A.J., *Proceedings and Report of the Liverpool Inquiry, conducted by A.J. Ashton, under the Police Act of 1909.* Liverpool Records Office.
Behan, Brendan, *Borstal Boy*, London: Hutchinson, 1958.
Belchem, John, ed. *Liverpool 800: Culture, Character & History*, Liverpool: Liverpool University Press, 2006.
Belchem, John, ed. *Popular Politics, Riot and Labour: Essays in Liverpool History, 1790-1940*, Liverpool Historical Studies, 8, Liverpool: Liverpool University Press, 1992.

Birkenhead, Earl of, *Famous Trials of History*, London: Hutchinson, 1926. Includes chapter on Liverpool Bank Fraud, pp. 229-236.

Biron, Chartres, 'Goudie Bank Frauds: F.E. Smith's Debut in London: A Baker Street Mystery'. Unreferenced essay found in *Police and Crime: 1931-June 1953. Press Cuttings Scrapbook*, Liverpool Record Office, Hq 352.2 CUT.

Braddock, Jack and Elizabeth, *The Braddocks*, London: Macdonald, 1963.

Brogden, Mike, *On the Mersey Beat: Policing Liverpool Between the Wars*, Oxford: Oxford University Press, 1991.

Brogden, Mike, 'Troubles in Toxteth, 1909', *Police Review* (August 6, 1982), 1506-7, 1534.

Cockcroft, W.R., *From Cutlasses to Computers: the Police Force in Liverpool, 1836-1989*, Market Drayton: S.B. Publications, 1991.

Crime in the City: Report of the Steering Group, November 1974.

Dunning, Eric, Murphy, Patrick, Williams, John, *The Roots of Football Hooliganism: an Historical and Sociological Study*, London: Routledge, 1988.

Fletcher, Colin, 'Beat and Gangs on Merseyside', in Raison, Timothy (ed.) *Youth in New Society*, London: Rupert Hart Davis, 1966, pp. 148-59.

Frosdick, Steve and Marsh, Peter, *Football Hooliganism*, Cullompton: Willan, 2005.

Gannon, John, 'The Bank Clerk from Shetland Who Stole a Fortune', *Shetland Life* (November, 1987) 39-43.

Greene, Joshua, *Here Comes the Sun: the Spiritual and Musical Journey of George Harrison*, London: Bantam, 2006.

Hernon, Ian, *Riot!: Civil Insurrection from Peterloo to the Present,* London: Pluto Press, 2006. Includes chapter on the 1919 police strike.

Humphries, Steven, *Hooligans or Rebels?: An Oral History of Working-Class Childhood and Youth, 1889-1939*, Oxford, Blackwell, 1981.

Lowson, David Murray, *City Lads in Borstal: a Study Based on 100 Lads Discharged to Addresses in Liverpool*, Social Research Series, Liverpool: Liverpool University Press, 1970.

Lucas, Norman, *Britain's Gangland*, London: W.H. Allen, 1969.

Mays, John Barron, *Growing up in the City: a Study of Juvenile Delinquency in an Urban Neighbourhood*, rev. ed., Social Research Series, Liverpool: Liverpool University Press, 1964.

Morton, James, *Gangland: vol.2: The Underworld in Britain and Ireland*, London: Warner Books, 1995.

Murphy, Andrea, *From the Empire to the Rialto: Racism and Reaction in Liverpool 1918-1948*, Birkenhead: Liver Press 1995.

Nott-Bower, Sir William, *Fifty-Two Years a Policeman*, London: Edward Arnold, 1926.

O'Mara, Pat, *The Autobiography of a Liverpool Irish Slummy*, London: Martin Hopkinson, 1934.

Royal Commission on the Liquor Licensing Laws, P.P. 1898, XXXVI, 26310, 26311.

Samuelson, James, *The Children Of Our Slums: Their Sufferings, Protection, Rescue, Training, & Afterlife*, Liverpool: The Liverpool Booksellers, 1911.

Seiga, Charlie, *A Liverpool Streetwise Kid: the Early Years*, The Picture Book Corporation Limited, 2005.

Shaw, Frank, *My Liverpool*, London: Wolfe Publishing, 1971.

Shortall, Barry, *The Cameo Murders*, Liverpool: Bluecoat Press, 1999.

Simpson, Charlie, 'Tragic story of Lerwick man', *Shetland Times* (28 December 2001) 20-21.

Skelly, George, *The Cameo Conspiracy: the Real Story of the Cameo Murders*, Upstage Entertainment, 2001.

Taplin, Eric, *Near to Revolution: The Liverpool General Transport Strike of 1911*, Liverpool: Bluecoat Press, 1994.

Toulmin, Vanessa, *Electric Edwardians: the Story of the Mitchell & Kenyon Collection*, London: British Film Institute, 2006.

Waller, P.J., *Democracy and Sectarianism: A Political and Social History of Liverpool, 1868-1939*, Liverpool: Liverpool University Press, 1981.

Watch Committee, *Report on the Police Establishment and the State of Crime, For the Year Ending …*

Whittington-Egan, Richard, *Liverpool Roundabout*, Manchester:

E.J. Morten, 1976. Originally published by Philip Son &
Nephew, 1957.